Beyond Barriers

Women's Progress from Mid-Twentieth Century to Today

Maria L. Ellis, BBA, MBA

Ellis Publishing House

Washington, DC, USA

Published 2025

DISCLAIMER

Cover Design: Jennifer Stinson

Editing: Cory Hott

DEDICATION

To my daughters-in-law, Dominique and Kathryn:
Your strength, intelligence, and grace inspire me daily.
You are building lives filled with purpose,
courage, and love.

And to my precious granddaughter, Maven Rose:
May you grow up in a world with fewer barriers and
limitless possibilities.
May you always know that your voice matters, your dreams
are valid, and your future is bright.
This book is for you, and for every woman who dares to
move beyond what was toward what can be

TABLE OF CONTENTS

FOREWORD

There are books that inform and books that transform, **"Beyond Barriers: Women's Progress from Mid-Twentieth Century to Today"** does both: it illuminates the past with rigor and lights up the present with purpose. From the ashes of the postwar era to the vibrant tide of twenty-first-century digital activism, these pages show how women have redefined what it means to lead, create, and fight for justice—not as a footnote to history, but as its driving force.

Whoever opens this book steps onto a hand-drawn map of paths: classrooms opened where there were once closed doors; courts and tracks where women's excellence ceased to be tolerated and began to be celebrated; parliaments and peace tables that learned to hear new voices; co-operatives, companies, and networks where the economy became more human; screens and algorithms contested so visibility depends not on concession but on rights. Art, politics, education, economics, technology, sport, environment, and spirituality: the journey Maria L. Ellis traces is broad—and above all, deeply human.

This is not a tally of "the first women to…," though it honors pioneers. It is a choral score: the well-known and the unnamed, from cities and peripheries, from majorities and margins, weave a story in which every advance is born from the meeting of conviction and community. Here, numbers matter—more girls in school, more women in parliaments, more peace agreements with a gender lens—but the ultimate metric is dignity: who is seen, who decides, who thrives, who tells the story.

Ellis writes as both chronicler and architect. She reminds us that barriers don't fall by statements alone, but by structures: laws like Title IX that opened playing fields; court rulings and reforms that turned equality into practice rather than promise; microfinance networks that converted "it can't be done" into "it's already happening"; digital platforms where a single testimony ignited millions of voices. She also names what hurts: political violence, pay gaps, online harassment, and the climate crisis that first strikes those who polluted the least. There is no triumphalism here; there is truth, memory, and work to do.

There are breathtaking moments: silence breaking into a rallying cry; the scientist who challenges a biased standard; the athlete who redefines the limits of body and mind; the leader who, in the midst of crisis, shows that empathy is not weakness but public strategy. And there are gestures that seem small—a neighborhood workshop, a care network, a gathering of neighbors, a prayer that becomes a march—but which, added together, change a community's trajectory.

May this book accompany you as a thoughtful companion through the stories of courage, creativity, and change. And when you finish it, may you carry not only a deeper understanding of women's progress—but a renewed resolve to continue advancing it.

Dr. Chigurupati Rani

Assistant Professor
Deputy Chairperson
Computer Information Systems

Borough of Manhattan Community College
The City University of New York

PREFACE

When I first began writing this book, I was struck by a simple but profound realization: the history of women's progress is not a side story to modern history – it is modern history. Every breakthrough in art, politics, science, economics, or culture carries the imprint of women who refused to stay silent, who imagined something better, and who worked tirelessly to bring it to life.

This book was born out of both gratitude and responsibility. Gratitude for the generations of women who broke barriers before us – often at great personal cost – and responsibility to ensure their stories are remembered, honored, and built upon.

As I traveled, read, researched, and reflected, I was moved again and again by how universal these struggles are. Whether in a Ghanaian marketplace, an American courtroom, an Indian temple, or an online feminist campaign, women everywhere are pushing against limits, lifting one another, and transforming societies in ways both visible and invisible.

My hope is that this book serves as more than history – it is also an invitation. An invitation to reflect, to question, and most importantly, to act. Because the work of progress is never finished. It asks something of each of us: to advocate, to mentor, to vote, to create, to stand in solidarity, and to believe in equity not as an abstract value but as a daily practice.

I believe deeply that the next chapters of women's progress will be even more transformative than the last. But they will not write themselves. They will be written by us – together, across generations and borders, with courage, creativity, and conviction.

Thank you for taking this journey with me. May the stories in these pages inspire you to carry the torch forward, to break barriers in your own life and community, and to build a world where equality is not the exception but the expectation.

Historical Roots (1910 to 1950)

The story of women's progress in the mid-twentieth century did not emerge in isolation. Its foundations were laid in the first half of the century, when women artists, thinkers, and activists challenged cultural boundaries and began reshaping expectations.

Between 1910 and 1950, modernist women artists across Europe and the United States experimented boldly with form and subject matter, often pushing against social norms that confined women to narrow roles. Figures such as Hannah Höch, Frida Kahlo, and others in the modernist movement demonstrated both creative resilience and cultural defiance. Their work paved the way for the artistic freedom women would claim in later decades.

In the United States, the ratification of the Nineteenth Amendment in 1920 gave women the right to vote, embedding their voices more firmly in the nation's democratic life. During World War II, millions of women entered factories, shipyards, and offices, upending assumptions about gender and capability. Although many were displaced after the war, the record of their competence endured and became a rallying point for the changes that followed.

Across Europe, similar milestones unfolded. In the United Kingdom, women more than thirty gained the right to vote in 1918, with full suffrage extended to all women a decade later. In France, women secured the vote in 1944, a landmark moment following their critical contributions to the Resistance during the war. In both Europe and America, women's wartime labor not only kept economies and communities functioning but also reshaped the cultural imagination of what women could do.

By 1950, the stage was set. These early pioneers, though not always recognized in their time, carved pathways that made the postwar decades ripe for transformation. The chapters ahead pick up the story after World War II, tracing how women's lives, opportunities, and influence accelerated in ways previously unimaginable.

Reader's Guide to the Appendices

Throughout this book, you will find references to women pioneers, leaders, and movements across politics, culture, economics, and spirituality. To preserve the flow of the narrative, detailed tables cataloging these figures have been relocated to the appendices at the back of the book.

- Appendix I highlights early pioneers and trailblazers.
- Appendix II covers political and social leaders.
- Appendix III presents cultural and economic innovators.
- Appendix IV catalogs contemporary global movements.
- Appendix V is a selected bibliography.
- Appendix VI is a reader's reflection guide.
- Appendix VII is a reader's discussion guide.

Each appendix is designed as a supplemental companion providing consolidated reference material for readers who wish to explore names, dates, and contributions in greater detail. In the narrative chapters, you will see callouts directing you to the relevant appendix.

With gratitude and hope,
Maria L. Ellis, BBA, MBA

CHAPTER 1:
REDISCOVERING
THE UNWRITTEN LEGACY

"Well-behaved women seldom make history."
— Laurel Thatcher Ulrich

The central question of this book is simple yet profound: How have women from 1950 onward reshaped society, and what remains to be done? For centuries, women's contributions have been overlooked, their stories scattered at the margins of history. To move forward, we must first uncover the past – not just the official record, but the lived experiences that defined generations.

To rediscover women's legacy is to broaden our historical lens. It means tracing the rise of women in education, politics, culture, and the economy while also asking what obstacles kept their stories from being told. It requires acknowledging both the visible victories and the invisible sacrifices that have defined women's progress since the mid-twentieth century. By reclaiming the unwritten legacy of the past, women laid the foundation for a future where progress would no longer be measured by presence alone but by power, influence, and transformation.

The story of women in the twentieth century has often been told in fragments – moments of progress celebrated, setbacks quietly endured, and contributions overlooked or erased. Too frequently, women's roles have been pushed to the margins of history rather than placed in its central chapters. Yet, beginning in the mid-twentieth century, a profound shift unfolded. From the aftermath of World War II to the rise of second-wave feminism and beyond, women began not only to claim space but also to reshape the very structures of society.

This book begins with a central question: How have women since 1950 reshaped society, and what remains to be done? By asking this, we acknowledge both the progress achieved and the unfinished work that lies ahead. Women's influence has extended across every sphere – politics, science, art, literature, business, sports, and social movements – transforming institutions once closed to them and redefining what power, leadership, and creativity look like. At the same time, persistent inequalities remind us that the legacy is still unwritten, still unfolding.

To rediscover this unwritten legacy is to look closely at the women who dared to cross boundaries, challenge assumptions, and insist that their stories belonged at the center of the human story. Some led movements or broke barriers in public life; others reshaped society more quietly through research, invention, entrepreneurship, or cultural work whose importance only later came to light. Together, their actions reveal a tapestry of progress that is neither linear nor complete – but undeniably transformative.

Consider, for instance, the contradictions of the 1950s. In the wake of World War II, millions of women who had filled factories, offices, and laboratories during the war were urged to return home, to trade their uniforms and tool belts for aprons and suburban kitchens. Advertisements celebrated the ideal of the cheerful housewife, while magazines reinforced the image of feminine fulfillment through marriage and motherhood. Yet beneath the polished surface of postwar domesticity, a quiet revolution was brewing. Many women remained in the workforce, unwilling to relinquish financial independence or professional identity. Others turned to grassroots action. In Freedom Summer of 1964, for example, Fannie Lou Hamer and local women canvassed Mississippi homes, registered Black voters, and ran freedom schools – organizing that built skills and networks later carried into the feminist, antiwar, and education movements that erupted in the years that followed.

Some of these women became defining figures of their time. In 1955, Rosa Parks, a quiet yet determined seamstress in Montgomery, Alabama, refused to surrender her bus seat to a white passenger. Her act of defiance ignited the Montgomery Bus Boycott and catalyzed the civil rights movement, demonstrating the power of one woman's courage to shift the course of history. Across the Atlantic, Rosalind Franklin was conducting groundbreaking research that produced the X-ray diffraction images crucial to identifying the double-helix structure of DNA. Though her contributions were long overshadowed, her work laid the foundation for one of the most significant scientific discoveries of the century. Together, Parks and Franklin represent the spectrum of women's impact in the 1950s – one through public protest, the other through scientific innovation – both challenging systems that sought to keep them invisible.

This chapter opens the door to that rediscovery. It situates women's voices within the broader landscape of the mid-twentieth century, a time of both entrenched norms and radical change. It asks readers to consider not just what women achieved but also how their struggles illuminate what still must be achieved for equality to become not an aspiration but a reality.

The mid-twentieth century marked a global turning point. Women – long relegated to the margins of power – began breaking through barriers in politics, education, the arts, and sports. This book was inspired by the exhibition *Radical! Women* Artists and Modernism 1910 to 1950, which brought to life the overlooked genius of women artists shaping modernism against the odds. Their courage and creativity reflect a broader truth: that the full story of progress cannot be told without the voices of women.

Beyond Barriers explores how women, from mid-century to today, have challenged restrictive norms and carved out new spaces for agency, visibility, and leadership. From the art studios of Vienna to the sports fields of the United States, from boardrooms to grassroots movements, this book traces a timeline of transformation – and honors the work that still lies ahead.

I didn't expect to be so moved by an art exhibition. As I walked through the rooms of the Belvedere in Vienna, surrounded by works from women artists who dared to defy the norms of their time, I felt a stirring I couldn't shake. *Radical! Women* Artists and Modernism 1910 to 1950 wasn't just a presentation of creativity – it was a quiet rebellion made visible. These artists, many of whom had been erased from the pages of art history, told stories not just with their brushes and film but with their presence. They lived and created despite not being invited to the table. Their work, once relegated to the shadows, is now illuminating the legacy of a movement that transcended borders and expectations.

That experience inspired this book.

I've lived through decades of social and cultural shifts as a woman, entrepreneur, and lifelong learner. I've seen the slow but steady dismantling of invisible walls that held women back – from boardrooms to sports arenas. But I've also seen how much of our progress remains unrecognized, how many stories go untold. We tend to celebrate the icons – Ruth Bader Ginsburg, Serena Williams, Malala Yousafzai – but behind every historic figure are thousands of women who pushed boundaries in quieter, sometimes less celebrated ways.

This book is for them – and for those continuing the work.

Beginning in the post–World War II era, *Beyond Barriers* traces the evolving role of women in public and private life: in art, education, politics, sports, science, and the home. These chapters explore not just what women have accomplished but what they've had to overcome: systemic exclusion, cultural silence, unequal access to opportunity, and persistent stereotypes.

I was particularly moved by how women's sports in the United States changed after Title IX – not only because it opened doors for athletes but because it symbolized something bigger. For generations, women were told that competition, strength, and ambition didn't belong to them. That narrative is being rewritten – just like the one in art, business, and leadership.

Each chapter of this book explores a different frontier of female progress. You'll meet pioneers who reshaped their fields, women who challenged cultural assumptions, and young changemakers preparing the way forward. While this book begins in the twentieth century, it is ultimately about today – and tomorrow.

Beyond Barriers is both a tribute to women's overlooked contributions and a call for action. It is a reminder that the freedom to create, to lead, and to define our own destinies is never a given – it is something we must earn, protect, and extend to those who follow.

As you turn the page, I invite you to reflect not just on how far women have come – but on where we must go from here.

Women and Modernism: Art as Resistance and Voice

Part I: Breaking Ground (1950s to 1970s)

In the quiet halls of Vienna's Belvedere Museum, I stood face-to-face with a revolution I had never fully seen before. *Radical! Women* Artists and Modernism 1910 to 1950 pulled back the veil on a truth long buried: women were not passive observers of the modernist era – they were its architects, disruptors, and visionaries. Yet history had chosen to forget many of their names.

What struck me most was not just the talent on display but the courage. These women created in defiance of a system that dismissed their work as decorative, derivative, or overly emotional. They pushed the boundaries of form, subject, and style – not to conform, but to express truths that could not be silenced. In a world still structured by patriarchal norms, their art became a form of resistance and voice.

The Shadowed Foundations of Modernism

Modernism, as an art movement, was born of rupture – of war, displacement, industrialization, and the desire to break with the past. Between the 1910s and 1950s, artists rejected tradition and sought new ways to express the fractured, complex world around them. Yet even as the movement embraced radical change, it remained bound by gender exclusion.

While male artists like Picasso, Kandinsky, and Matisse were widely celebrated, women were often relegated to the background. Some, like Georgia O'Keeffe or Frida Kahlo, achieved recognition – but they were the exceptions. Others, equally talented, were erased, overlooked, or remembered primarily as muses or companions to their male counterparts. Their contributions to Cubism, Expressionism, Surrealism, Dada, and Constructivism remained hidden or attributed to others.

But the reality was different.

Women like Sonia Delaunay, Natalia Goncharova, Hannah Höch, and Toyen were central to the avant-garde. They challenged both artistic conventions and societal norms. They painted, collaged, filmed, and performed as innovators – not imitators. Their work captured the chaos and vitality of the modern world through a distinctly female lens – exploring themes of identity, sexuality, motherhood, war, and labor.

Art as Survival and Protest

In the mid-twentieth century, the political landscape was volatile. Women artists faced not only sexism but also fascism, communism, displacement, and war. For many, art became a lifeline – a way of making sense of trauma, asserting agency, and preserving personal and cultural identity.

Consider the work of Austrian artist Maria Lassnig, who developed the concept of "body awareness" painting, where the canvas became a mirror of the internal self. Or the haunting photomontages of Hannah Höch, who used the fragmented images of Weimar society to critique gender roles and nationalism. These women weren't just making art; they were making statements about who controls the image – Lassnig insisting a woman's interior sensations be seen, Höch ripping open the glossy masks of patriarchy and nationalism.

Their media were as diverse as their messages. Embroidery, film, performance, and textile arts – often dismissed as "feminine" crafts – were reclaimed as instruments of protest: stitches that spelled slogans across cloth, performances that recast housework as refusal, and films cut to lay bare the politics of the everyday. In the hands of artists like Sophie Taeuber-Arp and Anni Albers, weaving became a language of abstraction and resistance, its warp and weft reading like coded messages smuggled into domestic space.

Many of these women faced exile, censorship, or poverty. Yet they persisted, and in doing so, laid the groundwork for the feminist art movements of the 1970s.

Reclaiming the Narrative

The erasure of women from the modernist canon was not accidental – it was systemic. Curators, critics, and institutions often ignored or devalued their work. For decades, art history books told a half-truth: that modernism was a male revolution.

Over the last two decades, scholars and museums have steadily rewritten that narrative. The Belvedere's Radical! Women Artists 1900 to 1950 was part of this wave – a call to remember, restore, and rethink what we mean by "modern."

And remembering matters. Because when we

acknowledge that women helped shape one of the most important artistic revolutions in history, we also open the door to seeing women's contributions in every sphere – with new eyes and deeper respect.

From Canvas to Catalyst

This chapter isn't just about forgotten art. It's about what's lost when women are denied recognition – and what becomes possible when they're finally heard. The modernist women artists showed us that creation itself is a political act when you're told not to create.

Their stories remind us that change often begins in quiet acts of defiance – in brushstrokes, in performances, in unspoken truths captured on canvas. They taught us that to be radical is not just to be different, but to make the work undeniable: to bring "women's work" onto museum walls, to write yourself into catalogues and labels, and to demand eye-level placement where women were once absent.

As we turn the page to examine how women challenged systems in education, politics, and sport, we carry with us this foundational truth: the act of expression – especially in the face of exclusion – is where progress begins.

Their stories remind us that change often begins in quiet acts of defiance – in brushstrokes, in performances, in unspoken truths captured on canvas. They taught us that to be radical is not just to be different – but to be seen, to insist on your place in the world.

The following highlights some of the groundbreaking women artists mentioned in this chapter. Their lives and work offer visual testimony to the ideas explored in these pages.

Breaking Frames – Women and Modernism, 1910 to 1950

The early twentieth century marked a seismic shift in the world of art, culture, and politics. The rise of modernism between 1910 and 1950 challenged centuries-old traditions, giving rise to avant-garde movements such as Dada, Constructivism, Surrealism, and Expressionism. Yet within this artistic revolution, many women faced a double bind: they were creators of new visual languages and radical aesthetics, yet they were marginalized, often viewed as muses rather than makers.

This chapter tells the story of women who didn't just participate in modernism – they reshaped it. Their lives and works offer a window into the struggles and breakthroughs of a generation determined to speak in its own voice, against a backdrop of war, repression, and the evolving struggle for gender equality.

In the Weimar Republic of post-World War I Germany, Hannah Höch carved a space for herself within the male-dominated Dada movement. Known for her photomontages that cut and reassembled mass media images, Höch turned the tools of propaganda against themselves. Her 1919 piece *Cut with the Kitchen Knife Dada through the Last Weimar Beer-Belly Cultural Epoch of Germany* critiques the chaos of postwar German society and the gender politics within it. But beyond the sharp edges of satire was a woman navigating her own complex identity – as a bisexual artist, as someone resisting traditional roles, and as a public intellectual during a volatile time. She once said, "I would like to show the world today as an ant sees it and tomorrow as the moon sees it." That multiplicity – of perspectives, of roles, of belonging – was the heart of her practice.

Meanwhile in Zurich, Sophie Taeuber-Arp was defying all boundaries: between art and craft, between high culture and applied design, between dancer and visual artist. A trained textile designer, she brought geometric abstraction to embroidery, beading, and furniture design. Her vertical-horizontal compositions – precise yet joyful – met wartime viewers like an architecture of calm: crisp crossings and buoyant color blocks that offered rhythm and refuge while headlines screamed. She danced at the Cabaret Voltaire, home of the Zurich Dada movement, then retreated into silence when her work was dismissed as merely decorative. But for Taeuber-Arp, the act of creating – whether a beaded bag or an abstract painting – was inherently political. Her sudden death from accidental carbon monoxide poisoning in 1943 cut short a career that had quietly but powerfully challenged the hierarchy of the arts.

In Russia, Lyubov Popova embraced revolution not only politically but visually. As a leading figure in Russian Constructivism, Popova experimented with abstract compositions that abandoned representation altogether. Her bold color blocks, sharp diagonals, and layered forms embodied the energy of a society undergoing radical transformation. In the 1920s, she shifted her talents to industrial design and theater, producing dynamic stage sets that merged art with communal purpose. Yet behind the utopian ideals was a woman who suffered personal loss and systemic limitations. Popova's life was tragically brief – she died of scarlet fever in 1924 at just thirty-five – but her vision of art as a tool for social construction endured long after her passing.

The French Dadaist Suzanne Duchamp, sister to Marcel Duchamp, often wrestled with being overshadowed by her famous brother. Yet she was an accomplished artist in her own right. Her collages and paintings explored themes of identity, war, and womanhood through fragmented imagery and mechanical motifs. Works like *Marcel's Unhappy Readymade* and *Multiplication Broken and Restored* played with irony, language, and gendered expectations. She was one of the few Dadaists who directly referenced the experiences of women during World War I. In a movement that sought to dismantle meaning, Suzanne Duchamp injected a deeply personal – and often feminist – layer into the nonsense.

As the Nazis rose to power, the avant-garde faced a dark reckoning. Charlotte Salomon, a German-Jewish artist, fled to the south of France to escape persecution. There, she began her monumental work *Life? or Theatre?*, a semi-autobiographical series of more than 700 paintings accompanied by texts and musical cues. In a unique synthesis of painting, theater, and memoir, Salomon captured the torment of her family's history and the impending horror of the Holocaust. Her style – vibrant, raw, emotionally charged – embodied both trauma and hope. In 1943, at the age of twenty-six and five months pregnant, Salomon was arrested and deported to Auschwitz, where she was murdered. Her work survives as a haunting testimony to art's power to preserve memory when life itself is extinguished.

These women – Höch, Taeuber-Arp, Popova, Duchamp, and Salomon – transcended the frames placed around them by society and even by their artistic circles. They were painters, designers, writers, performers, and thinkers whose contributions to modernism are finally being recognized not as footnotes but as foundational.

Their work was not created in isolation but emerged from intense interaction with the social upheavals of their time: revolutions, wars, the collapse of empires, the birth of new ideologies, and the slow advance of women's rights. Through scissors, stage sets, color planes, collages, and painted stories, they shaped a new way of seeing the world – and of imagining a woman's place within it.

As we reflect on this foundational moment, let us recognize that their work laid the groundwork for generations of women artists. Their courage to create – when a curator pinned "decorative" to a wall label, when a signature vanished from a catalog entry, when a show was closed under pressure – still echoes in the barriers women face in the art world today.

For a fuller catalog of pioneering women artists of modernism from 1910 to 1950 – including their countries, works, and defining contributions – see Appendix I: Pioneers and Trailblazers.

Voices of Defiance

Throughout history, women have not only acted – they have spoken, written, protested, and created with fierce conviction. Their words endure as testaments to courage, clarity, and a refusal to remain silent in the face of injustice. In this section, we highlight the voices of those who challenged the status quo through thought, expression, and unapologetic self-definition. These are the echoes of resistance – raw, poetic, timeless – that continue to inspire change across generations.

"I want to be famous so that I may get to paint. And I want to paint so that I may get to be famous."
— Suzanne Valadon,
quoted in *Suzanne Valadon: A Biography by June Rose*

Valadon's defiance lay in her insistence on being seen as a serious painter, not a muse or model. This quote reflects her savvy understanding of the gendered art world she had to navigate – and subvert – to be recognized.

"I paint self-portraits because I am so often alone… because I am the person I know best."
— Frida Kahlo, diary entry (early 1940s)

Though Kahlo's influence permeates later chapters, her early defiance of colonial, gender, and class norms through both image and word grounds her firmly in the modernist moment.

Each of these artists not only made remarkable contributions to the modernist movement – they also used their work to challenge cultural expectations, engage with political realities, and expand what was possible for women in art. You are encouraged to explore their works online or in art books for a fuller appreciation of their bold, transformative visions.

In conclusion, by reclaiming an unwritten legacy, women built a future where progress is measured not by presence but by power, influence, and transformation. Women of faith have long walked the line between silence and song; each step toward equality turns tradition into liberation.

Reflection Prompts

1. What stories from your own family or culture have been overlooked or forgotten?
2. Think about the women whose names are rarely mentioned but whose influence was quietly profound.
3. Which artists or cultural figures from this period stood out to you, and why?
4. Consider what made their contributions meaningful in spite of social or political barriers.
5. How does reclaiming hidden histories change our understanding of progress?
6. Reflect on how this broader, more inclusive view might shift your definition of legacy.
7. What creative or intellectual contributions are you making today that could serve as a legacy for future generations?
8. Explore the idea that your everyday actions – your voice, your art, your decisions – are part of a larger, living history.

CHAPTER 2:
POST-WAR SOCIETY AND
THE RISE OF FEMALE ACTIVISM

"The future depends entirely on what each of us does every day; a movement is only people moving."
— Gloria Steinem

Breaking Ground (1950s to 1970s): Post-War Society and the Rise of Female Activism

The end of World War II ushered in a period of reconstruction, not only of nations but also of gender roles. In many parts of the world, the war had drawn women into public life – into factories, farms, offices, laboratories, and resistance movements – only to see them urged back into domestic spaces once peace was declared. Advertisements in the United States and Western Europe celebrated the ideal of the suburban homemaker, signaling a return to "normalcy." Yet this postwar vision, polished and promoted as universal, masked a much more complex global reality. Across continents, women were questioning old hierarchies, challenging expectations, and laying the groundwork for movements that would reshape the second half of the twentieth century.

The end of World War II ushered in a period of reconstruction – not only of nations but also of gender roles. In many parts of the world, the war had drawn women into public life – into factories, farms, offices, laboratories, and resistance movements – only to see them urged back into domestic spaces once peace was declared. Advertisements in the United States and Western Europe celebrated the ideal of the suburban homemaker, signaling a return to "normalcy." Yet this postwar vision, polished and promoted as universal, masked a more complex reality. In Abeokuta, Nigeria, for example, thousands of market women led by Funmilayo Ransome-Kuti crowded the Alake's palace in 1947 to 1949, rattling tins and singing protest songs until the head tax on women was scrapped – an early crack in the supposed 'return to normalcy.'

But activism was not confined to the West. In India, women had played a pivotal role in the independence movement, from organizing mass protests to leading underground networks. Figures such as Aruna Asaf Ali, who hoisted the Indian National Congress flag during the Quit India Movement, continued to influence political life in the newly independent nation. Indian women activists carried forward the ethos of collective resistance into campaigns for education, healthcare, and women's political representation, ensuring that independence was not solely a matter of sovereignty but also of social transformation.

In Africa, the aftermath of colonialism and the stirrings of liberation movements created new avenues for activism. In Ghana, women traders and market leaders were central to mobilizing communities against British colonial policies, culminating in independence in 1957 under Kwame Nkrumah. Women like Hannah Kudjoe emerged as national organizers – serving as the Convention People's Party's National Propaganda Secretary, touring towns to stage rallies during the Positive Action campaign, and later founding the All-African Women's League (later the Ghana Women's League). In South Africa, women resisted apartheid through mass protests such as the 1956 Women's March on Pretoria, where 20,000 women of all races – led by Lilian Ngoyi, Helen Joseph, Rahima Moosa, and Sophia Williams-De Bruyn – demanded an end to discriminatory pass laws. Their chant – "You strike a woman, you strike a rock" – resonated far beyond South Africa, symbolizing women's collective strength in the face of systemic oppression.

In Latin America, women were equally central to postwar transformations. In Argentina, Eva Perón mobilized women's suffrage campaigns – culminating in the 1947 vote – and helped found the Female Peronist Party, then one of the world's largest women's political organizations. *Her cultural celebrity as a radio and stage star amplified recruitment through mass rallies and nationwide broadcasts, but it also personalized the movement around her image, complicating independent leadership.* In Mexico and Brazil, women pressed for labor rights and expanded access to education through unions, teachers' leagues, neighborhood committees, and student federations. Taken together, these campaigns tied gender equality to wage struggles, land reform, and democratization, borrowing shared strategies – strike kitchens, literacy circles, cross-border conferences, and union newspapers – that knit gender, political, and economic liberation into a single, practical agenda.

Together, these global movements reveal a striking pattern: while women were often encouraged – or compelled – to return to domestic roles after the war, they simultaneously carved out new spaces for activism and leadership. Whether in Birmingham, Alabama, or Pretoria, South Africa; in Delhi, India, or Buenos Aires, Argentina, women recognized that the postwar order offered both opportunities and obstacles. Their activism was not uniform, but it was interconnected – linked by shared tactics (boycotts, strike kitchens, literacy circles), by union and church networks, and by women's congresses and radio/print campaigns that carried ideas across borders – driven by common aims of dignity, recognition, and autonomy.

The rise of female activism in the postwar era was thus not a side story to the political upheavals of the time; it was a central force shaping them. Women's voices and actions challenged the limits of the possible, linking questions of gender equality to decolonization, civil rights, labor justice, and democratization. This was the beginning of a global conversation, one that continues today: how can women not only participate in society but transform it?

The end of World War II marked both relief and a reckoning. Across Europe, Asia, and the Americas, countries faced the monumental task of rebuilding their economies, political institutions, and social fabrics. Amid this reconstruction, women emerged not just as helpers in the healing process but as leaders, thinkers, and organizers reshaping the postwar world.

During the war, women had stepped into roles long denied to them – factory workers, engineers, farmers, soldiers, codebreakers, resistance fighters, and caregivers. They proved, by necessity, that they could hold societies together during their most fractured moments. But peace brought a complicated reality. Instead of celebration or promotion, many women were told to step back. They were expected to return quietly to domestic life.

This tension – between what women had proven they could do and what society expected of them – fueled a wave of consciousness that would give rise to decades of activism.

A Return to the Kitchen – or a Refusal?

In the U.S. and Western Europe, the 1950s are often remembered as an era of domesticity. Television shows, advertisements, and public policy all encouraged women to embrace a "return to normalcy," which meant marriage, motherhood, and homemaking. The "ideal woman" of the era was expected to be obedient, supportive, and self-sacrificing. Women were told they had fulfilled their patriotic duty during the war – but now, it was time to make way for returning men.

But many women did not go quietly.

They had experienced independence. They had earned wages. They had run farms and businesses. They had tasted agency – and they were not willing to give it up. Picture, for example, a Black entrepreneur in 1946 Birmingham who kept her beauty salon open through the war – ordering supplies on rationed credit, training younger women, and paying two assistants every Friday; an ad telling her to "return home" had no place to land. For women of color, immigrant women, and working-class women, the "return to domesticity" was a myth that never applied. They had always worked – and continued to do so – in canneries and laundries, as domestics and field hands, and in small shops and service businesses, often in roles that were underpaid and undervalued.

It was this shared sense of being pushed back into a mold that no longer fit that planted the seeds of what would become a multi-decade feminist movement.

Seeds of a Movement

In 1949, French intellectual Simone de Beauvoir published *The Second Sex*, a groundbreaking philosophical treatise that analyzed how women had been historically constructed as the "Other" in a male-dominated world. Her assertion that "one is not born, but rather becomes, a woman" shook cultural assumptions across continents.

In the United States, Betty Friedan's *The Feminine Mystique* (1963) gave voice to what she called "the problem that has no name" – the silent discontent of middle-class housewives. The book became a bestseller, and more importantly, a catalyst. It struck a chord with women who felt trapped in roles that denied their intellect, creativity, and autonomy.

Key Contribution: Authored *The Feminine Mystique* (1963), which sparked the second wave of feminism by addressing "the problem that has no name." After interviewing housewives across America, Betty Friedan gave voice to the silent desperation of women confined to domestic roles. Her work catalyzed a wave of questioning: "Is this all?" Her intellectual activism led to the founding of the National Organization for Women (NOW) in 1966.

Around the same time, women were organizing at the grassroots for civil rights, reproductive rights, labor protections, and access to education. In Montgomery, Rosa Parks – secretary of the local NAACP and adviser to its Youth Council, freshly trained at Highlander Folk School in 1955 – refused to surrender her seat on December 1, 1955; working with E.D. Nixon, she helped launch the Montgomery Bus Boycott, a spark for the modern Civil Rights Movement.

In Latin America, women were mobilizing against dictatorships and advocating for land reform. In Asia and Africa, anti-colonial movements often saw women leading protests, writing manifestos, and demanding inclusion in new national narratives. Activism was not confined to any one region; it was global, interconnected, and deeply personal.

Building Institutions for Change

By the late 1960s, the energy of activism had led to the creation of formal organizations dedicated to women's rights. In the U.S., the National Organization for Women (NOW) was founded in 1966, calling for full equality between the sexes. Similar movements arose across Europe, including the Women's Liberation Movement in the UK and student-led feminist collectives in France, Germany, and Italy.

These groups demanded equal pay, access to contraception and abortion, better childcare, protection from sexual harassment, and the right to pursue careers and education without discrimination. Their protests were sometimes met with ridicule or backlash – but they persisted.

At the center of this story are Black feminists, Chicana organizers, and Indigenous women, who built the conferences, presses, and collectives that reshaped the agenda. The Combahee River Collective and the National Black Feminist Organization articulated a politics that linked race, gender, sexuality, and class; Chicana activists convened the 1971 National Chicana Conference in Houston and launched newspapers and student groups; Indigenous women formed organizations such as Women of All Red Nations (WARN) to fight for sovereignty, health, and land. Through books and presses – *This Bridge Called My Back* and Kitchen Table: Women of Color Press – they challenged a single-issue feminism and insisted on what we now call intersectionality. Their leadership made the movement not monolithic but a broad, evolving coalition capable of speaking to many realities at once.

Culture, Art, and Visibility

Art and media became vital tools for spreading feminist ideas. Magazines like *Ms.*, launched by Gloria Steinem and others in 1972, challenged traditional narratives and celebrated women's voices. Female artists, writers, musicians, and filmmakers began using their platforms to tell new stories – ones that reflected the realities of women's lives, struggles, and dreams.

The feminist slogan "the personal is political" was not just a rallying cry; it was a radical reframing of how society understood power. Women began to speak publicly about issues long kept private: domestic violence, marital inequality, sexual identity, and mental health. As this chapter showed in Montgomery, Rosa Parks's refusal to surrender her seat – rooted in the daily indignity of segregated buses – became a 381-day citywide boycott and, ultimately, the *Browder v. Gayle* ruling, turning a personal affront into a public shift in power. The ruling effectively declared bus segregation unconstitutional and became a key legal victory of the early Civil Rights Movement.

From Protest to Policy

While cultural shifts were essential, real progress required institutional change. And slowly, the political system began to respond.

In the United States, Title VII of the Civil Rights Act of 1964 prohibited gender-based employment discrimination. In 1972, Title IX was passed, banning sex-based discrimination in federally funded education – opening the doors for a new era in women's athletics and academia.

In other countries, women gained suffrage, joined parliaments, and formed women-led political parties. Scandinavian nations, in particular, became leaders in implementing family-friendly policies like paid maternity leave, childcare subsidies, and equal parental leave.

The Legacy of the Post-War Activists

By the end of the 1970s, women's activism had reshaped the world. What began as frustration and marginalization evolved into one of the most impactful social movements of the twentieth century. The gains made were not perfect or complete, yet they laid the groundwork for future generations to build upon.

Women proved that their experiences, insights, and voices were not secondary – they were essential to any vision of justice, equality, and human dignity.

This chapter highlights notable female activists from the post-war period and provides historical depth and context to reinforce the chapter's content.

Post-War Society and the Rise of Female Activism

The conclusion of World War II ushered in a period of reconstruction, reckoning, and redefinition. As nations rebuilt their cities, economies, and identities, women artists around the world began to rise not only as creators but as cultural activists – women who challenged social norms, reimagined gender roles, and demanded a space in both the gallery and society. The trauma of war, the momentum of modernism, and the growing international conversation around civil rights and feminism combined to catalyze a new wave of female expression.

This chapter traces the stories of women who brought activism into their art and art into their activism. Through paint, sculpture, abstraction, portraiture, and pedagogy, they advocated for change, visibility, and voice.

In postwar Britain, Barbara Hepworth navigated grief, motherhood, and professional marginalization — and poured that experience into work that radiated serenity. In postwar Britain, she redefined modern sculpture with elegant, abstract forms drawn from nature and quiet spiritual discipline. Installed in public spaces, her large bronzes proposed harmony and balance as civic values. As a single mother who lost a son in the war, she turned private sorrow into shared healing. In 1956, *Meridian* set a modernist axis in motion — an arc suggesting the planet's tilt and a human reach toward the cosmos — an insistence on connection against the era's fragmentation and loss.

Alma Thomas, an African American artist and educator, rose to prominence later in life but left a lasting impact on the Washington Color School. A former schoolteacher in segregated D.C., Thomas's abstract works celebrated joy, color, and nature while subtly protesting racial and gender exclusions in the art world. Her 1966 painting *Resurrection* — the first work by a Black woman to enter the White House permanent collection — offered not only aesthetic beauty but symbolic rebirth. Thomas's late-in-life success proved that visibility can be a radical form of activism.

In New York, Lee Krasner fought for recognition within the Abstract Expressionist movement, often overshadowed by her husband, Jackson Pollock. Krasner's powerful canvases were not only technically masterful but emotionally raw, reflecting her insistence that women could produce large-scale, monumental work on par with any male peer. Her work broke with feminine stereotypes and expanded the vocabulary of abstraction to include grief, resilience, and self-reclamation.

A fellow New York School artist, Grace Hartigan blended abstraction and figuration, drawing from pop culture, mythology, and literature. Her paintings, often riotous in color and layered in meaning, challenged both academic elitism and commercial art's superficiality. She once stated,

"I want an art that is not 'abstract' or 'realistic' but both; a shattering unity of experience." Hartigan's refusal to conform made her a formidable activist for artistic independence.

Helen Frankenthaler, one of the pioneers of color field painting, introduced the "soak-stain" technique that would influence a generation of male painters. While her technique appeared lyrical and fluid, her presence in the art world was anything but passive. Frankenthaler pushed the boundaries of medium and scale, asserting that softness did not equal weakness. Her activism lay in technique – in proving that innovation could emerge from intuition, and that feminine expression was valid, visionary, and essential.

Elaine de Kooning, an artist and critic, advocated for both the creation and interpretation of art by women. Her action-filled portraits and abstract works pulsed with vitality, capturing the essence of motion and personality. A frequent contributor to *ARTnews*, de Kooning used writing to elevate other women's voices and to challenge the patriarchal art historical canon. Her dual role as artist and critic positioned her at the front of feminist art discourse.

The work of Louise Bourgeois, rooted in memory, trauma, and the body, exploded into public consciousness in the 1970s, though she had been making groundbreaking art for decades. Her iconic sculpture *Maman* – a towering spider – reflected both maternal strength and psychological complexity. Bourgeois confronted subjects like domesticity, rage, and childhood abuse with unsparing honesty. In doing so, she became a pioneer of the confessional mode that would define feminist art in decades to come.

In China, Pan Yuliang broke barriers by embracing Western oil painting techniques at a time when such forms were rare and discouraged. Trained in France, Pan integrated Chinese calligraphy and ink sensibilities with European modernism. A former sex worker turned professor and professional artist, Pan's nude female figures were bold statements of bodily autonomy in a conservative society.

Her life and work – often produced in exile – embodied resistance and reclamation.

Georgette Chen, working in postwar Singapore, contributed to the development of the Nanyang style, a synthesis of Chinese ink traditions and Western oil techniques. Her portraits and still lifes centered on local identity, tropical culture, and the quiet dignity of everyday life. Through teaching and painting, Chen helped build a Southeast Asian modernism that recognized women's perspectives as foundational, not supplementary.

The women of this postwar generation expanded the definition of what it meant to be both artist and activist. Their diverse media, geographies, and messages shared one underlying goal: to give form to female experience in all its complexity.

They made visible what was hidden. They carved space where there was none. They transformed private struggle into public truth.

These women stood not just at the edge of art movements but at the heart of social transformation – challenging conventions, building institutions, and mentoring new generations.

Their legacy is not only visual but institutional – visible in museum collections and leadership, academic programs and curricula, and even public policy. The world they envisioned on canvas, in sculpture, and in silence now shapes how activism is taught, funded, and practiced.

A detailed listing of notable female activists of the mid-twentieth century, along with their movements and lasting impact, is provided in Appendix I.

Voices of Defiance

In the wake of war, women were expected to retreat – back to kitchens, quiet lives, and conventional roles. But many refused. The post-war era ignited a firestorm of female activism as women began to name the injustices, challenge the expectations, and demand more than society was willing to give. Their words – fierce, articulate, and unrelenting – captured the pulse of a generation no longer willing to be silent. These voices did not just echo through protest halls or legislative chambers – they rang out in books, courtrooms, diaries, and letters, reshaping the social fabric and laying the foundation for modern feminism.

> *"Each suburban wife struggled with it alone. As she made the beds, shopped for groceries… she was afraid to ask even of herself the silent question – 'Is this all?'"*
> — Betty Friedan, *The Feminine Mystique*, 1963.

Friedan's question shattered the illusion of postwar domestic bliss, giving language to a generation of women suffocating in silence.

> *"If they don't give you a seat at the table, bring a folding chair."*
> — Shirley Chisholm, *Unbought and Unbossed*, 1970.

With wit and clarity, Chisholm captured the spirit of female agency – asserting space, power, and presence where none was offered.

In conclusion, from kitchens to picket lines, women in the post-war world proved that activism was not a side story but the heartbeat of social change.

Reflection Prompts

1. How did the aftermath of war reshape gender expectations in your country or culture?
2. Reflect on how these shifts affected opportunities – or restrictions – for women.
3. Which female activist from this period most inspires you, and why?
4. Consider what personal qualities or actions defined their leadership.
5. What systems today are being rebuilt – and how are women participating in that process?

6. Think about crises (economic, environmental, social) and how women are shaping recovery or resistance efforts.
7. In your own life, where have you stepped into leadership during a time of change or instability?
8. Identify moments when your own voice or action made a difference, however small.

CHAPTER 3:
EDUCATION AND ACCESS: OPENING THE DOORS TO KNOWLEDGE

"When you educate a woman, you educate a nation."
— African Proverb

Education has always been both a place of exclusion and a tool of liberation. For women, the right to learn – and to use knowledge as a path to equality – was one of the most contested and transformative struggles of the twentieth century. To understand how education became a cornerstone of women's progress, we must trace its evolution from the postwar years to the present, following the global arc of reform, resistance, and resilience.

The Postwar Landscape: 1950s to 1960s

In the aftermath of World War II, education systems around the world were being rebuilt. In the United States, the GI Bill expanded access to higher education, but largely for men, reinforcing gender disparities. Women were funneled toward teaching, nursing, or domestic sciences – fields seen as "appropriate" extensions of their roles at home. In Western Europe, education reforms expanded secondary and university access, but gender tracking persisted, steering young women into limited career paths.

Meanwhile, in newly independent nations across Asia and Africa, education became a symbol of national renewal. In India, Prime Minister Jawaharlal Nehru's government established new universities and technical institutes, and activists like Savitribai Phule's intellectual descendants carried her legacy by advocating for girls' schools, particularly in rural regions. In Ghana and other parts of Africa emerging from colonial rule, leaders recognized that women's education was essential for building new democratic societies. Yet deeply ingrained cultural and economic barriers meant progress was uneven, with urban girls often advancing faster than those in rural areas.

Expanding Rights: 1970s to 1980s

The global women's rights movements of the 1970s pushed education to the forefront. In the United States, Title IX (1972) banned sex discrimination in federally funded education, opening new pathways in academics and athletics alike. Across Latin America – where authoritarian regimes curtailed civil liberties – education became a form of political resistance: clandestine literacy circles doubled as civic training, rights education, and organizing hubs. In Chile and Brazil, women's groups ran parish- and neighborhood-based programs that taught reading and writing alongside how to document abuses, coordinate mutual aid, and plan safe protests – classrooms that quietly seeded the networks that later helped challenge dictatorship.

In parts of Africa, activists like Graça Machel in Mozambique linked women's education to national development by pairing adult literacy classes with maternal health visits and agricultural co-ops – so a village session might end with a reading primer, a vaccination appointment, and a plan for the next market day. Similarly, in South Korea and Japan, rapid industrial growth spurred governments to expand girls' secondary and university places; yet hiring tracks often channeled women into clerical "office lady" roles or school-to-factory pipelines, with strong norms to quit at marriage – expanding credentials but narrowing the path to leadership.

Breaking Boundaries: 1990s to 2000s

By the late twentieth century, education reform had become a global priority. The 1990 World Conference on Education for All in Jomtien, Thailand, set international goals for universal primary education, with special emphasis on reducing the gender gap. In many countries, grassroots initiatives filled gaps where government programs fell short. For example, in Bangladesh, the BRAC movement launched non-formal schools that educated millions of girls who had been excluded from traditional schooling.

By the early 2000s, women were a majority of university students in countries such as Argentina and Mexico, yet fields remained sharply gendered: women clustered in education, nursing, psychology, social work, and communications, while men dominated banking, engineering (civil, mechanical, petroleum), computer science, physics, and programs tied to construction and mining. Even in medicine and law, women's numbers thinned in surgical specialties, economics, and senior academic posts. I felt those currents personally: in the 1970s, when it was my turn to choose a career, Jenny, my sweet and loving mother, urged me toward teaching – the expected path for women then. I chose international banking instead; after earning my MBA from the University of Massachusetts, I joined Bank of America's International Department as a Corporate Lending Officer – a career that served me well throughout my professional life.

The Contemporary Moment: 2010s to Present

Today, women's access to education is higher than at any point in history, yet stark inequalities remain. In the United States and Europe, women now outnumber men in higher education, but the "STEM gap" continues to limit their presence in science and technology fields. Globally, UNESCO reports show that girls' primary school enrollment has nearly reached parity with boys, but regions of Sub-Saharan Africa, South Asia, and the Middle East still face persistent barriers – from child marriage to conflict-driven displacement.

Activists and educators have responded with creativity and urgency. The global advocacy of Malala Yousafzai – who survived a Taliban attack and went on to win the Nobel Peace Prize – has reignited worldwide commitment to girls' education. Meanwhile, digital platforms have expanded specific kinds of learning: adult literacy and numeracy; secondary school catch-up courses; English and digital skills; coding, data, and bookkeeping certificates; health worker and teacher training; and entrepreneurship and financial literacy modules. In remote or underserved areas, WhatsApp/SMS tutoring, downloadable offline lessons, radio classes, and community Wi-Fi hubs let women study after work or childcare and sit for recognized exams and micro-credentials – bridging gaps that once seemed insurmountable.

Looking Ahead

The story of women's education is one of undeniable progress but also unfinished work. The postwar vision of limited opportunity has given way to unprecedented access, yet systemic barriers – economic inequality, cultural norms, and political instability – continue to close doors for millions of women worldwide. To open those doors fully, education must be seen not just as a right but as a foundation for equality in every sphere of life.

The Shifting Landscape: From Primary School to PhDs

In countries like Sweden, the United Kingdom, and the United States, new policies expanded access to public education for girls. Secondary education enrollment began to climb, and more women pursued college degrees than ever before. The U.S. GI Bill indirectly supported this shift by freeing up men to attend university, which over time necessitated more infrastructure and eventually included more women.

In developing nations, the push for girls' education

became linked with national progress. The United Nations and UNESCO began to emphasize literacy programs for women, recognizing the far-reaching social benefits: lower infant mortality, higher family incomes, and more stable communities.

Still, the barriers were formidable – especially for rural girls, ethnic minorities, and those living under authoritarian regimes. Schools remained distant, poorly funded, or explicitly patriarchal. Some governments, fearing the "radicalization" of women, censored educational content or punished those who pushed for reform.

Yet women persisted. And educators – many of them women themselves – began changing not just who learned but what was taught.

Education as Liberation

For women's movements around the world, education became central to the fight for rights. Knowledge wasn't just power – it was defense, offense, and a means of collective organization. Feminist consciousness-raising groups, study circles, and women's colleges offered more than instruction – they offered transformation.

In the United States, women's studies departments began appearing in universities in the early 1970s, providing a platform for interrogating the male-centered curriculum and developing a more inclusive approach to history, literature, economics, and sociology. This was mirrored in Europe, Canada, and Australia.

In Latin America, popular education movements – such as those inspired by Brazilian educator Paulo Freire – taught women to read not only words but the "world," challenging traditional hierarchies and encouraging participation in social change.

In Africa and Asia, local women-led initiatives brought learning to communities neglected by colonial or national institutions. These efforts often wove together literacy, health education, and political awareness in ways that were culturally rooted and community driven.

Education was no longer just about textbooks; it was about consciousness, agency, and belonging.

When Girls Learn, Societies Thrive

One of the most well-documented truths of the twentieth century is that when girls are educated, entire societies benefit. Educated women marry later, have fewer children, and participate more in civic life. Their children are healthier, and their families are more resilient.

Economists, sociologists, and development experts have all confirmed what activists already knew: access to education is the single most powerful lever for female empowerment.

Yet, despite this, the struggle continues. In many parts of the world – even today – girls still face forced marriage, limited schooling, and systemic inequality. The post-war period marked incredible progress, but it also revealed how fragile that progress can be without vigilance and commitment.

The Women Who Opened the Doors

None of these changes happened by accident. Teachers, policymakers, activists, and ordinary mothers campaigned for girls' education. They raised funds, built schools, defied laws, and taught their daughters to dream beyond the boundaries imposed on them.

Women like Malala Yousafzai's mother, Ziauddin, fought for girls' schools in rural Pakistan. In the U.S., figures like Shirley Chisholm – the first Black woman elected to Congress – championed education equity as a tool for liberation. In Kenya, Wangari Maathai insisted that environmental sustainability and female literacy must go hand in hand.

Each step forward was paved by countless untold stories – of women learning under candlelight, walking miles to reach classrooms, and teaching others what they had barely learned themselves.

Education and Access: Opening the Doors to Knowledge

The mid-twentieth century witnessed a quiet revolution, one that began not on the canvas or in the gallery, but in classrooms, workshops, and art schools. As societies reckoned with inequality and the legacies of colonialism, women artists increasingly turned their focus toward education – as both learners and leaders. In doing so, they expanded access to knowledge, redefined who could be an artist, and laid the groundwork for new feminist and multicultural frameworks in the arts.

This chapter follows the women who used teaching, mentorship, and institutional reform as creative tools – those who viewed access to knowledge as a fundamental right, not a privilege.

Anni Albers, trained at the Bauhaus and later a key figure at Black Mountain College in the United States, transformed textile arts into a language of modernist innovation. Barred from the Bauhaus's painting workshop because she was a woman, Albers turned to weaving and elevated it into a serious and experimental practice. At Black Mountain, she taught generations of students to see structure and thread as conceptually rich and intellectually rigorous. Her writings and curriculum reshaped art education globally and gave voice to a medium long dismissed as "women's work."

Corita Kent, a Catholic nun turned pop artist and educator, revolutionized the Immaculate Heart College art department in Los Angeles during the 1960s. Her printmaking combined vivid color, typography, and political messages drawn from civil rights, anti-war movements, and spiritual teachings. Kent taught her students that art could be a tool for social change and encouraged them to see beauty every day. Her innovative pedagogy blended joy, protest, and devotion, breaking down barriers between art and activism.

Faith Ringgold, an artist, author, and activist, used storytelling and education as tools for empowerment. Her story quilts, like *Tar Beach*, combined painting, fabric, and narrative to explore themes of race, family, and Black girlhood. As a professor, Ringgold challenged institutions to include African American artists in their canons and curricula. Through her children's books and classroom presence, she nurtured future artists by showing that their stories, too, belonged in the center of art history.

In Japan, Yayoi Kusama's art school education was a springboard to a career that defied convention. Though her early instructors tried to suppress her avant-garde impulses, she persisted, moving to New York in the 1950s and developing a visual language that merged repetition, obsession, and personal trauma. Kusama's installations and performances later became spaces of experiential learning, where audiences confronted infinity, selfhood, and mental health. Her foundation in Japan continues to fund educational programs for young artists, reinforcing her commitment to accessibility.

Lygia Clark, a Brazilian artist and educator, broke down the boundaries between art and life. Her later work focused on participatory experiences and therapeutic exercises, viewing the viewer as co-creator. As a teacher at the Sorbonne, Clark developed "relational objects" and sensory-based practices that influenced contemporary art education. She taught that the body was not just a tool of perception but a source of creation.

Judy Chicago, a pioneer of feminist art education, created the first Feminist Art Program in the United States, first at Fresno State and later at CalArts. Her collaborative projects, such as *Womanhouse* and *The Dinner Party*, emerged directly from this educational ethos. Chicago's curriculum emphasized consciousness-raising, collaborative production, and a critique of patriarchal structures. She taught women to make art about their own lives – and insisted the world take it seriously.

In South Africa, Esther Mahlangu, a Ndebele artist, has turned her traditional knowledge into a platform for cultural education. Her vividly painted geometric murals –

rooted in a heritage passed from mother to daughter – have adorned everything from gallery walls to BMWs. But Mahlangu is not only a practicing artist; she has opened an art school in her home village to ensure the transmission of Ndebele techniques to future generations. For Mahlangu, education is preservation.

Mildred Thompson, an African American artist and teacher, worked across disciplines – painting, printmaking, music – to explore scientific and metaphysical themes. After years of working in Europe due to racial barriers in the U.S., she returned to teach at institutions like Spelman College, where she mentored young Black artists to think expansively about abstraction and identity. Her lessons fused rigor with curiosity, encouraging students to experiment without apology.

In India, Nasreen Mohamedi taught at the Maharaja Sayajirao University in Baroda, where her minimalist ink drawings inspired a generation of Indian artists. Though quiet in demeanor and often working in isolation, her classroom was a space of radical freedom. Mohamedi's teachings emphasized restraint, rhythm, and introspection – lessons that transcended the visual and reached into the philosophical.

These educators, in their studios and classrooms, reshaped the very foundations of the art world. They questioned who could be taught, what could be taught, how teaching itself could become an act of liberation, and where learning could happen – from kitchen tables and union halls to community centers and museum studios after hours.

Their classrooms extended far beyond walls – into streets, galleries, books, quilts, rituals, and digital archives. They opened doors for others while creating pathways for themselves.

Through education, they did not just teach technique. They taught power, presence, and possibility.

A detailed listing of Female Pioneers in Access and Reform (Post-WWII Era) is provided in Appendix I.

Voices of Defiance

Education has long been a battleground where power, opportunity, and equality are either withheld or unlocked. For women around the world, the pursuit of learning was often met with closed doors, cultural resistance, and systemic exclusion. Yet, time and again, women broke through – demanding access not just for themselves, but for generations to follow. Their words reflect the urgency, resilience, and unshakable belief that knowledge is a right, not a privilege. These voices echo from classrooms, courtrooms, and protest lines, reminding us that education is the foundation of freedom.

"Until we get equality in education, we won't have an equal society."
— Sonia Sotomayor,
U.S. Supreme Court Justice, *My Beloved World*, 2013

As the first Latina Supreme Court Justice, Sotomayor's journey from a Bronx housing project to the nation's highest court underscores the transformative power of education.

"No woman can call herself free who does not own and control her own body. No woman can call herself free until she can choose consciously whether she will or will not be a mother."
— Margaret Sanger, 1920

While controversial, Sanger's advocacy for women's education about their own bodies laid the early groundwork for sexual health literacy and reproductive freedom.

"I believe that education is the single most powerful tool we can use to change the world."

— Oprah Winfrey, educator and philanthropist

Winfrey's personal story – from poverty to global influence – makes her commitment to educating girls in South Africa a continuation of her belief in dignity through learning.

In conclusion, education did more than open doors for women; it unlocked worlds, proving that knowledge is the most enduring form of power.

Reflection Prompt

1. Historical Context: What surprised you most about the early struggles women faced in gaining access to education? How do those struggles mirror or differ from the educational barriers girls face today in other parts of the world?

2. Personal Experience: How has access to education shaped your own life or the lives of women you know? Were there key moments when access – or lack of access – played a decisive role?

3. Global Perspective: In many developing countries, girls still struggle to attend and complete school. What responsibilities do more privileged societies have in supporting global education efforts for girls and women?

4. Call to Action: What are some tangible actions you can take – locally or globally – to promote educational equity for women and girls? How can education be used as a tool for breaking cycles of poverty and oppression?

CHAPTER 4:
TITLE IX, U.S. LEGAL REFORMS, AND THE TRANSFORMATION OF WOMEN'S SPORTS

"Champions keep playing until they get it right."
— Billie Jean King

When Title IX was signed into law in 1972, it revolutionized women's sports in the United States. By prohibiting sex-based discrimination in federally funded educational programs, it required schools and universities to provide equal opportunities for women in athletics. The results were dramatic. High school girls' participation rose from under 300,000 in 1972 to more than 3.4 million today, while athletic scholarships opened doors to college and professional sports. Scholarships became a pathway to higher education and professional sports careers.

Title IX reshaped the American athletic landscape. It also sent a powerful message: that equity in sport is not a privilege granted at will, but a right guaranteed by law.

What Is Title IX?

At its heart, Title IX is a single sentence with extraordinary consequences:

"No person in the United States shall, on the basis of sex, be excluded from participation in, be denied the benefits of, or be subjected to discrimination under any education program or activity receiving federal financial assistance."

Although not originally drafted with athletics in mind, its application to sports became one of its most visible and transformative arenas. Because nearly all educational institutions receive federal funding, they are now required to provide equal opportunities in everything from team offerings to facilities, coaching, and scholarships.

Title IX opened the door, making access non-negotiable.

Resistance and Pushback

The backlash was immediate. Critics claimed Title IX would "ruin" men's sports, especially non-revenue teams at smaller colleges. Others insisted that women simply weren't interested in competing at the same level as men, framing investment in women's athletics as wasteful.

But activists, athletes, and advocates fought back. Bernice Sandler, often called the "Godmother of Title IX," worked tirelessly to clarify and enforce the law. Donna de Varona, an Olympic swimming champion, and Billie Jean King, a tennis legend, used their public platforms to rally support. Legal challenges and compliance battles stretched into the 1980s, but the women's movement was prepared — armed with lawsuits, advocacy campaigns, and grassroots pressure.

The result was not the demise of men's sports; instead of destroying men's sports, Title IX unlocked a generation of women's opportunities.

When Title IX was signed into law in 1972, it did more than guarantee equal access to athletic fields and locker rooms — it unlocked a revolution. The law turned gymnasiums, stadiums, and courts into arenas where women could prove their power, skill, and determination.

Billie Jean King and the "Battle of the Sexes"

One year after Title IX, on September 20, 1973, Billie Jean King faced Bobby Riggs at the Houston Astrodome;

an estimated 90 million viewers watched her win 6–4, 6–3, 6–3 – a cultural inflection point that affirmed women athletes as equals and propelled her push for equal pay and the co-founding of the Women's Tennis Association.

Cheryl Miller and College Basketball's Explosion

In the 1980s, Cheryl Miller turned USC women's basketball into appointment viewing – back-to-back NCAA titles (1983 to '84), packed arenas, an '84 Olympic gold, and highlight reels leading sports segments. Fueled by Title IX–era scholarships, travel budgets, and training resources, she and her teammates played a fast-break, pressure-defense style that felt unmistakably big-time. It became a cultural turning point, proving to sponsors and broadcasters that women's sports could command prime time and equal respect.

The 1999 U.S. Women's World Cup Victory

On a hot July day in 1999, more than 90,000 fans packed the Rose Bowl in Pasadena for the Women's World Cup Final. After 120 scoreless minutes, the U.S. defeated China 54 in a penalty shootout, with Brandi Chastain converting the decisive kick – and her celebratory jersey strip becoming an indelible image of women's empowerment. The victory was a direct outgrowth of Title IX, which had built a generation of female athletes ready for the global stage; it also helped spur investment in professional women's soccer and proved women's sports could fill stadiums.

Global Echoes: From Brazil to Nigeria

While the U.S. had Title IX, women around the world fought their battles for access. In Brazil, women were banned from playing football until 1979, yet stars like Marta Vieira da Silva rose to global prominence, forcing institutions to recognize women's talent. In Nigeria, the Super Falcons women's national team became a continental powerhouse, winning championships and challenging the idea that sport was men's territory alone. These global stories show that the demand for equality in sport has many expressions but one shared spirit.

The Larger Pattern

From King's symbolic victory to Miller's collegiate dominance, from the World Cup triumph to grassroots battles across continents, women's sports have moved from the margins to the mainstream. Title IX was a catalyst, but the global transformation rests on women insisting that sport is about more than games. It is about justice, visibility, and dignity. Title IX also showed that when women are given the chance to play, they learn to lead.

A New Era for Girls and Women in Sports

The statistics tell the story:

- By 1980, girls' high school sports participation had quadrupled.
- By 1990, it topped 2 million.
- Today, it's over 3.4 million, with hundreds of thousands competing in college.

Athletic scholarships opened pathways to higher education that were once unthinkable for women. Entire athletic departments began investing in women's programs, creating a pipeline not just for athletes but for coaches, trainers, administrators, and sports media professionals.

Title IX's ripple effect extended far beyond the playing field; it created a generation of female leaders in business, politics, and culture who often credit their confidence, resilience, and teamwork to athletics.

Cultural Impact

Title IX didn't just change opportunities; it changed perceptions. Joyner-Kersee, Hamm, Williams, and Biles redefined excellence, turning sport into a stage for power and inspiration. Americans recalibrated what women could achieve.

The 1999 U.S. Women's Soccer World Cup victory – watched by more than 90,000 in the stadium and millions more on television – was widely seen as a "Title IX moment," the culmination of decades of investment that turned girls who had grown up with equal sports access into world champions.

Professional leagues soon followed, from the WNBA to the National Women's Soccer League, giving women opportunities to compete and be recognized at the highest levels.

Pioneering Figures of the Title IX Era

- Billie Jean King – Tennis champion, equal pay advocate, and co-founder of the Women's Tennis Association, whose "Battle of the Sexes" victory in 1973 symbolized the growing power of women athletes.

- Wilma Rudolph – Overcame polio to win three Olympic golds in 1960, paving the way for Black female athletes before Title IX and inspiring those who would follow.

- Pat Summitt – Legendary University of Tennessee coach whose over 1,000 wins brought women's basketball national respect and visibility.

- Cheryl Miller – NCAA basketball star in the 1980s who elevated women's college sports with her dominance and charisma.

- Mia Hamm – Soccer icon and 1999 World Cup champion, whose career reflected Title IX's promise fulfilled.

- Flo Hyman – Volleyball star and outspoken advocate for gender equity in Olympic sports.

- Donna de Varona – Co-founder of the Women's Sports Foundation, tireless defender of Title IX in policy and media.

- Nancy Lieberman – One of the first female athletes to benefit from scholarships, later a pioneer in professional play and coaching.

- Sarah Fuller – In 2020, became the first woman to play and score in a Power Five college football game, showing how far Title IX's influence has reached.

Each of these women carried forward the spirit of Title IX. When access expands, excellence follows.

Beyond Sports: Broader Implications

Though athletics became its most visible battleground, Title IX's reach extended further. It laid the groundwork for broader gender equity in education, including protections against sexual harassment and assault in schools and colleges. In this way, it has helped redefine not only what women could play, but what they could expect.

The Work Ahead

Despite its transformative impact, disparities remain:

- Women's sports receive only about 5 percent of total sports media coverage in the U.S.

- Female athletes are consistently paid less and offered fewer sponsorships than their male peers.

- Women remain underrepresented in coaching and sports administration – in 2024, women held about 45 percent of NCAA Division I head-coach roles for women's teams and only 16 percent of Division I athletic director posts.

New debates – such as policies on transgender athletes

– test the law's evolving meaning, reflecting ongoing tensions about inclusion and fairness.

The story of Title IX is one of extraordinary progress, but also unfinished business. It taught the world that gender equity in sport is possible when guaranteed by law. The next challenge is ensuring that opportunity is matched by visibility, respect, and true equality.

For a more complete list of Women Who Changed Sports and Equity Through Title IX, see Appendix I.

Voices of Defiance

For generations, women were told that sports were not for them – that competition was unladylike, unnecessary, even dangerous. But the passage of Title IX in 1972 cracked open the gates of the athletic world. With sweat, skill, and relentless determination, women began to take the field, the court, the track – not just to play, but to claim equality. These voices capture the fight for access, the joy of victory, and the courage to challenge a culture that long excluded them. In sports, as in life, they proved that opportunity changes everything – and they were never going back.

> *"Somewhere behind the athlete you've become and the hours of practice… is a little girl who fell in love with the game and never looked back."*
>
> — Mia Hamm,
> U.S. Soccer legend and two-time Olympic gold medalist

Mia Hamm inspired a generation by turning passion into performance – and by showing young girls that they belonged on the world stage.

> *"I think that Title IX is the most important piece of legislation for women in this country."*
>
> — Billie Jean King,
> tennis champion and activist

More than a tennis icon, King used her platform to advocate for equity in sports and education, championing Title

IX's transformative power.

> *"We have to teach our girls that they*
> *can reach as high as humanly possible."*

— Serena Williams, tennis champion

Williams broke records and defied expectations – not just in tennis, but in how society views power, motherhood, and grace under pressure. "With each whistle and each barrier shattered, Title IX proved that when women are given the chance to play, they learn to lead. The work now is matching opportunity with visibility, respect, and real equality."

Reflection Prompts

1. Historical Impact: How did the introduction of Title IX reshape societal expectations about women's physical abilities, leadership, and competitiveness? In what ways did it challenge traditional gender roles?

2. Personal Connection: Have you or someone you know been personally impacted by Title IX in sports, education, or career opportunities? What was the outcome?

3. Global Comparison: How do opportunities for female athletes in the United States (post–Title IX) compare with those in other countries without similar legislation? What lessons can be learned or shared globally?

4. Advocacy and Accountability: Title IX is only effective if it is enforced. What can individuals, schools, and communities do to ensure compliance and continued progress toward gender equity in sports and education?

CHAPTER 5:
OPENING DOORS: EARLY
POLITICAL BREAKTHROUGHS

"Early women leaders did not inherit power; they carved space where none existed, leaving behind a blueprint of courage for those who would follow."

— Maria L. Ellis

A New Political Era

After World War II, women didn't just enter politics. They changed its rhythm. While suffrage had been secured in many countries by the mid-twentieth century, meaningful representation remained elusive. For decades, women's names rarely appeared on ballots, and even more rarely in positions of national leadership. Yet step by step, women began to break through, carving out political space that reshaped democracies across the world.

The First Elected Voices

In the United States, Margaret Chase Smith became the first woman elected to both the House and the Senate (1940 to 1973). In 1950, she delivered her "Declaration of Conscience," denouncing "the Four Horsemen of Calumny — Fear, Ignorance, Bigotry, and Smear." Her stand in the McCarthy era showed what independent authority looked like.

Momentum gathered globally.

In 1960, Sirimavo Bandaranaike of Ceylon (Sri Lanka)

became the world's first female prime minister, shattering assumptions about women's ability to lead nations. Soon after, Indira Gandhi rose to power in India, serving as prime minister for over a decade and shaping both domestic policy and international relations.

These early figures were trailblazers, often navigating extraordinary resistance, but their leadership signaled that the era of male-only politics was ending.

The Rise of Women in Parliaments

In the late twentieth century, women's representation in parliaments grew steadily. In Scandinavia, political parties introduced quota systems, dramatically increasing female participation. By the 1970s, Sweden and Norway had some of the highest proportions of women legislators in the world, laying the groundwork for gender equality policies that became models internationally.

In the United States, progress was slower, but the women's rights movement of the 1960s and 1970s pushed more women into local and state offices. Trailblazers like Shirley Chisholm, elected in 1968 as the first Black woman to Congress, challenged both racial and gender barriers. Chisholm's 1972 presidential campaign, though unsuccessful, broke ground and inspired generations to follow.

Political Power and Policy Impact

As women gained seats, they influenced agendas. Women legislators pushed childcare, healthcare access, education, and workplace protections to the center. Their advocacy reframed policy debates, proving that representation is substantive, not symbolic.

The United Nations' International Women's Year in 1975, followed by the UN Decade for Women, spotlighted global inequalities and mobilized governments to act. Conferences in Mexico City, Copenhagen, and Nairobi amplified women's political voices and created a transnational dialogue that fueled progress.

Breaking Executive Glass Ceilings

By the late twentieth century, women were not only legislators but heads of government. Beyond Bandaranaike and Gandhi, leaders like Golda Meir in Israel and Margaret Thatcher in the United Kingdom showed that women could hold the highest offices over time. While each embodied different ideologies and leadership styles, their elections shattered the notion that women could not command political power on the world stage.

Setting the Stage for the Twenty-First Century

The breakthroughs of the mid-to-late twentieth century did not come easily, nor did they immediately dismantle entrenched systems of male power. But they opened doors. Women moved from being token figures to recognized political actors whose presence altered policy, institutions, and global expectations.

The foundations built in this era created the conditions for the transformations – and setbacks – that would mark the twenty-first century. As we will see in Chapter 19, the struggle for equality in political representation continues, but the ground gained in these early decades made the fight possible.

For centuries, politics was framed as the preserve of men – whether in parliaments, presidencies, or party leadership. Women were expected to influence quietly, if at all, from behind the scenes. Yet since the mid-twentieth century, women have entered political office in unprecedented numbers, altering not just who sits at the table, but what gets discussed when power is exercised.

This chapter examines how women leaders have changed institutions – not simply by their presence, but by redefining priorities, reshaping policy, and broadening the meaning of representation.

Breaking Barriers: Symbolic Firsts

The arrival of women into top political roles carried

symbolic power but also triggered institutional shifts.

Indira Gandhi, elected Prime Minister of India in 1966, demonstrated that women could command the largest democracy in the world. Her centralization of power and foreign policy maneuvers made her one of the most formidable Cold War figures. Yet her controversial declaration of Emergency (1975 to 1977) revealed that women, like men, could wield power in authoritarian ways.

Margaret Thatcher, the United Kingdom's first woman Prime Minister (1979), reshaped the British state through economic liberalization and a combative leadership style. Her tenure proved that women could dominate political life at the highest level, though critics argued her policies did little to advance women collectively.

These firsts proved women could ascend. They also raised a deeper question: Does individual success translate into institutional transformation? The answer lies in distinguishing symbolic breakthroughs from systemic change – and measuring shifts in rules, budgets, and leadership pipelines, not just who stands at the podium.

From Presence to Power

- Women's political leadership reveals a dual lesson. On one hand, electing women does not guarantee feminist outcomes – leaders like Gandhi and Thatcher prove that women, like men, are shaped by ideology and circumstance. On the other hand, when women's presence becomes widespread and institutionalized – as in Rwanda or the Nordic states – political culture itself shifts.

- The question is no longer whether women can lead. The pressing challenge is how institutions can evolve so that women's leadership translates into equity, justice, and durable reform.

The Power Gap: Historical Roots of Exclusion

Until the mid-twentieth century, few women in the world held formal political power. In many countries, they lacked the right to vote, let alone run for office. Political participation was seen as a male duty – an extension of manhood, intellect, and rationality. Women were expected to serve the nation through the private sphere: raising children, maintaining homes, and supporting husbands.

But World War II mobilization, the U.S. Civil Rights Movement of the 1950s to 60s, and the wave of anti-colonial struggles from Ghana to India – alongside the expansion of higher education (including Title IX in 1972) – began to erode that belief. As women moved onto factory floors and into newsrooms, classrooms, and laboratories – and organized through churches, unions, and student groups – they demanded seats in the political institutions that shaped their lives.

Still, barriers remained from cultural stereotypes, discriminatory laws, lack of party support, limited access to campaign financing, and the persistent belief that women weren't "tough enough" for politics.

Cracking the Glass Ceiling: Milestones from the 1980s to 2000s

The late twentieth century marked a series of breakthroughs. Women began rising in political ranks – not just as symbols, but as serious contenders and effective leaders.

- **Margaret Thatcher** became Prime Minister of the UK in 1979, the first woman to lead a major Western democracy.
- **Benazir Bhutto** became the first female Prime Minister of a Muslim-majority country, Pakistan, in 1988.
- **Corazon Aquino** rose to the Philippine presidency in 1986, leading a peaceful revolution.

- **Gro Harlem Brundtland** of Norway, elected Prime Minister in 1981, became a global voice for sustainable development and gender equality.

- In the U.S., **Geraldine Ferraro** became the first woman nominated for Vice President by a major party in 1984.

Representation Matters: The Power of Visibility

When women hold political office, they bring different lived experiences, priorities, and leadership styles to the table. Studies show that female lawmakers are more likely to advocate for education, healthcare, child welfare, and gender-based violence prevention. They also tend to work more collaboratively across party lines and are often more attuned to marginalized voices in their constituencies.

Just as importantly, female political leaders serve as civic signals – especially to girls watching. They show that leadership means steering a country's course: setting budgets, appointing judges, negotiating treaties, and writing laws; it also means claiming one's own destiny and shouldering the rights and responsibilities of citizenship. By doing so, they expand the imagination of what is possible – and who gets to decide it.

When Ellen Johnson Sirleaf became President of Liberia in 2006 – the first elected female head of state in Africa – she helped steer the country out of civil war, secured debt relief, and built institutions that invited women into public life. Angela Merkel governed Germany for sixteen years with a different register of power – steady, data-driven crisis management rather than theatrics. In 2008, she went on television with her finance minister to guarantee bank deposits, calming panic during the financial crisis. In 2011, after Fukushima, she brokered a cross-party nuclear phase-out and redirected energy policy. In 2015, she held a humane line during the refugee crisis – "Wir schaffen das" – while negotiating European burden-sharing. In 2020, the trained physicist explained exponential spread and the R-number in plain language, building public compliance without alarm.

And in 2008, when Hillary Clinton ran a competitive race for the Democratic nomination – and again in 2016 as the first woman to lead a major party's ticket – the change was measurable: a woman could raise national money, win 18 million primary votes, carry big states, secure the nomination, and win the popular vote by nearly three million. The resistance was just as visible: gendered scrutiny over "likability" and "tone," chants of "Lock her up," the "nasty woman" moment – and the enduring fact that the United States has yet to elect a woman president.

Challenges Within the System

Despite these gains, women in politics still face formidable challenges.

- **Underrepresentation**: As of 2000, women held only about 13 percent of parliamentary seats worldwide. That number has improved, but parity is far from achieved.

- **Sexism and harassment**: Female candidates often endure gendered criticism, media bias, and threats of violence at higher rates than men.

- **Double standards**: Women are often expected to appear strong but not aggressive, smart but not intimidating, likable but not "too ambitious."

- **Work-life balance pressures**: Political life often involves long hours, travel, and public scrutiny – demands that collide with family responsibilities disproportionately carried by women.

These barriers fall hardest on women of color, LGBTQ+ women, Indigenous women, and women from lower-income backgrounds. For women of color, party gatekeeping and "electability" bias often mean higher credential bars and less early money, alongside racialized online abuse that chills speech. Indigenous candidates contend with distant polling sites, ID/address rules that can disenfranchise reservation voters, and jurisdictional hurdles when organizing on tribal lands. LGBTQ+ women face doxxing, threats, and media fixation on identity rather than policy. Candidates without wealth run into filing fees, unpaid campaign time, childcare costs, and thin donor networks, making a run financially risky. In practice, intersectionality looks like this: the same barriers – fundraising, media bias, voter access – cut deeper when race, sexuality, indigeneity, and class overlap.

Building Momentum: Grassroots to Global Impact

While national office draws the spotlight, many of the fastest, most tangible gains have come from women leading locally. On school boards and city councils, they hold the levers that shape daily life – zoning codes and building permits, water and sanitation contracts, school budgets, bus routes, policing protocols, and procurement. That proximity lets them act quickly and with detail: funding twenty-four-hour domestic-violence intake, mandating lead testing in schools and pipes, directing dollars to after-school programs, rewriting eviction rules, and green-lighting mixed-income housing near transit. Because they meet constituents in PTA meetings, clinic waiting rooms, church basements, and neighborhood councils, they pair granular data with trust – turning problems into policy.

Organizations such as EMILY's List, She Should Run, and the Center for American Women and Politics have helped train, fund, and support women candidates across the political spectrum. Meanwhile, countries like Rwanda, Iceland, and Finland have implemented gender quotas or parity laws, resulting in some of the world's highest levels of female parliamentary representation.

The global rise of feminist foreign policy, gender-responsive budgeting, and intergovernmental gender equity frameworks shows that this shift isn't isolated – it's part of a broader rethinking of governance and justice.

The Road Forward

As we move further into the twenty-first century, women are redefining power – not just occupying positions but reimagining the systems themselves. They're demanding accountability, transparency, compassion, and inclusion. They're running not only for office but for *impact*.

Progress has not been linear, and backlash is real. But the women who have entered the political arena – whether as firsts, pioneers, or part of growing waves – have expanded what's possible for everyone.

Because when women gain seats, budgets and laws change: Childcare and clean water move up the agenda; domestic-violence prevention gets funded; oversight tightens; and services reach the neighborhoods that need them most.

These women did not simply join politics – they remade it. Their victories were not always electoral; sometimes, just being present in rooms where decisions were made was revolutionary.

They proved that representation matters, but that presence alone isn't enough – policy must reflect the people it serves.

Their stories remind us that leadership isn't about likeness or legacy. It's about courage, clarity, and commitment to the public good.

For a more complete list of pioneers and changemakers (1980s to 2000s), see Appendix II.

Voices of Defiance

Politics has long been the stronghold of male power – structured, gatekept, and protected by centuries of exclusion. But determined women across the globe rose to challenge this status quo, demanding not only a seat at the table but the power to reshape the table itself. These leaders navigated hostility, broke historical barriers, and redefined what leadership could look like. Their words speak to boldness, resilience, and the unshakable belief that democracy is incomplete without the voices of women. In every campaign, protest, and policy battle, they proved that representation is not a privilege – it's a right.

"When they go low, we go high."
— Michelle Obama,
Democratic National Convention speech, 2016

With poise and clarity, Michelle Obama reminded the world that moral leadership is its own form of power – and one women have always carried with strength and grace.

*"Women belong in all places where decisions are being made.
It shouldn't be that women are the exception."*
— Ruth Bader Ginsburg,
Associate Justice of the U.S. Supreme Court

Ginsburg's quiet tenacity and sharp intellect reshaped the legal landscape – and inspired generations of women to pursue justice from the bench to the ballot. "I do not wish for [women] to have power over men; but over themselves."

*"You may not be interested in politics,
but politics is interested in you."*
— Pericles, as often quoted by Alexandria Ocasio-Cortez

This quote, revived by modern leaders like AOC, captures the reality that disengagement is a luxury – one many women have never been afforded.

In conclusion, as women moved from the margins to the chambers of power, they redefined not only who leads but how leadership itself is measured.

Reflection Prompts

1. Historical Progress: Which political figures or movements stood out to you as pivotal in advancing women's rights and representation?

What risks did they take, and what legacies did they leave?

2. Barriers to Entry: What are some of the obstacles that still keep women – especially from marginalized communities – out of political office? What strategies or reforms might help address these barriers?

3. Global Context: Compare the political representation of women in different countries. What lessons can be learned from nations that have achieved gender parity – or made significant strides – in political leadership?

4. Call to Action: If you were mentoring a young woman interested in politics, what advice would you offer her? What do you believe is the most important contribution women can make in political life today?

CHAPTER 6:
ECONOMIC EMPOWERMENT
– FROM DOMESTIC WORK
TO CORPORATE LEADERSHIP

"A woman's place is in the boardroom."
— Sheryl Sandberg

The end of World War II left women at a crossroads. During the war years, they had stepped into factories, shipyards, and offices, sustaining industries while men fought overseas. When the war ended, many were told to relinquish their positions and return to the home. Yet something had shifted. Having experienced independence, wages, and the dignity of professional contribution, millions of women were reluctant to retreat entirely into domestic life. By the early 1950s, women were re-entering the workforce in growing numbers, though most often funneled into clerical, teaching, and service-sector jobs that mirrored the social expectations of the time.

Despite the restrictions, the seeds of long-term change were sown. By 1960, more than a third of American women were active in the workforce, and their presence would only grow in the decades to follow. The paradox of postwar America was clear: while cultural norms celebrated the suburban homemaker, the economy was increasingly reliant on women's labor.

The "Pink-Collar" Economy

The 1950s and 1960s saw an explosion of "pink-collar" work – teaching, nursing, retail, and office administration. These jobs kept society running yet offered limited mobility and far less pay than comparable men's roles. In offices, secretaries triaged switchboards, typed contracts from shorthand at ninety words a minute, booked travel, ran meeting calendars, and kept filing systems legible. Receptionists greeted clients, routed calls and telexes, and kept the front desk moving. Bookkeepers balanced ledgers by hand, reconciled inventories, and cut payroll checks on deadline. They kept the machinery of business humming – yet few were seen as candidates for management.

Nevertheless, women gained valuable skills and workplace experience during this period. Many viewed these roles as stepping stones, even if advancement was slow. For some, clerical jobs became a form of economic independence; for others, they served as training grounds for leadership that would emerge later.

Legal and Policy Breakthroughs

The 1960s ushered in a wave of laws that reshaped women's work – the Equal Pay Act (1963) and Title VII of the Civil Rights Act (1964) – and women quickly put them to use. In 1969, Lorena Weeks, a Georgia telephone operator denied a higher-paying "switchman" job under a rule barring women from lifting more than 30 pounds, won on appeal against Southern Bell, forcing the company to open the job and pay back wages – proof that the new statutes could pry open promotion ladders, not just make statements. The Equal Pay Act of 1963 was an early milestone, mandating equal pay for equal work – though enforcement lagged. Even more significant was the Civil Rights Act of 1964, particularly Title VII, which outlawed employment discrimination on the basis of sex, race, religion, and national origin.

These legal frameworks gave women tools to challenge

systemic barriers. Lawsuits brought against discriminatory employers, though difficult and slow-moving, began to create precedents that widened access to professional and managerial roles. For the first time, the notion of women as permanent participants in the labor force – not just temporary workers or wartime substitutes – was written into law.

Breaking the Glass Ceiling

By the 1970s, the phrase "glass ceiling" entered the cultural vocabulary, describing the invisible barriers that kept women from rising into senior management and executive ranks. The concept captured a frustrating reality: women were present in the workforce in unprecedented numbers, but few had ascended to positions of real decision-making power.

Still, there were pioneers who defied the odds. Katharine Graham became the first woman CEO of a Fortune 500 company when she took the helm of the Washington Post Company in 1972, guiding it through both Watergate and the Pentagon Papers. Carly Fiorina broke another barrier in 1999, becoming CEO of Hewlett-Packard, the first woman to lead a major American technology company. Ursula Burns, who rose from an intern at Xerox to become its CEO in 2009, became the first Black woman to lead a Fortune 500 firm.

Their stories illustrate both progress and persistence. Progress came at a cost: unpaid overtime, a second shift at home, and stalled pay while training the men promoted above them – yet together they widened boardrooms and reshaped what leadership looks like.

A Global Perspective

The movement toward female leadership was not confined to the United States. In Europe, women also made strides, often propelled by legislation that mandated inclusion. Norway introduced corporate board quotas in 2003, requiring companies to fill at least 40 percent of board seats with women – a bold move that reshaped governance practices across Scandinavia. Other European nations soon followed with their versions of quota laws, leading to a sharp rise in female board representation.

In contrast, the United States relied on market and cultural pressures rather than legal quotas – an approach rooted in a governance tradition that favors disclosure and shareholder activism over mandates and is shaped by constitutional/Title VII concerns about sex-based quotas. The result was slower but steady gains: by the early 2000s, American women still held under 20 percent of board seats at major corporations, compared with 40 percent+ in several Nordic countries that adopted statutory quotas. In Asia, progress varied widely: Japan and South Korea lagged despite government campaigns, while India accelerated change by requiring at least one-woman director on many listed company boards.

Persistent Barriers

Despite these breakthroughs, challenges remain. The gender pay gap persists; in 2024, women earned about 85 cents for every dollar men earned across all workers (and 83 percent among full-time, year-round workers in 2023). The "double burden" is measurable: in 2024, women spent 2.7 hours per day on household work versus 2.3 for men, and among households with children under 6, women provided 3.0 hours of primary childcare versus 2.0 for men. In corporate pipelines, the "broken rung" still blocks advancement: in 2024, for every 100 men promoted to manager, only 81 women were – and just 54 Black women.

Representation in STEM and finance – industries that often drive the highest-paying leadership positions – also lags. Women may now occupy C-suites, but they are still underrepresented in the most influential CEO and board chair roles.

The Twenty-First Century Workplace

The twenty-first century has seen renewed focus on diversity, equity, and inclusion. Companies increasingly recognize the business case for gender-diverse leadership: studies consistently show that companies with more women executives outperform those without. Mentorship and sponsorship programs have helped women climb corporate ladders, and role models in tech, finance, and politics have broadened the public's image of female leadership.

The COVID-19 pandemic further transformed the workplace. Remote and hybrid models provided some women greater flexibility but also underscored the disproportionate caregiving responsibilities they carry. These changes have sparked broader debates about workplace design, leadership, and the future of women in employment.

The trajectory of women's employment and leadership since World War II is one of persistence and resilience. From pink-collar jobs to corner offices, women have fought for recognition, equal pay, and leadership roles in the face of systemic barriers. The glass ceiling, while cracked, has not entirely disappeared – but it is thinner than ever before.

Economies are shaped not just by policies and profits but by people – and for centuries, women's contributions were invisible. From unpaid domestic work to low-wage labor, women's economic role was dismissed as secondary. Yet as women entered workplaces, launched businesses, and climbed into boardrooms, they transformed economies and redefined leadership.

Rosalind Brewer – Breaking Barriers in the Corporate World

When Rosalind Brewer became CEO of Walgreens Boots Alliance in 2021, she was one of the few Black women to lead a Fortune 500 company. Brewer's journey – from chemist at Kimberly-Clark to executive leadership at Starbucks and Walmart – shows how women can rise in male-dominated corporate spaces. She championed diversity initiatives and advocated for inclusive workplace practices, proving that leadership is not just about profit margins but about shaping culture.

Corporate Leadership: The Long Climb

Despite growing participation in the workforce, leadership roles remained elusive for many women. In 1995, only a handful of Fortune 500 companies had female CEOs. Boardrooms remained predominantly male, especially in finance, technology, and manufacturing.

Women in leadership faced higher bars – expected to deliver more for less credit just to be taken seriously. They navigated double binds: be assertive, not abrasive; confident, not arrogant; strong – and still nurturing.

Those who broke through – like Indra Nooyi (PepsiCo), Anne Mulcahy (Xerox), and Sheryl Sandberg (Meta/Facebook) – became symbols of possibility. Yet even they acknowledged the pressure, isolation, and personal sacrifices that came with climbing to the top.

Meanwhile, the gender pay gap persisted across virtually every industry, with women – particularly women of color – earning significantly less than their male counterparts for similar work.

In 1995, at the Beijing World Conference on Women, economic empowerment was declared a critical area of concern for global gender equality. The conference's call to "remove the persistent barriers" to women's full participation in the economy became a global mandate.

Redefining Leadership

Today, women are not just working within systems – they are redesigning them. Female executives are challenging outdated corporate cultures, emphasizing emotional intelligence, work-life balance, and inclusive decision-making. Many are pioneering social enterprises that prioritize sustainability, ethics, and impact over profit alone.

Women are leading fintech companies, climate ventures, global startups, and investment firms. They are proving that leadership is not about mimicking male models of success but about creating new ones. For example, Kathryn's fintech caps fees, publishes plain-language APRs, seats a customer advocate on the board, and ties executive bonuses to customer savings and lower default rates – measuring success by outcomes, not extraction.

At the same time, working-class and informal-sector women are building power through cooperatives, digital platforms, and mutual aid networks. Their labor, often unpaid or underpaid for generations, is finally being recognized as essential to local and global economies.

The Path Ahead

Economic empowerment is not a finish line – it is a foundation. When women control income, wealth, and capital, they not only improve their lives but uplift families, communities, and nations. Yet gaps persist in pay, access to credit, and representation in leadership.

As the world faces new economic challenges – automation, climate change, and demographic shifts – the inclusion of women's voices is not just a matter of fairness. It's a strategic imperative.

Women have moved from domestic margins to economic engines. The next frontier is ownership – leading and redesigning the systems that shape our financial future.

Economic Empowerment – From Domestic Work to Corporate Leadership

Economic empowerment has been one of the most transformative frontiers of gender equality. For centuries, women's labor was either unpaid or undervalued, whether in the home, on farms, or in factories. But across the twentieth and twenty-first centuries, women began to demand financial independence, entrepreneurial opportunity, and leadership roles in boardrooms and banking halls. From labor rights to global finance, their presence and power continue to reshape the world's economic landscape.

This chapter traces the arc from survival to strategy – from washing floors to managing Fortune 500s – through the lives of the women who redefined what economic participation looks like.

Madam C.J. Walker, born to formerly enslaved parents in 1867, became the first female self-made millionaire in America. Her line of haircare products for Black women not only built a private enterprise but also empowered other women through jobs, training, and ownership. Walker's business model included a nationwide network of sales agents, and she used her success to support civil rights causes, educational scholarships, and women's economic independence.

Dolores Huerta, co-founder of the United Farm Workers alongside César Chávez, championed the rights of agricultural workers – most of them women and immigrants – who endured low pay and unsafe conditions. Her leadership in labor organizing helped secure fair wages, maternity rights, and union protections for countless working-class families. Her rallying cry "Sí, se puede" still echoes in movements for justice today.

Rosalind Brewer, one of the first Black women to lead a Fortune 500 company, rose through the ranks of corporate America to become CEO of Walgreens Boots Alliance. Brewer's leadership is marked by a commitment to diversity, ethical sourcing, and customer-centered strategy. Her rise represents both a breaking of glass ceilings and a beacon for inclusive corporate culture.

Indra Nooyi, the former CEO of PepsiCo, brought strategic vision and global insight to one of the world's largest food and beverage companies. Born and educated in India, Nooyi integrated sustainability and health-conscious product innovation into the company's long-term strategy. Her leadership redefined the expectations placed on women executives – and on how corporations define success.

Oprah Winfrey, media mogul and philanthropist, turned a career in broadcast journalism into a billion-dollar multimedia empire. As the first Black woman billionaire in America, Oprah leveraged storytelling to influence culture, politics, and public health. Her investment in schools, scholarships, and entrepreneurship for women – especially women of color – transformed visibility into action.

Katharine Graham, publisher of *The Washington Post* during its groundbreaking coverage of Watergate, shattered stereotypes about women in media and business. Inheriting the paper in a male-dominated industry, she learned on the job and led with moral clarity, courage, and conviction. Under her watch, the Post became a model of investigative journalism and press freedom.

Ruth Handler, co-founder of Mattel and creator of Barbie, transformed toy marketing and sparked – controversial as it was – new conversations about gender, aspiration, and commercial power. The throughline was agency: if Barbie provoked debate about how girls imagine their bodies and futures, Handler's next venture asked how women reclaim their bodies after surgery. A breast-cancer survivor, she founded Nearly Me, one of the first widely marketed prosthetic breasts – showing how entrepreneurship could merge profit with purpose.

Weili Dai, co-founder of semiconductor company Marvell Technology Group, stands as one of the few women to lead in the male-dominated tech sector. Her work helped revolutionize digital storage, and she has consistently advocated for women in STEM (science, technology, engineering, and math). Dai's journey from immigrant to tech executive exemplifies the potential of innovation and inclusion.

Luisa Moreno, a Guatemalan-born labor organizer, mobilized Latinx workers across the U.S. in the 1930s and 1940s, especially in garment factories and agricultural fields. Fluent in multiple languages, she bridged ethnic divides to demand fair wages, healthcare, and education for immigrant laborers. Her economic vision was "union plus community": contracts with wage floors, grievance procedures, and safety standards paired with clinics, night schools, and legal aid. In 1939, she helped convene El Congreso de Pueblos de Habla Española in Los Angeles, tying shop-floor goals to civil-rights demands – ending segregation, curbing police abuses, and securing equal access to public services – making clear that prosperity and citizenship had to advance together.

These women did more than climb the ladder – they rebuilt it. Each, in her own way, expanded the definition of success, shifted economic power, and modeled how women could lead industries, redefine work, and multiply opportunity.

Their legacies remind us that economic empowerment is not just about profit – it's about equity, impact, and the freedom to define one's own path.

For a more complete list of Women Who Redefined Work and Leadership (1980s to 2000s), see Appendix II.

Voices of Defiance

Economic power has always been a lever of control – and liberation. For centuries, women labored in homes, fields, and factories without recognition, fair pay, or agency. But from organizing domestic workers to breaking boardroom barriers, women have fought to reclaim their value in the marketplace. These voices reveal the quiet grit of survival, the collective strength of unions, and the trailblazing force of corporate pioneers. They are reminders that true empowerment begins when women can earn, invest, and lead on their terms.

> *"Don't sit down and wait for the opportunities to come. Get up and make them."*
> – Madam C.J. Walker,
> America's first self-made female millionaire

Walker built a business empire in the early twentieth

century by creating products for Black women – and opportunities for Black women to build wealth and self-respect.

*"I tell my daughters to have their voice in this world,
and it became clear I needed to role-model that."*

– Melinda French Gates,
philanthropist and advocate for
women's economic empowerment

From the tech world to global development, Gates has used her platform to champion women as economic decision-makers at every level of society.

*"I'm not going to continue knocking on that old
door that doesn't open for me. I'm going to create
my own door and walk through that."*

– Ava DuVernay,
filmmaker and entrepreneur

While from the creative industry, DuVernay's entrepreneurial spirit embodies the same defiance and independence fueling women's rise in business.

This chapter has traced the arc of women's roles in employment and corporate leadership across the twentieth and early twenty-first centuries. The chapters that follow will continue to explore how these gains intersect with broader social, cultural, and political struggles, shaping a more complete picture of women's progress in the modern era.

The journey from invisible labor to boardroom influence reveals that women's economic power is not supplemental – it is foundational to prosperity.

Reflection Prompts

1. Personal Economics: Think about your own career or the careers of women in your family. What barriers or opportunities have shaped those paths? How have expectations changed across generations?

2. Wage Gap and Equity: The gender pay gap continues to affect women around the world. What are the root causes of this gap, and what actions – policy, organizational, or personal – can help close it?

3. Entrepreneurship as Empowerment: How does starting a business empower women economically and socially? What barriers still exist for women entrepreneurs, and how can these be overcome?

4. Building a Better Future: If you could redesign a workplace or economic system to support women's full participation and leadership, what would it look like? What values would be at its core?

CHAPTER 7:
MEDIA, REPRESENTATION, AND THE FEMALE GAZE

*"The media's the most powerful entity on earth…
they control the minds of the masses."*
— Malcolm X

Representation in media has always been more than entertainment. It reflects society's values and shapes its possibilities. The twentieth century saw women slowly move from being portrayed as objects of desire or domestic caretakers to becoming storytellers, producers, directors, and cultural critics in their own right. Their entrance into media industries not only widened opportunities but also transformed how stories were told, who was seen, and what issues gained public attention.

Defining the "Female Gaze"

The term female gaze emerged as a counterpoint to the influential concept of the male gaze, first articulated by film theorist Laura Mulvey in her 1975 essay "Visual Pleasure and Narrative Cinema." Mulvey argued that much of classical cinema was constructed around a male viewer: women were framed as passive objects of beauty, existing primarily to please male desire and advance male-centered narratives.

The female gaze describes a perspective that disrupts this paradigm. It is not simply about reversing roles – objectifying men instead of women – but about reshaping storytelling altogether. Through the female gaze, women become full subjects – with agency, inner lives, and complex desires.

It emphasizes empathy over objectification, relationship over domination, and authenticity over stereotype. This framework has since expanded beyond film to literature, television, advertising, and digital media, influencing how gender dynamics are understood in popular culture.

Breaking Into Media Industries

From the mid-twentieth century onward, women gradually gained ground in industries historically closed to them. In Hollywood, pioneers like Ida Lupino, one of the first women to direct studio films, challenged gender norms by portraying working-class women and taboo subjects such as bigamy and unwed motherhood. In television, producers like Barbara Walters and Shonda Rhimes transformed both the newsroom and scripted drama by bringing women's voices and experiences into prime-time prominence.

Globally, progress was equally significant. In India, filmmaker Mira Nair's *Salaam Bombay!* (1988) spotlighted street children and social inequality, challenging sanitized portrayals of urban life. In Iran, Samira Makhmalbaf and Marjane Satrapi redefined cinema under restrictive conditions, making women's experiences central to national and global conversations. In Nigeria, the rise of Nollywood brought new opportunities for women producers and actresses to craft local stories for mass audiences.

Changing Public Perception – and Policy

Women's breakthroughs in media did more than diversify storytelling; they reshaped public discourse and sometimes catalyzed change. In the United States, television shows like *Murphy Brown* (1988 to 1998) challenged stereotypes of single motherhood and career-driven women. The show even sparked a political debate when then-Vice President Dan Quayle criticized its lead character's choice to raise a child alone – unintentionally amplifying conversations about family structures, gender roles, and workplace equity.

Similarly, *Will & Grace* (co-created by Max Mutchnick and David Kohan but shaped by women executives and activists) played a role in shifting U.S. public opinion on LGBTQ rights, which later influenced policy debates leading up to marriage equality reforms. In Latin America, telenovelas such as *Simplemente María* (Peru, 1969) and *Vale Tudo* (Brazil, 1988) portrayed women navigating work, class, and morality in ways that resonated across societies – sparking conversations about labor rights, education, and corruption.

In South Africa, women journalists and filmmakers used media as a tool against apartheid, documenting abuses and amplifying calls for justice. In more recent years, the #MeToo movement – first voiced by activist Tarana Burke and later amplified globally by journalists and actresses – revealed the power of digital and traditional media in reshaping laws, workplace practices, and public awareness around harassment and gender violence.

Beyond Visibility: Reimagining Power

What makes the female gaze transformative is not only the presence of women behind the camera or at the editorial desk but the ripple effects of their perspectives. Stories told differently invite audiences to see differently. They can make invisible labor – caregiving, eldercare, and the planning/emotional load that keeps households running – visible; they can normalize new family structures, validate marginalized identities, and challenge unjust laws.

From Ida Lupino's films to Shonda Rhimes's dramas, from Mira Nair's social realism to Satrapi's autobiographical animation, the female gaze has been less about exclusionary politics than about expansion – broadening who belongs in the story and what counts as important. And as women gained footholds in media worldwide, the power of representation became undeniable: it is both a cultural force and a lever for social change.

For most of modern history, media presented women as objects of desire or symbols of domesticity. Rarely were women allowed to shape the lens through which they were seen. The rise of women creators, however, redefined representation – not just by adding more female voices, but by challenging the assumptions behind the gaze itself.

Ava DuVernay – Reframing Hollywood Narratives

When Ava DuVernay directed *Selma* in 2014, she became the first Black woman nominated for a Golden Globe for Best Director. But her influence extends beyond awards. Through her production company ARRAY, DuVernay has championed underrepresented filmmakers, ensuring that stories about women and people of color are told with authenticity. Her Netflix series *When They See Us* reshaped public understanding of criminal justice, race, and gender – showing how storytelling can move policy conversations.

Shonda Rhimes – Changing Television from the Inside Out

As the creator of *Grey's Anatomy* and *Scandal,* Shonda Rhimes transformed television by placing women of color in leading roles – something almost unheard of in network primetime. Her characters were ambitious, flawed, and powerful, reflecting real women's complexity. Rhimes didn't just tell stories – she disrupted casting norms, broadened representation, and demonstrated how visibility on screen could change how viewers saw race, power, and gender.

Chimamanda Ngozi Adichie – Storytelling Across Borders

Nigerian writer Chimamanda Ngozi Adichie's TED Talk *We Should All Be Feminists* went viral and was later sampled in Beyoncé's "Flawless," reaching millions worldwide.

Her novels – from *Half of a Yellow Sun* to *Americanah* – bring African women's stories into global focus, weaving themes of migration, identity, and power. She reminds us that the female gaze is not just visual – it is narrative, cultural, and political.

When women hold the pen, the camera, or the microphone, they do not just tell different stories – they redefine what stories are possible.

Women Behind the Scenes: Rewriting the Script

The rise of female directors, producers, journalists, editors, and media executives began to shift the landscape. As women gained positions of creative control, they began telling stories that reflected the complexity of women's lives – not as caricatures, but as full human beings.

In film, Penny Marshall, Kathryn Bigelow, and Nora Ephron emerged as influential directors, telling stories about female friendship, war, ambition, and love.

- In television, Diane English created Murphy Brown, a show about a single, career-driven journalist, while Shonda Rhimes would later pioneer complex storytelling around women of color in shows like Grey's Anatomy and Scandal.

- In journalism, women like Barbara Walters, Christiane Amanpour, and Gwen Ifill broke barriers in newsrooms and foreign reporting.

- In music, artists such as Madonna, Tina Turner, and Lauryn Hill redefined female performance and agency in a male-dominated industry.

These creators challenged traditional narratives by centering women as thinkers, leaders, lovers, and rebels – often not idealized, but complex and fully real.

Advertising and the Politics of Image

Advertising has long been one of the most powerful – and problematic – platforms for shaping gender roles. From the 1950s through the 1980s, women were routinely shown as housewives, beauty objects, or accessories to male success.

But feminist criticism, consumer activism, and cultural backlash in the 1990s began to shift expectations. Companies that adapted – creating inclusive, empowering messages – were rewarded with loyalty and credibility. Others, clinging to outdated tropes, faced public critique and backlash.

Campaigns like Dove's "Real Beauty," launched in 2004, broke new ground by showcasing women of all ages, sizes, and ethnicities. It was one of the earliest global attempts to disrupt narrow beauty standards and invite real conversations around body image.

However, progress was often co-opted. "Femvertising" – the use of feminist themes to sell products – walked a fine line between empowerment and exploitation. Femvertising is a marketing and advertising strategy that uses pro-female messages, imagery, and narratives to promote products or brands while also aligning with gender equality values. Questions emerged: Was representation enough? Or was it another layer of commodification?

The Rise of the Female Gaze

As women gained more control over content production and distribution, the female gaze began to emerge – not simply as the inverse of the male gaze, but as a more nuanced, empathetic way of seeing.

The female gaze in media emphasizes:

- Emotional depth over visual objectification
- Internal experience over external validation
- Relational context over isolated beauty

Films like *The Piano*, *Lost in Translation*, *Whale Rider*, and

Frida exemplified this shift – highlighting women's perspectives and inner lives without reducing them to tropes.

Authors and critics began championing media that portrayed women's desires, struggles, and transformations without male-centered filters. Feminist film festivals, women-run production companies, and indie publishers emerged as platforms for authentic storytelling.

Pop Culture and Identity Formation

Representation in media isn't just about fairness – it's about identity. What we see on screen affects how we see ourselves. For generations, many women – especially women of color, LGBTQ+ women, and women with disabilities – saw few reflections of their realities in mainstream media.

But by the late 1990s and early 2000s, change was gaining speed:

- The L Word (2004) brought lesbian narratives to prime time.

- Girlfriends, Living Single, and Ugly Betty offered stories centering women of color.

- Buffy the Vampire Slayer gave rise to a new feminist archetype: the emotionally complex, physically powerful heroine.

- Documentaries and memoirs exploded in popularity, giving women control over their narratives – from Aileen: Life and Death of a Serial Killer to My Life on the Road by Gloria Steinem.

The digital age, still in its early stages, hinted at the coming explosion of user-generated content and social media platforms – spaces where women would further challenge gatekeepers and create media on their terms.

Looking Ahead

By the early 2000s, the groundwork was laid for an even more profound shift in media. The rise of streaming, online publishing, podcasts, YouTube, and social networks would give women the tools to bypass traditional institutions altogether.

It became less about whether women could shape media and more about how they used that power – and what new standards they would set.

As we continue to challenge outdated frameworks and expand representation across race, gender, ability, and identity, the media remains one of the most powerful tools for shaping the world we imagine – and the one we inherit.

Chapter 7 highlights influential women across film, television, journalism, music, and advertising who redefined media, shattered stereotypes, and expanded the spectrum of female representation.

In the twentieth and twenty-first centuries, control over visual narratives became a central front in the struggle for gender equity. Women were long depicted by others – painted, filmed, photographed, or written about through a patriarchal lens. But as access to media production expanded, women seized the tools of storytelling and began to define themselves.

Laura Mulvey, a British film theorist, catalyzed the conversation about the "male gaze" with her groundbreaking 1975 essay, *Visual Pleasure and Narrative Cinema*. Her work exposed how classical Hollywood films were structured to center male desire and female objectification. By naming the gaze, Mulvey empowered generations of filmmakers, critics, and scholars to challenge it. She made visible what had long been assumed and gave feminist film theory a foundational vocabulary.

Ava DuVernay, a former publicist turned filmmaker, created space for Black women behind the camera and on the screen. Her films, including *Selma*, *13th*, and *When They See Us*, center Black stories with emotional depth and political clarity. DuVernay also founded ARRAY, a distribution collective for women and filmmakers of color. She not only directs films; she also builds platforms, fostering a more equitable media ecosystem.

Agnès Varda, the French New Wave pioneer, approached cinema with curiosity, humor, and an unapologetically feminist lens. Her hybrid documentaries blurred boundaries between fiction and reality, public and personal. In works like *Cléo from 5 to 7* and *The Gleaners and I*, she centered female subjectivity and everyday moments, challenging the cinematic status quo. Varda's playful aesthetic and lifelong activism made her a beloved godmother of feminist film.

Shonda Rhimes, a powerhouse television producer, redefined what leadership and diversity looked like in American media. Through shows like *Grey's Anatomy*, *Scandal*, and *Bridgerton*, she populated prime time with women of color, complex female leads, and narratives that challenged stereotypes. Rhimes's "Shondaland" empire proved that inclusive storytelling was not only necessary – it was wildly successful.

Laverne Cox, an Emmy-nominated actress and documentary producer, became one of the most visible transgender women in American media. Her breakout role on *Orange Is the New Black* was followed by outspoken advocacy for trans rights, representation, and safety. Through projects like *Disclosure*, she examines how trans people have been portrayed on screen and how they can reclaim their stories.

Nan Goldin, an American photographer, used her camera to document queer communities, addiction, intimacy, and survival in unflinching detail. Her *Ballad of Sexual Dependency* series redefined the boundaries of documentary photography. In recent years, Goldin became an activist, founding the group P.A.I.N. to protest the opioid crisis and hold the Sackler family accountable. Her work merges personal truth with political urgency.

Mira Nair, an Indian American filmmaker, explored themes of identity, diaspora, and globalization in films such as *Monsoon Wedding* and *The Namesake*. Her work highlights the nuances of South Asian womanhood and the multiplicity of postcolonial identities. Nair's films bridge continents, offering global audiences intimate portraits of cultural negotiation.

Issa Rae, a digital media trailblazer, leveraged YouTube success (*The Misadventures of Awkward Black Girl*) into mainstream acclaim with HBO's *Insecure*. Rae writes, produces, and stars in stories that challenge monolithic depictions of Black women. She has also founded media and music companies, investing in community storytelling and talent development.

Julie Dash, director of the seminal 1991 film *Daughters of the Dust*, became the first African American woman to release a widely distributed feature film in the U.S. Her poetic cinematography and lyrical narrative style opened space for African American women to tell their stories through an Afrocentric lens. Dash's influence can be seen in everything from Beyoncé's *Lemonade* to indie cinema worldwide.

These women are not simply artists – they are architects of meaning. They challenged how women and marginalized communities are seen, and, more importantly, who gets to do the seeing.

By placing the camera in their hands, they redefined power in the digital age. They taught us that stories are not just entertainment – they are how cultures dream, grieve, and imagine justice.

The female gaze is more than a perspective; it is a revolution in focus.

For a more complete list of Women Who Transformed Media and Representation (1980s to 2000s), see Appendix II.

Voices of Defiance

For too long, women were portrayed through a lens

not their own, flattened into stereotypes, silenced in scripts, and overlooked behind the camera. But with bold vision and unwavering intent, women began to challenge those narratives, insisting on being the subject, not the object. These voices represent a radical reclamation of image and identity. Whether behind the pen, the lens, or the mic, they confronted systems that distorted their stories and demanded space to define themselves. Through defiance, they reshaped culture – and invited the world to see women as they truly are.

> *"I'm not going to apologize for who I am. I'm going to shine as bright as I can, and if you don't like it, you can look away."*
>
> — Laverne Cox,
> actress and LGBTQ+ advocate

As the first openly transgender woman nominated for a Primetime Emmy, Cox challenged media norms and broadened public understanding of womanhood and representation.

> *"The most revolutionary thing one can do is always to proclaim loudly what is happening."*
>
> — Rosa Luxemburg,
> political theorist and writer

Though not traditionally part of the media industry, Luxemburg's insistence on truth-telling resonates with women journalists and filmmakers who use media to expose injustice.

> *"I will not have my life narrowed down. I will not bow down to somebody else's whim or to someone else's ignorance."*
>
> — Bell Hooks,
> cultural critic and author

Hooks redefined feminist and media discourse, exposing how race, gender, and power intersect in storytelling – and insisting on the validity of the Black female gaze.

By reshaping the lens through which stories are told,

women claimed not just visibility but the authority to define culture itself.

Reflection Prompts

1. Stereotypes and Silences: What common stereotypes of women have you noticed in mainstream media? Which voices or identities do you feel are still underrepresented or misrepresented?

2. Emotional Truths: Have you ever encountered a piece of media – a film, book, or show – that made you feel truly seen or understood as a woman or as someone who supports women? What made it powerful?

3. Creating Your Own Narrative: In the age of digital storytelling and social platforms, anyone can share their voice. How might you use media to tell your story – or amplify others'?

4. Call to Awareness: How can consumers become more mindful of the media they support? What role does media literacy play in shaping a more just and inclusive cultural narrative?

CHAPTER 8:
INTERSECTIONALITY AND THE INCLUSIVE FEMINIST MOVEMENT

"Intersectionality reminds us that no woman walks a single path; her journey is shaped by the many identities she carries."
— Maria L. Ellis

The concept of intersectionality, first articulated by Kimberlé Crenshaw in the late 1980s, became a defining hallmark of the Third Wave of feminism. This wave, emerging in the 1990s, pushed beyond earlier feminist frameworks by insisting that gender could not be examined in isolation from race, class, sexuality, and other identities. Third Wave feminists broadened the movement's inclusivity. Their work created space for multiple voices – particularly those historically marginalized – to reshape what feminism meant.

Kimberlé Crenshaw and Legal Visibility

In a landmark 1989 paper, Kimberlé Crenshaw analyzed legal cases where Black women suing for discrimination were dismissed because courts considered "race" and "gender" separately. Her insight – that overlapping identities create unique forms of oppression – reframed both feminist and civil rights movements. Crenshaw's work gave activists and policymakers a framework to argue for protections that recognized the complexity of women's lives.

Indigenous Women and Land Rights in Latin America

In Guatemala, Indigenous Maya women have been at the forefront of land rights struggles. Women like Rigoberta Menchú, who won the Nobel Peace Prize in 1992, linked gender justice to Indigenous sovereignty. Menchú's testimony about violence against Indigenous women during Guatemala's civil war galvanized international human rights advocacy and pushed land and cultural rights into the feminist agenda. These struggles highlight how gender, colonialism, and economic injustice are deeply intertwined.

A Brief History of Intersectionality

The term intersectionality was coined in 1989 by legal scholar Kimberlé Crenshaw, who argued that Black women face forms of discrimination that cannot be understood by looking at race and gender separately. Her landmark paper, "Demarginalizing the Intersection of Race and Sex," showed how the law often failed to protect women of color because it treated race and gender as isolated categories.

But intersectional thinking existed long before the word itself. In the nineteenth century, Sojourner Truth's famous 1851 speech, "Ain't I a Woman?" challenged the narrow definitions of womanhood that excluded Black women. In the 1970s, the Combahee River Collective, a group of Black feminist lesbians, articulated a vision of liberation that accounted for race, gender, class, and sexuality simultaneously. Crenshaw's contribution gave a lasting name and analytical framework to a reality activists had long described.

Timeline at a Glance

- o **1851:** Sojourner Truth delivered her "Ain't I a Woman?" speech.
- o **1977:** The Combahee River Collective issued its statement on interlocking systems of oppression.
- o **1989:** Kimberlé Crenshaw coined the term

intersectionality.

- o **1990s to 2000s:** Intersectionality became central to feminist theory, legal scholarship, and activism.
- o **2010s to present:** Intersectionality informed global movements from climate justice to LGBTQ+ rights.

Intersectionality in Practice: Case Studies

Indigenous Women and Land Rights

In Canada, Indigenous women have been at the forefront of land rights struggles that intertwine gender, race, and sovereignty. Leaders such as Winona LaDuke in the United States and Indigenous women activists across Latin America have emphasized that the fight for environmental justice cannot be separated from women's rights. For example, in Ecuador, Indigenous women's organizations like CONAIE's Mujeres played pivotal roles in resisting oil extraction projects that threatened both the environment and Indigenous communities' survival. Their activism reframed feminist politics to include ecological sustainability, cultural preservation, and anti-colonial resistance.

Black Trans Women and the Fight for Visibility

In the United States, Black trans women have long been leaders in movements for LGBTQ+ rights, though their contributions were often marginalized. Marsha P. Johnson and Sylvia Rivera were central figures in the 1969 Stonewall uprising, sparking a movement that reshaped global understandings of queer liberation. Today, activists like Raquel Willis continue that legacy, advocating for policy reforms on issues from housing discrimination to healthcare access. Their activism demonstrates how intersectionality illuminates vulnerabilities at the sharpest points of oppression: where race, gender identity, and sexuality converge.

The Global South: Domestic Workers' Movements

Across Asia, Africa, and Latin America, women in

domestic work have organized to demand recognition and rights, highlighting the intersections of gender, class, and migration. In the Philippines, groups like the United Domestic Workers of the Philippines have linked labor rights to women's rights, showing how economic exploitation, gender discrimination, and migration policies interact. Their advocacy led to the International Labour Organization's Convention on Domestic Workers (C189, 2011), a landmark global treaty.

Beyond Theory: Why Intersectionality Matters

What intersectionality offers is a way to see how systems of power overlap, creating unique struggles but also unique forms of resilience. It also clarifies why feminist movements that fail to address racism, class inequality, homophobia, or colonial legacies risk leaving many women behind.

Intersectionality has reshaped not only feminist scholarship but also activism, broadening the scope of who feminism is for and what liberation means. From Indigenous land defenders to trans activists, from domestic workers to climate justice leaders, the most transformative movements of recent decades have been those that embraced the intersections of struggle.

For much of modern history, the mainstream women's movement has been critiqued – often rightly – for centering a narrow, privileged perspective: white, Western, middle-class, and heterosexual. While it advanced meaningful progress for some, many women stood at the margins of that movement, feeling unseen, unheard, and left behind. Their realities were different. Their challenges were layered. And their liberation required more than just gender equality – it required the recognition of how race, class, ability, sexuality, and culture intersect with gender in complex, often compounding ways.

This chapter explores the emergence of intersectionality as both a concept and a catalyst, tracing how inclusive feminism took shape in the late twentieth century and began reshaping the fight for justice in broader, deeper, and more transformative ways.

The Limits of One-Size-Fits-All Feminism

Second-wave feminism of the 1960s and 70s made important strides: advocating for reproductive rights, workplace equality, and protection against gender-based violence. But many women of color, working-class women, Indigenous women, and LGBTQ+ women found that their experiences were missing from the conversation.

While white feminists rallied around the right to work outside the home, Black women had always worked – often in poorly paid domestic or service roles. While middle-class feminists advocated for reproductive freedom, Indigenous and Latina women were fighting against forced sterilizations. Queer women were often made to feel invisible or unwelcome in mainstream feminist circles.

The result? Many chose to build their movements – movements that reflected their whole identity, not just their gender.

Defining Intersectionality

In 1989, legal scholar Kimberlé Crenshaw coined the term *intersectionality* to describe how systems of oppression are interconnected and cannot be examined separately. She used the concept to explain how Black women were often excluded from both feminist and antiracist discourse, their experiences lost in the gap between race-only and gender-only frameworks.

Intersectionality wasn't just a theory. It was a lens that revealed what had long been ignored.

- That a poor, undocumented immigrant woman faces different risks than a wealthy white executive.

- That a trans woman of color may experience violence and discrimination in ways profoundly different from her cisgender peers.
- That Black mothers face higher maternal mortality not because of race alone or gender alone, but the interaction of both in medical systems.

Crenshaw's framework was revolutionary because it didn't just ask, "What do women face?" It asked, *Which women? Where? Under what systems of power?*

Movements Within the Movement

The rise of intersectionality inspired a wave of activism that challenged monolithic feminism and expanded its reach:

- Black feminist collectives like the Combahee River Collective (founded in 1974) had already laid groundwork with their statement: "If Black women were free, it would mean that everyone else would have to be free since our freedom would necessitate the destruction of all the systems of oppression."
- Chicana feminists like Gloria Anzaldúa and Cherríe Moraga explored the complexity of living between cultures, languages, and sexual identities.
- Queer feminism gained visibility as women like Audre Lorde, Adrienne Rich, and Judith Butler argued for the inclusion of diverse sexual identities and gender expressions.
- Disability rights activists highlighted how ableism and gender bias intersected to exclude disabled women from economic, social, and political life.
- Global South feminists challenged the West's assumption of being the center of feminist

theory – offering perspectives rooted in colonialism, war, displacement, and indigenous knowledge.

Each of these movements added depth to feminism and reminded the world that there is no single story of womanhood.

Intersectionality in Practice

Intersectional feminism began showing up in new spaces and forms:

- In advocacy, where coalitions tackled issues like domestic violence, police brutality, and environmental racism as interconnected problems.

- In academia, where feminist studies began to include race, postcolonialism, queer theory, and disability rights.

- In activism, where organizers used inclusive language, created safe spaces for marginalized voices, and practiced shared leadership.

- In policy, where legal frameworks began to recognize overlapping identities in cases of discrimination, asylum, and education.

Intersectional practice meant recognizing that *who* leads matters – and so does *how* they lead. It was not just about adding more voices, but about shifting power.

Cultural Catalysts and Public Awareness

Popular culture helped expand intersectional awareness. The works of Bell Hooks, Roxane Gay, Laverne Cox, and Maya Angelou reached global audiences and invited people to think differently about identity, love, oppression, and belonging.

Music, poetry, film, and fashion became tools for challenging stereotypes and setting new norms: from the unapologetic lyrics of Missy Elliott and Salt-N-Pepa to the genre-bending poetry of Audre Lorde to the activism of public figures like Janet Mock and Alicia Garza.

The explosion of digital platforms allowed marginalized voices to speak without filters. Blogs, zines, online forums, and later, social media, democratized discourse and made it harder to ignore the diversity of feminist thought.

Challenges and Backlash

As intersectional feminism grew, so did pushback. Critics accused it of being "divisive" or "too complicated." Some mainstream institutions resisted changes in leadership or narrative. Even within feminist circles, tensions emerged over who was being centered and whose experiences were still being overlooked.

It is not about identity politics; it is about power, and who gets to define the terms of justice. It calls feminism to a higher standard – one that refuses to replicate the systems it seeks to dismantle.

Toward a More Just Movement

Today, intersectional feminism is no longer a fringe idea. It is foundational to any serious conversation about equity and justice. It informs the policies of global NGOs, shapes the language of protest, and animates youth movements across the world.

It challenges us not just to ask, "What do I fight for?" but also, "Who do I fight alongside?"

As we move forward, intersectionality reminds us that real liberation doesn't leave anyone behind. It teaches us that the most inclusive movements are also the most powerful – because when the most marginalized rise, we all rise.

Chapter 8 features key thinkers, writers, activists, and organizers who helped shape and expand the feminist movement through the lens of intersectionality – bringing race, class, sexuality, ability, and nationality into the center of the conversation.

Intersectionality and the Inclusive Feminist Movement

Feminism has never been a single story. From its earliest waves to the present, the movement for gender equity has been marked by tensions, contradictions, and breakthroughs. The concept of *intersectionality*, coined by legal scholar Kimberlé Crenshaw in 1989, articulated a vital truth: that gender does not exist in a vacuum. Race, class, sexuality, disability, and other identities intersect to create unique experiences of oppression and resilience.

This chapter explores the women who have centered intersectionality in their activism, scholarship, and leadership – redefining feminism to be not only more inclusive but more effective.

Kimberlé Crenshaw, a law professor and theorist, introduced the concept of intersectionality to explain how traditional feminist and anti-racist frameworks often failed to address the specific experiences of Black women. Her work illuminated how legal systems, media, and public policy often rendered these experiences invisible. Crenshaw's insights transformed feminist thought and laid the groundwork for more inclusive activism and advocacy.

Audre Lorde, a self-described "Black, lesbian, mother, warrior, poet," believed that difference should be a source of strength, not division. Through her essays and poetry, Lorde challenged white feminism's blind spots and called for feminism rooted in lived experience and radical empathy. Her book *Sister Outsider* remains a foundational text in intersectional feminist literature.

Gloria Anzaldúa, a Chicana writer and theorist, brought forth the idea of the "borderlands" – both geographic and metaphorical – as a space of resistance and hybridity. Her groundbreaking work *Borderlands/La Frontera* explored how culture, language, sexuality, and colonial history intersect. Anzaldúa's concept of "mestiza consciousness" encouraged a fluid, inclusive vision of self and society. Bell Hooks – a prolific writer, educator, and cultural critic –

insisted that feminism be anti-racist and anti-classist, rooted in love and justice. Her accessible prose and critique of patriarchy as a system built on domination made her one of the late twentieth century's most influential feminist voices, and works like *Feminism Is for Everybody* helped democratize feminist theory.

Patricia Hill Collins, a sociologist, developed the concept of the "matrix of domination" to explain how various forms of oppression are interconnected. Her book *Black Feminist Thought* examined how Black women create and pass on knowledge through lived experience, oral tradition, and community leadership. Collins positioned intersectionality as a tool not only for analysis but for empowerment.

Angela Davis – a scholar, prison abolitionist, and activist – has long advanced a feminism that links gender justice to racial, economic, and carceral justice. Since the 1970s, her work has exposed how the prison-industrial complex, capitalism, and misogyny intertwine. Davis embodies a feminism that is as intellectually rigorous as it is politically urgent.

Lydia X. Z. Brown, a disability justice advocate, writer, and organizer, has expanded intersectional feminism to include neurodiversity and the experiences of disabled queer people of color. Brown's work in academia, policy, and activism underscores that inclusion must account for the entire spectrum of identity – not just the most visible axes.

Tarana Burke, founder of the #MeToo movement, emphasized that sexual violence disproportionately affects women of color, especially in marginalized communities. Her activism predates the viral hashtag and focuses on survivor-led healing and justice. Burke's grassroots work reframed conversations around consent, power, and structural accountability.

Ai-jen Poo, director of the National Domestic Workers Alliance, has advocated for the labor rights of immigrant women, care workers, and low-wage workers – those too often left out of traditional feminist priorities. Her organizing connects feminism to economic justice, aging, and immigration, demonstrating how intersectionality can build cross-movement solidarity.

Intersectionality is not a trend or a buzzword – it is a lens that reveals the deeper architecture of inequality. These women did not simply add voices to the movement; they reoriented it entirely.

They showed that true liberation requires listening, co-alition-building, and confronting privilege within feminist spaces.

Their leadership reminds us that feminism must evolve to survive – and that inclusion strengthens, rather than di-lutes, its transformative power.

For a more complete list of Pioneers of Intersectional Feminism and Inclusive Activism (1960s to 2000s), see Appendix II.

Voices of Defiance

The feminist movement has never been monolithic – and for too long, it excluded the voices of women of color, LGBTQ+ individuals, disabled women, and those outside Western frameworks. The rise of intersectionality reframed the struggle for gender equality as one bound to race, class, sexuality, and beyond. These voices did more than speak – they shook the foundation of mainstream feminism and made space for a movement rooted in justice for all. Their defiance was not just against patriarchy but against partial liberation. Through their words, we are reminded that no movement is truly free until it includes everyone.

"Intersectionality is a lens through which you can see where power comes and collides, where it interlocks and intersects."

— Kimberlé Crenshaw,
legal scholar and originator of the term "intersectionality"

Crenshaw gave language to layered oppression and challenged the legal system – and feminism – to recognize the full complexity of identity.

*"I will not have my life narrowed down. I will not bow down
to somebody else's whim or to someone else's ignorance."*

— Bell Hooks,
author of *Ain't I a Woman?*

Hooks dismantled the myth of a singular feminist experience, calling for love, inclusion, and liberation that encompasses class, race, and patriarchy's hidden forms.

*"It is not our differences that divide us. It is our inability
to recognize, accept, and celebrate those differences."*

— Audre Lorde,
Sister Outsider, 1984

This truth continues to challenge institutions and individuals alike – to move beyond tokenism and into transformative inclusion.

Intersectionality teaches us that justice that excludes is not justice at all.

Reflection Prompts

1. Who's Centered? Who's Missing?: Think about feminist movements past and present. Whose voices have historically been centered, and whose have been left out? What are the consequences of that exclusion?

2. Your Role: How can you practice intersectionality in your own community, workplace, or activism? What might it look like to challenge exclusionary practices or amplify marginalized voices?

3. Conflict and Growth: Intersectional spaces can sometimes be messy, with disagreements and growing pains. How can we navigate conflict with grace and commitment to shared goals?

4. Vision for the Future: Imagine a feminist movement ten years from now. What do you hope it

looks like? Who is leading it? What issues are at
its heart?

CHAPTER 9:
WOMEN AND TECHNOLOGY – FROM DIGITAL PIONEERS TO TECH FOUNDERS

"The future never just happens; it is created."
— Mae Jemison

In the early 1940s, in a room filled with the hum of massive machines, six women programmed the world's first electronic computer, the ENIAC. Among them was Jean Jennings Bartik, a mathematician who, with her colleagues, turned rows of cables and switches into a system capable of calculating ballistic trajectories during World War II. Their groundbreaking work went unrecognized for decades, overshadowed by the men credited with designing the hardware. Only much later were Bartik and her peers recognized as some of the first true programmers.

Their story is emblematic of women's role in technology: present at the foundation, often invisible in recognition, yet indispensable in shaping the digital age. From wartime codebreaking to Silicon Valley start-ups and today's global founders, women have been pioneers, innovators, and leaders – pushing technical limits while reshaping who is seen as belonging in tech.

Early Computing: The Hidden Figures

The history of modern computing is intertwined with women's intellectual labor. During World War II, thousands of women served as "computers," performing complex mathematical calculations by hand. At Bletchley Park in Britain, women like Joan Clarke played key roles in code-breaking efforts that shortened the war, even as their contributions were obscured for decades.

In the United States, Grace Hopper pioneered programming languages, developing COBOL, one of the first high-level computer languages, which helped make programming more accessible and laid the foundation for modern software development. These women demonstrated not only technical skill but vision, shaping computing into a field that touched science, business, and daily life.

Yet as the industry professionalized, many were sidelined, reinforcing the perception of computing as a male domain.

Silicon Valley and the Tech Boom

By the 1970s and 1980s, Silicon Valley had become the epicenter of technological innovation. While male founders like Steve Jobs and Bill Gates dominated headlines, women were quietly shaping the industry. Radia Perlman, often called "the mother of the internet," developed the Spanning Tree Protocol, which made modern networks possible. Anita Borg created platforms to connect and support women in computing, advocating for equity in a rapidly expanding industry.

In the same era, companies like IBM and Hewlett-Packard began to hire women engineers and programmers in larger numbers, though often into lower-status roles. Despite barriers, many drove real influence — leading project teams, filing patents, setting internal coding standards, designing user interfaces, and shaping training and hiring practices — contributing directly to both hardware and software breakthroughs.

Tech Start-Ups and Global Founders

The rise of the internet and start-up culture in the

1990s and 2000s opened new opportunities for women entrepreneurs. In the United States, Meg Whitman built eBay into a global e-commerce powerhouse, while Sheryl Sandberg became one of the most visible women in Silicon Valley as COO of Facebook, sparking debates on women's leadership with her book *Lean In*.

Globally, women began building companies that redefined technology's reach. In Africa, Rebecca Enonchong, founder of AppsTech in Cameroon, became a leading voice in enterprise software and advocacy for African tech ecosystems. In China, Zhou Qunfei rose from a factory worker to the billionaire founder of Lens Technology, a key supplier of smartphone glass. In Latin America, entrepreneurs like Silvina Moschini of Argentina have driven digital platforms that expand access to work for women across borders.

The Continuing Struggle for Equity

Despite these achievements, women remain underrepresented in technology. According to UNESCO, women make up only 28 percent of the global STEM workforce, and in venture capital, less than 3 percent of funding goes to women-led start-ups. Cultural stereotypes, structural barriers, and systemic biases continue to limit opportunities.

Yet, grassroots initiatives are pushing back with new energy and visibility.

Organizations such as Girls Who Code, Black Girls Code, and global networks like Women in Tech Africa are building pipelines of diverse talent. Their work suggests that the next generation of digital pioneers will be more inclusive, redefining not only technology but the culture surrounding it.

Technology has long been imagined as the domain of men in lab coats or hoodies, yet women were present at every stage of the digital revolution. From coordinating rapid-response legal aid to livestreaming protests, online networks now move faster than traditional news cycles.

From coding the first algorithms to founding startups, their stories show how innovation is not only about machines but about who gets to imagine the future.

Ada Lovelace – The First Programmer

In the 1840s, long before the word "computer" existed, Ada Lovelace wrote what is considered the first algorithm intended for a machine – the Analytical Engine. Though her work was dismissed or ignored for generations, Lovelace foresaw that machines could go beyond numbers to create music and art. Today, she is celebrated as the first programmer, her story a reminder that women were present at technology's very birth.

Grace Hopper – The Mother of COBOL

During World War II, Grace Hopper became one of the first programmers of the Harvard Mark I computer. Later, she developed the COBOL programming language, which brought computing into business and government on a massive scale. Hopper's insistence on making coding accessible helped shape modern computing as we know it. Known for her wit and tenacity, she famously said, "The most dangerous phrase in the language is, 'We've always done it this way.'"

Radia Perlman – The Mother of the Internet

In the 1980s, Radia Perlman invented the Spanning Tree Protocol, a breakthrough that made modern computer networks – and eventually the internet – possible. Her contributions are foundational, even if her name isn't widely known: STP underpins the web as we know it. Perlman's work proves that women were not only users of technology but its architects.

Whitney Wolfe Herd – Tech Startup Leadership in the twenty-first Century

Fast forward to the twenty-first century: Whitney Wolfe Herd founded Bumble, a dating app where women make the first move. Launched in 2014, Bumble challenged tech's male-dominated culture by embedding feminist principles of agency and safety directly into its design – women initiate conversations, and in-app tools prioritize consent and harassment prevention. In 2021, Wolfe Herd became the youngest self-made female billionaire after Bumble's IPO, showing how women could transform not just code but company culture.

Women in Global Tech Ecosystems

Beyond the West, women are pioneering in technology ecosystems worldwide. In Africa, Rebecca Enonchong, a Cameroonian entrepreneur, founded AppsTech and became a leading voice for African tech innovation. In India, Roshni Nadar Malhotra became the first woman to lead a listed IT company, HCL Technologies, one of the largest in the country. Their stories highlight how women in tech are driving global economic transformation.

From Ada Lovelace's notebooks to Wolfe Herd's IPO, women in technology have shaped every era. Yet barriers remain – women are still underrepresented in STEM education, receive a fraction of venture capital funding, and face gender bias in tech workplaces.

Women in technology are not a footnote. They are the authors of its story.

Without women's vision and labor, the digital world would look different.

Looking Ahead

From Jean Jennings Bartik's quiet genius to Zhou Qunfei's entrepreneurial ascent, women have shaped the digital age at every turn. Their stories remind us that progress in technology is not just about machines and code but about who gets to imagine the future. The task ahead is not merely to celebrate past pioneers but to ensure that equity and inclusion drive the next wave of innovation.

In the collective imagination, the technology industry

is often seen as the domain of men – brilliant, hoodie-clad coders shaping the future from Silicon Valley garages. But that vision erases a far more complex truth: women have always been at the forefront of technological innovation – often in invisible or undervalued roles. From early computing to today's AI revolution, women have contributed not just as workers but as visionaries, coders, designers, engineers, and entrepreneurs.

This chapter explores the overlooked history of women in tech, the systemic challenges they've faced, and the ways women today are redefining the tech landscape – not by fitting in but by transforming it.

The Hidden History of Women in Computing

Long before computers fit in our pockets, women were doing the calculations. In fact, the term "computer" once referred to the women who did the work.

- Ada Lovelace, in the 1840s, wrote what is now recognized as the first computer algorithm for Charles Babbage's proposed Analytical Engine, earning her the title of the world's first computer programmer.

- During World War II, thousands of women worked as codebreakers and calculators for military intelligence and weapons development.

- The ENIAC (Electronic Numerical Integrator and Computer), one of the first general-purpose electronic computers, was programmed by six women in the 1940s – Kay McNulty, Jean Jennings Bartik, and others – yet their role was nearly erased from the historical record.

In the mid-twentieth century, programming was considered "women's work," often likened to clerical tasks. But as the field became more prestigious and profitable, men increasingly dominated, and women were systematically pushed out.

The Silicon Ceiling

As the personal computer industry took off in the 1980s and 1990s, gender disparities widened. Marketing campaigns targeted boys and men, reinforcing stereotypes about who "belonged" in tech. Tech workplaces – shaped by intense competition, long hours, and exclusionary cultures – became increasingly hostile to women.

Despite this, many broke through.

- Radia Perlman, known as the "Mother of the Internet," invented the Spanning Tree Protocol that made modern Ethernet networks possible.

- Dr. Shirley Ann Jackson conducted breakthrough research in telecommunications, paving the way for innovations in caller ID and fiber optics.

- Ellen Pao, a venture capitalist and former Reddit CEO, became a national figure after suing her firm for gender discrimination – sparking a public reckoning in Silicon Valley.

But these successes were rare exceptions in an industry with staggering gender imbalances. As late as 2018, women made up only about 25 percent of computing jobs in the U.S. – and women of color represented a fraction of that; for example, Black women held about 3 percent and Latinas roughly 1 percent of computing roles. This gap is why, for the past twenty-two years, I have led *Girls for STEM* workshops as an active member of the American Association of University Women (AAUW), organizing programs that teach young girls about science, technology, engineering, and math – work I've run with great success at Barnard College and the University of Mount Saint Vincent in New York – so they see mentors, build skills, and know they belong.

The Rise of the Female Tech Founder

In the early 2000s, something began to shift. Tired of waiting for a seat at someone else's table, women started building their own.

- Reshma Saujani founded Girls Who Code to close the gender gap in tech by empowering a new generation of girls through coding education.

- Tracy Chou, a software engineer, launched Project Include to advocate for diversity and inclusion in tech hiring and culture.

- Ankiti Bose co-founded Zilingo, a fashion tech company that raised millions in venture funding before she turned thirty.

Globally, women are launching health tech platforms, climate data firms, edtech startups, and AI labs. They are disrupting not just industries but the gendered norms of innovation itself.

Coding as Empowerment

Today, learning to code is not just about career paths – it's about power. Programming is the new literacy of the twenty-first century. Women's access to that literacy has enormous implications for economic mobility, civic engagement, and leadership.

Organizations around the world are closing the digital divide:

- Black Girls Code, Kode With Klossy, and Technovation Challenge offer coding education to girls from underrepresented communities.

- In sub-Saharan Africa, women-led incubators are training young tech entrepreneurs to solve local problems with global tools.

- In Latin America, platforms like Laboratoria are helping low-income women gain the skills needed to enter the tech workforce.

The message is clear: women aren't just users of technology – they are creators, engineers, critics, and change agents.

Online Harassment and Digital Inequality

The digital world creates real attack surfaces: Women – especially those who are vocal, visible, or marginalized – face doxxing, stalking, non-consensual image sharing (including deepfakes), threats of sexual violence, and coordinated pile-ons that can escalate to swatting and offline harm. Gamergate in 2014 exposed the depth of misogyny in gaming and tech subcultures, sparking broader debates about platform responsibility, safety versus free expression, and systemic bias in digital spaces.

There are also economic inequalities:

- Women-owned startups receive just a small percentage of venture capital funding.
- Algorithmic bias in AI and machine learning systems – often trained on biased datasets – can reinforce discrimination in hiring, healthcare, policing, and finance.
- Globally, women are less likely to have access to the internet, mobile devices, and digital literacy tools, limiting their ability to participate in the digital economy.

Closing these gaps requires more than representation; it requires rethinking who tech serves and how it is built.

Reimagining the Future of Tech

Women are not just fitting into existing tech structures – they are redefining what technology can be. Feminist technologists are designing tools that prioritize ethics, inclusion, and equity. They are challenging surveillance capitalism, questioning biased algorithms, and advocating for user privacy and consent.

Women are leading conversations on:

- Tech ethics and AI governance
- Cybersecurity and data sovereignty
- Digital storytelling and immersive media
- Human-centered design and accessibility

As technology becomes more integrated into daily life, these voices are not just important – they are essential to building a world that reflects our highest values.

The Next Generation

A global movement is underway. Girls and young women are learning to code, engineer, invent, and lead. They are building apps to stop harassment, designing AI tools for mental health, and hacking education systems to make learning more inclusive.

They are no longer waiting to be invited into the future. They are building it themselves.

And this time, they're bringing everyone with them.

Chapter 9 highlights pioneering women in technology – founders, engineers, educators, and visionaries – who have shaped the digital age, broken through barriers, and created space for future generations of innovators.

Women and Technology – From Digital Pioneers to Tech Founders

Technology has shaped the modern world – and yet, for much of its history, the contributions of women to computing, innovation, and entrepreneurship have been minimized or forgotten. From early programming to cutting-edge startups, women have helped define the digital era. They have cracked codes, launched billion-dollar ventures, and created technologies that reshape how we live, learn, and connect.

Ada Lovelace, often called the world's first computer programmer, developed the first algorithm intended for machine execution in the mid-1800s. Working with Charles Babbage's Analytical Engine, she foresaw computers going beyond calculation – to compose music, process images, and more. Her notes were far ahead of their time, setting in motion the logic behind modern computing.

Grace Hopper, a U.S. Navy rear admiral and computer scientist, helped develop the first computer compiler and laid the groundwork for the COBOL programming language. Known as "Amazing Grace," Hopper popularized the idea of machine-independent programming languages and inspired generations of technologists with her visionary thinking and mentorship.

Radia Perlman, often dubbed the "Mother of the Internet," invented the spanning tree protocol, a critical component in how networks route data efficiently. Her innovations enabled scalable, robust communication systems – making modern networking and the Internet itself possible. Perlman also championed ethical tech education and inclusivity throughout her career.

Katherine Johnson, a mathematician at NASA, played a crucial role in the success of the U.S. space program. Her calculations enabled the Apollo missions and John Glenn's orbital flight. Johnson's brilliance and perseverance, in the face of racial and gender segregation, made her a trailblazer in both STEM and civil rights history.

Carol Shaw, among the first women to both design and program video games, worked at Atari and later Activision. *River Raid*'s success showed that women could innovate in a male-dominated industry. Her influence endures across gaming and digital entertainment.

Reshma Saujani, founder of Girls Who Code, has worked to close the gender gap in technology by creating educational programs that reach thousands of girls across the U.S. Saujani's advocacy focuses on shifting cultural narratives around failure, perfectionism, and female ambition – encouraging girls to be brave, not perfect.

Kimberly Bryant, an electrical engineer and the founder of Black Girls CODE, created a movement to empower girls of color with coding skills, mentorship, and a sense of belonging in tech. Her vision challenges systemic barriers and builds new pathways for digital innovation that is inclusive by design.

Anne Wojcicki, co-founder of the personal genomics company 23andMe, helped pioneer direct-to-consumer DNA testing. By putting genetic information in the hands of individuals, Wojcicki sparked global conversations about ancestry, health, privacy, and the future of personalized medicine.

Fei-Fei Li, a computer scientist and AI researcher, led the development of ImageNet, a massive visual database that advanced artificial intelligence through deep learning. As an advocate for "human-centered AI," Li has consistently emphasized ethics, bias mitigation, and representation in tech development.

These women did more than disrupt industries – they designed new ways of thinking. They changed the culture of technology and helped it serve a broader, more inclusive vision of humanity.

They proved technology is a tool for imagination, problem-solving, and social change.

As we build the future, their legacies remind us to ask: Who gets to invent it?

For a more complete list of Women Who Changed the Tech World (1940s to Today), see Appendix II.

Voices of Defiance

In the world of technology, women were often erased from the narrative – written out of innovation's story despite being its architects. Even in the shadows of mainframes and algorithms, women-built systems, launched revolutions, and founded companies that changed the world.

Their voices speak to the quiet brilliance of early pioneers and the bold vision of today's founders. They defied gender bias, challenged stereotypes, and proved that genius is not defined by who's allowed in the room – but by what one creates when they get there.

> *"The most dangerous phrase in the language is: '*
> *We've always done it this way.'"*

— Rear Admiral Grace Hopper,
computer programming pioneer
and inventor of the compiler

Hopper's rebellious innovation laid the foundation for modern programming, challenging rigid thinking in both military and tech spaces.

> *"I learned that it is faith that decides whether*
> *something will happen, not statistics."*

— Katherine Johnson,
NASA mathematician and one of
the women featured in *Hidden Figures*

Johnson's brilliance helped launch astronauts into space, and her courage broke racial and gender barriers at the highest levels of science and exploration.

> *"I didn't get there by wishing for it or*
> *hoping for it, but by working for it."*

— Estée Lauder,
cosmetics innovator and business mogul

Though not a tech founder, Lauder's words resonate with today's female entrepreneurs navigating startup culture – where persistence is power.

In conclusion, from coding rooms to boardrooms, women in technology showed that innovation thrives when diversity is not an afterthought but a driving force.

Reflection Prompts

1. Representation and Reality: Why do you think

women's contributions to technology have historically been overlooked or erased? How does this impact how we perceive the tech industry today?

2. Entrepreneurship and Innovation: What challenges do women tech founders face when launching startups or seeking funding? How can the investment and innovation ecosystems become more supportive of women?

3. Mentorship and Role Models: Who are some contemporary women in tech you admire? How do their stories inspire future generations of girls to pursue careers in science, engineering, and innovation?

4. Your Relationship with Tech: Reflect on your own use of technology. How has it empowered or challenged you? In what ways might you advocate for more inclusive and equitable tech solutions in your personal or professional life?

CHAPTER 10:
GLOBAL MOVEMENTS
AND THE POWER OF SOLIDARITY

"Alone we can do so little; together we can do so much."
— Helen Keller

The history of women's activism since 1950 is not just a story of individual courage or national reform. It is also a story of solidarity – the ways women across borders have connected, shared strategies, and built coalitions to amplify their collective power. Global feminism has expanded the scale of activism, but it has also faced challenges, from unequal access to resources to critiques of cultural dominance. Understanding both its strengths and limits shows how solidarity wins reforms (for example, anti-violence laws across countries) even as movements wrestle with who sets the agenda and who benefits.

In September 1995, the streets of Beijing filled with the voices of women from every corner of the world. Delegates carried banners in dozens of languages, their chants echoing across the conference grounds: demands for equality, justice, and recognition. Inside the halls, rural farmers from Africa spoke alongside corporate executives from Europe, and Indigenous leaders from the Americas debated policy with government ministers from Asia. Despite their different backgrounds, they shared one conviction: that women's voices must shape the global agenda.

This gathering – the Fourth World Conference on Women – brought together more than 30,000 activists and representatives from 189 countries. Out of it came the Beijing Platform for Action, a landmark framework for advancing women's rights globally. But perhaps its most lasting achievement was not the document itself – it was the sense of connection forged among women who realized their struggles were not isolated. They were linked, and together, they were stronger.

Women's rights movements have often emerged from the soil of national struggle – fighting local injustice, challenging cultural norms, and demanding systemic change. But over the past few decades, women's activism has grown global. What began as local flashpoints – like Iceland's 1975 Women's Day Off strike – has become interconnected movements, powered by digital tools, international networks, and a shared understanding: what happens to one of us affects us all.

In the face of authoritarianism, environmental collapse, economic injustice, and gender-based violence, women have led cross-border campaigns grounded in solidarity, sisterhood, and collective power. This chapter explores how global feminism evolved, the role of transnational movements, and the strategies women have used to build unity without erasing difference.

Solidarity is more than sympathy; it is the act of linking arms across differences to demand justice. In the late twentieth and early twenty-first centuries, women's movements learned that local struggles could not be isolated. Globalization, digital networks, and transnational activism turned feminist causes into worldwide mobilizations, reshaping both awareness and policy.

Ni Una Menos in Latin America

In 2015, thousands of women in Argentina filled the streets chanting "Ni Una Menos" ("Not One [Woman] Less"), protesting femicide and gender-based violence. The movement spread rapidly across Latin America, from Mexico to Chile, galvanized by the viral hashtag #NiUnaMenos, which broadcast testimonies and organizing calls across borders. Ni Una Menos proved how a local rallying cry could become a transnational movement through cultural resonance and shared struggle.

African Women's Peace Networks

In Liberia, the Women of Liberia Mass Action for Peace, led by Leymah Gbowee in the early 2000s, organized sit-ins, prayers, and nonviolent protests that pressured warring factions to end a brutal civil war. Their grassroots activism was instrumental in the peace agreement that followed, and Gbowee was awarded the Nobel Peace Prize in 2011. This story highlights how women's solidarity not only mobilizes protest but helps secure peace agreements and open paths to democratic elections.

Digital Solidarity Across Borders

Movements like #MeToo showed the role of social media in linking experiences worldwide. First gaining momentum in the United States in 2017, the hashtag quickly spread globally, adapted into local languages and contexts. In France, it became #BalanceTonPorc ("Expose Your Pig"); in China, activists used emojis to evade censorship. These digital adaptations revealed both the universality of sexual harassment and the unique risks activists face in different countries.

These examples demonstrate the mechanics of solidarity: shared language, shared space, and shared risk. Movements succeed not only by inspiring but by sustaining networks – through marches, hashtags, coalitions, and community ties. Yet challenges remain; accusations of Western dominance sometimes overshadow Global South leadership, and grassroots voices risk being drowned out by more visible elites. Still, the power of solidarity is undeniable: when women stand together across borders, their collective force reshapes not just politics, but the imagination of what justice can look like worldwide.

Networking Across Borders

Networking is the backbone of global solidarity. Conferences, workshops, and now digital platforms have enabled women to connect across geography, language, and politics. From the United Nations Decade for Women conferences (1975 to 1985) to today's social media–driven networks, women have forged bonds that make local struggles visible on a global stage. For example, the 2014 #BringBackOurGirls campaign began on Twitter in Nigeria and spread to Facebook and Instagram, transforming local outrage into worldwide pressure that prompted government responses and drew international assistance. These networks amplify voices often silenced at home, providing legitimacy and visibility that can pressure governments or international organizations.

Information Sharing

Solidarity has also flourished through the exchange of knowledge – reports, testimonies, and data that expose injustices. During the 1970s, newsletters circulated among feminist groups worldwide, linking activists in Latin America with those in Europe and Africa. In the digital age, hashtags like #MeToo and #BringBackOurGirls have carried stories across borders in seconds, transforming private experiences into public calls for justice. For example, UN Women's Global Database on Violence Against Women and Girls compiles national laws and policies; organizers use it to compare countries, spot legal gaps, and arm campaigns with evidence. Information sharing not only mobilizes support but also builds archives of resistance that future generations can draw upon.

Coalition Building

Coalitions emerge when diverse groups unite around shared goals, despite differences. Examples include the Women's Environment and Development Organization (WEDO), which connected women activists to global climate negotiations, and the African Women's Development and Communication Network (FEMNET), which amplifies regional voices in policy debates. Coalitions can secure seats at negotiating tables, influence treaties, and ensure women's perspectives shape global priorities.

Successes of Global Solidarity

Solidarity has led to tangible victories. The 1995 Beijing Conference on Women mobilized over 30,000 activists, producing the Beijing Platform for Action, a landmark framework still guiding international gender policy. Campaigns to end practices like female genital mutilation gained traction by linking local activists with international NGOs, creating pressure that combined cultural sensitivity with global accountability.

Transnational alliances have also strengthened labor movements: Latin American and Asian garment workers, for instance, have coordinated campaigns against exploitative multinational corporations, leading to corporate codes of conduct and safer working conditions.

Critiques and Limitations

Yet solidarity is not without its critics. Many have pointed out that global feminism has too often reflected Western priorities and voices, sidelining women from the Global South. Activists in Africa, Asia, and Latin America have argued that Western frameworks sometimes impose solutions without attending to cultural contexts, echoing older patterns of colonial power.

Resource imbalances are a persistent barrier: groups with more funding and visibility often dominate agendas, while grassroots activists struggle for recognition. Even in digital spaces, inequalities in internet access create uneven participation, meaning some voices remain unheard.

There is also the challenge of sustaining solidarity across differences. Coalitions may fracture when priorities diverge, such as when economic development goals conflict with environmental sustainability, or when LGBTQ+ rights clash with more conservative local norms. These tensions highlight the ongoing negotiation required to build inclusive and effective movements.

The Future of Solidarity

Global solidarity is both fragile and powerful. Its mechanisms – networking, information sharing, and coalition building – have proven vital in amplifying women's voices and securing reforms. Yet its limits remind us that solidarity must be reflexive, attentive to power imbalances, and committed to inclusion. The power of solidarity lies not in erasing differences but in weaving them into a fabric strong enough to resist oppression in all its forms. When women in Mexico City march alongside women in Johannesburg or Seoul, and when hashtags link survivors in rural villages with advocates in global capitals, solidarity becomes more than a concept – it becomes a force capable of reshaping the world.

From Local Resistance to Global Connection

Historically, many feminist movements reflected national identity, the colonial aftermath, and cultural contexts. While twentieth-century Western feminism focused on workplace equality and legal rights, women in the Global South often organized against imperialism, economic exploitation, and patriarchal customs imposed by colonizers and local elites.

Hashtags and Human Rights

A single tag could mobilize across languages and time zones.

- #MeToo, started by activist Tarana Burke and later popularized globally, exposed the epidemic of sexual harassment and assault in every corner of society – from Hollywood to hospitals, parliaments to plantations.

- #BringBackOurGirls, led by Nigerian women including Oby Ezekwesili, mobilized global attention after Boko Haram kidnapped hundreds of schoolgirls.

- #NiUnaMenos in Latin America became a transnational rallying cry against femicide and gender-based violence, especially in Argentina, Mexico, and Peru.

- #MahsaAmini protests in Iran were sparked by the death of a young woman detained for "improper" dress, prompting nationwide marches, university walkouts, and solidarity rallies abroad under authoritarian rule.

- In India, South Africa, and Turkey, movements against rape culture and honor-based violence gained traction, with young women demanding change through digital platforms and street protests alike.

These were not just hashtag campaigns – they were political awakenings. They connected survivors, pressured states, and revealed transnational patterns of harm. They also established the infrastructure for the next fight: climate justice, where unequal exposure, recovery, and voice are deeply gendered.

Climate Justice, Indigenous Rights, and Feminist Environmentalism

Women have led the global environmental movement, especially in the Global South, where climate shocks reshape water access, food security, and migration.

- In Kenya, Wangari Maathai's Green Belt Movement mobilized thousands of women to plant trees, fight deforestation, and demand democracy.

- In the Amazon, Indigenous women like Nemonte Nenquimo led campaigns to protect ancestral lands from oil extraction.

- In Fiji, women-led groups such as femLINKpacific's Women's Weather Watch and the regionwide Shifting the Power Coalition organize early-warning networks and relocation advocacy, framing climate justice as a feminist issue.

- Globally, the Fridays for Future movement, led in part by activists like Greta Thunberg and Vanessa Nakate, illustrates the rise of young women leading planetary resistance.

Feminist environmentalism holds that the exploitation of nature and of women are linked, both driven by systems of domination that prioritize profit over life.

Feminist Solidarity in Humanitarian and Crisis Zones

Whether responding to war, disaster, or displacement, women have played essential roles in humanitarian response – often stepping in where formal institutions fail.

- In refugee camps, women form mutual aid groups, teach each other literacy, and care for orphaned children.

- In conflict zones, peace negotiations have higher success rates when women are meaningfully included – for example, as witnesses/signatories, mediators, or negotiators (2015) – yet they are often excluded from the table.

- Organizations like Women for Women International and MADRE work to amplify women's voices in places like Syria,

Afghanistan, Sudan, and Ukraine – ensuring aid addresses not just survival, but dignity.

Global feminism insists that no woman is "too far away" to matter. It is built on the understanding that human rights are universal and that solidarity means more than sympathy – it means action.

Building Inclusive Global Movements

True global solidarity must grapple with differences. It must respect local leadership, acknowledge privilege, and avoid imposing "solutions" that ignore culture or context.

Modern global feminist movements strive to:

- Center voices from the Global South
- Use intersectional analysis that includes race, class, ability, and sexuality
- Fund women-led initiatives rather than top-down aid
- Create multilingual, accessible spaces for collaboration
- Support both policy advocacy and grassroots organizing

This is feminism as plural, relational, and evolving. It doesn't always agree – but it is committed to liberation for all.

The Power of Collective Vision

In a world increasingly fractured by conflict, inequality, and misinformation, women-led movements remain some of the most visionary and effective forces for good. Their power comes not just from protest, but from proposition. They are building new ways of living, governing, and healing.

They imagine peace not just as the absence of war, but the presence of justice.

They envision economies that reward care and

cooperation, not just profit and exploitation.

They believe in leadership that is ethical, collaborative, and accountable to the most vulnerable.

And they know that no revolution lasts without love – and that solidarity, rooted in love, is the most radical tool of all.

Chapter 10 highlights influential leaders, organizations, and global movements that have shaped the modern feminist landscape through solidarity, activism, and cross-border collaboration.

Global Movements and the Power of Solidarity

Across borders, women have organized, resisted, and uplifted one another in the face of patriarchal, colonial, and authoritarian systems. These movements – sometimes quiet, sometimes loud – draw strength from solidarity: the conviction that individual liberation is bound to the collective.

This chapter traces the stories of women who built bridges across borders, languages, and struggles – reminding us that global feminism is both local and universal.

Wangari Maathai, a Kenyan environmentalist and human rights activist, founded the Green Belt Movement in 1977 to combat deforestation, poverty, and women's disenfranchisement. Her movement mobilized thousands of women to plant millions of trees – restoring ecosystems and building leadership from the ground up. In 2004, she became the first African woman to receive the Nobel Peace Prize.

Malala Yousafzai, a Pakistani advocate for girls' education, survived an assassination attempt by the Taliban and became a global symbol of resilience and youth activism. Through the Malala Fund, she campaigns for educational access worldwide, emphasizing the interconnection between gender equity, peace, and education.

These movements, from quiet organizing to mass uprisings, draw strength from solidarity – the belief that individual liberation is bound to the collective.

Leymah Gbowee, a Liberian peace activist, mobilized Christian and Muslim women in a nonviolent movement to end Liberia's second civil war. Her leadership helped force a peace agreement and paved the way for the election of Africa's first female president, Ellen Johnson Sirleaf. Gbowee's story is a testament to the moral authority of grassroots, interfaith, and women-led activism.

Rigoberta Menchú Tum, a K'iche' Maya woman from Guatemala, brought international attention to the oppression of Indigenous peoples and the violence of civil war. Her autobiography and activism helped secure her the Nobel Peace Prize in 1992. She advocated not only for Indigenous rights but for peace and justice throughout Latin America.

Sister Simone Campbell, an American Roman Catholic nun and lawyer, gained national recognition for organizing the "Nuns on the Bus" campaigns, which championed healthcare access, immigration reform, and economic justice. Her work represents a spiritual form of solidarity — bringing faith and feminism into progressive coalitions.

Huda Sha'arawi, a pioneering Egyptian feminist, founded the Egyptian Feminist Union in 1923 and fought for women's education, political participation, and the dismantling of colonial and patriarchal systems. Her decision to remove her veil in public became a symbolic act of resistance and marked the beginning of secular feminist organizing in Egypt.

Chimamanda Ngozi Adichie, a Nigerian writer and thinker, has amplified feminist discourse through literature and global lectures. Her essay *We Should All Be Feminists* and TED Talks have sparked global conversations about gender, identity, and power. Adichie's work bridges cultural divides, making feminism accessible and affirming to audiences across the globe.

Zainah Anwar, a Malaysian human rights advocate and co-founder of Sisters in Islam, has worked to reinterpret Islamic teachings through a feminist lens. Her efforts challenge both state and religious patriarchy, promoting legal reforms and women's autonomy in Muslim-majority societies. Anwar's vision is one of reform from within.

Maria Ressa, a journalist and co-founder of Rappler in the Philippines, has stood on the frontlines of the fight for press freedom in an era of authoritarianism and digital misinformation. Ressa is a Nobel Peace Prize laureate whose commitment to truth and transparency is inseparable from feminist solidarity; she insists on protecting women journalists worldwide.

These women didn't just lead movements – they embodied them. Their work reminds us that feminism cannot thrive in isolation. It grows through dialogue, alliance, and mutual respect across boundaries.

Solidarity, they teach us, is not an ideal; it is a practice. A hand extended. A voice raised. A tree planted, a book written, a veil lifted, a truth spoken.

In an age of global crisis and connection, their stories shine as road maps to collective freedom.

For a more complete list of Global Feminist Leaders and Movements (1990s to Today), see Appendix II.

Voices of Defiance

Across borders, languages, and ideologies, women have found one another in struggle – and in strength. From the factory floors of Bangladesh to the streets of Tehran, from Indigenous land defenders to Nobel laureates, global solidarity has become one of feminism's most powerful tools. These voices remind us that no victory is truly local, and no injustice too far removed. When women stand together – across nations and differences – they don't just resist oppression; they reshape the future. Their words are declarations of unity, courage, and the unstoppable force of collective action.

> *"Human rights are women's rights and*
> *women's rights are human rights."*

— Hillary Rodham Clinton,
UN World Conference on Women, Beijing, 1995

In one of the most iconic speeches in modern feminist history, Clinton's declaration ignited a global call to integrate gender justice into every human rights cause.

"Feminism is worthless without solidarity. We must listen, learn, and act – not just for ourselves, but for those most silenced."

— Aminatou Sow,
Guinean American digital strategist
and co-founder of Tech Lady Mafia

Sow's work bridges digital spaces with feminist organizing, reminding us that global connection requires humility and shared responsibility.

"You strike a woman, you strike a rock."

— South African women's anti-apartheid slogan,
Women's March, Pretoria, 1956

This rallying cry from Black South African women echoes through history as a powerful reminder of resistance rooted in dignity, community, and unyielding spirit.

Solidarity draws its power from unity, not uniformity; when women stand together across borders, barriers fall.

Reflection Prompts

1. Barriers to Solidarity: What challenges exist when trying to build solidarity across cultures, languages, or political systems? How might these challenges be addressed?

2. Personal Global Citizenship: How has learning about global feminist movements expanded your own understanding of feminism? What does being a "global feminist" mean to you personally?

3. Amplifying Voices: Are there feminist voices, movements, or stories from another country

that have moved or inspired you? How might you help amplify them in your community or network?

4. magining a United Future: If you could design a global summit for women's rights, what issues would be at the center? Who would be invited to lead the conversation, and what outcomes would you hope to achieve?

CHAPTER 11:
HEALTH, REPRODUCTIVE RIGHTS, AND AUTONOMY

"No woman can call herself free who does not control her own body."
— Margaret Sanger

From clinics and courtrooms to parliaments and protest lines, this chapter traces the fight for health, reproductive rights, and the autonomy that makes every other freedom possible.

Margaret Sanger and the Fight for Birth Control in the U.S.

In the early twentieth century, contraception was illegal in much of the United States. Margaret Sanger, a nurse, opened the nation's first birth control clinic in 1916, an act that led to her arrest. Her activism eventually helped secure the legalization of contraception and laid the foundation for Planned Parenthood. While her legacy is complex, Sanger's efforts spotlight how access to reproductive health care was – and remains – a cornerstone of women's autonomy.

Ireland's Repeal Movement

For decades, Ireland had some of the strictest abortion laws in Europe. In 2018, after years of grassroots organizing led largely by young women, the country voted to repeal the Eighth Amendment, which had banned abortion. Campaigners used storytelling – women sharing their personal experiences of traveling abroad for abortion care – to transform public opinion. Their success showed how personal narratives can shift national policy. Health is not only a biological condition – it is political. Access to contraception, maternal care, and freedom from violence determine whether women can live with dignity, opportunity, and choice. While progress has been made, the fight for health and autonomy remains uneven across the globe.

These stories – from Sanger's clinic in the U.S. to Ireland's Repeal movement and maternal health campaigns in Africa – highlight the diversity of struggles for women's autonomy. Yet they share common threads: the fight against stigma, the demand for recognition, and the insistence that women's health is a human right. When women claim control over their bodies, they claim control over their futures. Autonomy in health is the foundation of autonomy in every other sphere of life, the very measure of women's freedom.

In a rural clinic outside Kigali, Rwanda, a young woman named Amina waits nervously for her first prenatal checkup. A decade earlier, such a visit was rare in this region. Maternal mortality rates were so high that pregnancy was often a gamble with survival. But today, community health workers are present in nearly every village, and Amina is part of a new generation of women who can expect safe care during pregnancy. Her story is both hopeful and sobering: hopeful because progress is possible, sobering because for millions of women worldwide, such access remains out of reach.

Amina's experience illustrates the central theme of this chapter: women's health is inseparable from women's autonomy. Whether deciding if and when to have children, accessing safe and respectful maternal care, or living free from violence, health is not merely a medical issue but a fundamental human right.

From access to reproductive care to the fight against gender-based violence, women's ability to control their bodies and health outcomes has shaped not only personal lives but also broader social and political movements. Yet "women's health" is not a singular issue – it encompasses interconnected but distinct struggles. This chapter explores three critical dimensions: reproductive rights, maternal health, and gender-based violence.

Reproductive Rights: The Fight for Control

Reproductive rights remain one of the most visible battlegrounds in women's health. The right to decide whether, when, and how to have children has been central to women's economic independence and social equality.

- o **Global Legal Landscape:** In 1960, only a handful of countries had legalized contraception or abortion. Today, more than 90 percent of UN member states permit contraception, and around seventy countries allow abortion on request or broad social grounds. Yet in many parts of Latin America, Africa, and South Asia, restrictive laws still drive unsafe procedures, contributing to an estimated 39,000 maternal deaths annually, according to the WHO.
- o **Landmark Cases:** In the United States, Roe v. Wade (1973) expanded reproductive rights for decades, though it was overturned in 2022, reigniting global debates. In contrast, countries such as Ireland (2018 referendum) and Argentina (2020 legislation) have recently liberalized abortion laws, signaling shifting cultural norms.
- o **Access Inequalities:** Even where legal, access remains unequal. Rural women, low-income women, and women of color often face barriers to safe, affordable reproductive care.

The reproductive rights movement illustrates both victories and reversals, highlighting the fragile nature of gains that hinge on political climate.

Maternal Health: From Mortality to Well-Being

Maternal health is a cornerstone of women's health globally, yet disparities remain profound.

Global Trends: Since 2000, the global maternal mortality ratio has declined by about 40 percent (to 197 per 100,000 in 2023). Yet an estimated 260,000 women still died from pregnancy and childbirth in 2023, according to the WHO. Nearly 70 percent of those deaths occurred in sub-Saharan Africa and approximately 17 percent in Central and Southern Asia, underscoring stark inequities.

- **Access to Care:** In wealthier nations, maternal health is increasingly framed around holistic care, including mental health and postpartum well-being. By contrast, in low- and middle-income countries, basic access to skilled birth attendants and emergency obstetric care remains the defining challenge.

- **Case Example:** In Rwanda, government investment in community health workers and universal health insurance has significantly reduced maternal mortality, offering a model for resource-limited contexts.

- **Disparities Within Countries:** In the United States, Black women are three times more likely than white women to die from pregnancy-related complications, underscoring that wealth does not guarantee equity.

Maternal health reflects how women's well-being is shaped by both global inequalities and domestic systems of race and class.

Gender-Based Violence: Health as a Human Rights Issue

Gender-based violence is often treated as separate from health, though its physical and psychological impacts are profound.

- **Global Scope:** The World Health Organization estimates that one in three women worldwide have experienced physical and/or sexual violence in their lifetime. Gender-based violence is a global epidemic with health consequences ranging from physical injury to depression, anxiety, and maternal health complications.

- **Policy and Legal Responses:** Laws addressing domestic violence and marital rape have expanded since the 1970s, though enforcement remains uneven. In 1993, the UN declared violence against women a human rights violation, spurring global advocacy.

- **Case Example:** In India, the 2012 Delhi gang rape sparked nationwide protests and led to significant legal reforms, including stricter penalties for sexual violence. In Latin America, the Ni Una Menos movement has mobilized millions against femicide, linking gender-based violence to systemic inequality.

Autonomy as the Common Thread

Across reproductive rights, maternal health, and gender-based violence, autonomy is the throughline: progress is real but uneven, and only by treating health as a comprehensive human right can change endure. Whether choosing when to have children, surviving childbirth safely, or living free from violence, the right to health is inseparable from the right to dignity and self-determination.

The global picture is uneven – marked by both undeniable progress and persistent inequities. To achieve true autonomy, health must be approached not as a narrow medical issue but as a comprehensive human right.

To control one's body is to control one's life. And yet,

throughout history, women's bodies have often been controlled by others – by governments, institutions, families, religious authorities, and cultural norms. The fight for reproductive rights and bodily autonomy is one of the most enduring – and deeply personal – struggles of the women's movement. It is a battle for freedom, for dignity, and for the right to make decisions without fear, shame, or coercion.

This chapter explores the evolution of reproductive rights from the post-war era to the present day, the global inequities that persist, and how women have fought for health care not just as a service – but as a human right.

Reproductive Rights as Human Rights

In 1994, at the International Conference on Population and Development (ICPD) in Cairo, a global consensus was reached: reproductive rights are human rights. The conference redefined population policy, moving away from coercive control toward a rights-based approach that emphasized:

- The right to decide freely and responsibly the number and spacing of children
- Access to information, education, and means to do so
- The right to attain the highest standard of sexual and reproductive health

This declaration, championed by women from around the world, made it clear that reproductive freedom is central to gender equality, health, and development.

The Global Landscape: Uneven Access and Persistent Inequities

Despite progress, reproductive rights remain uneven and fragile worldwide.

In many African and South Asian countries, access to contraception, safe abortion, and maternal care is limited by poverty, distance, stigma, and underfunded health systems. In some places, women must seek permission from husbands or in-laws for basic care.

- In Latin America, countries like Argentina and Mexico have legalized abortion in recent years due to sustained feminist pressure, while others like El Salvador still impose total bans – with women imprisoned for miscarriages.
- In the United States, the 2022 reversal of Roe v. Wade ended a federal right and replaced it with a patchwork; activism surged, and legal whiplash followed.
- In the Middle East and parts of Asia, reproductive autonomy is often controlled through both religious and state policies, including forced veiling, sterilization, or denial of access to sexual health education.

Across the world, reproductive justice is not simply about legality – it's about access, equity, and agency.

The Maternal Health Divide

Another major aspect of reproductive justice is maternal health – and here, too, inequality is stark.

- In sub-Saharan Africa, a woman's lifetime risk of dying from pregnancy or childbirth complications is 1 in 37, compared to 1 in 3,800 in high-income countries.
- Black women in the United States are three times more likely to die from pregnancy-related causes than white women – regardless of income or education.
- Indigenous women in Canada, Australia, and the United States face systemic neglect, lack of culturally appropriate care, and significantly

worse outcomes. These gaps are built in, not incidental: rooted in racism, sexism, and austerity baked into health systems.

Activists and midwives worldwide are fighting for maternal health justice – advocating for:

- Skilled birth attendants and safe facilities
- Respectful, non-coercive care
- Postpartum support and mental health resources
- Recognition of traditional birthing knowledge and practices

The Politics of Contraception and Abortion

Access to contraception transformed the last century – and continues to reshape lives today. It has enabled women to:

- Pursue education and employment
- Plan families on their own terms
- Reduce poverty and maternal mortality
- Strengthen relationships and economic independence

But contraception remains highly politicized, with restrictions, misinformation, and cost barriers in many regions. In some countries, family planning programs still prioritize population control over consent and choice – targeting poor, rural, or minority women disproportionately.

Abortion access is even more contested. In some places, it is safe and legal; in others, it is criminalized, dangerous, or only available to the wealthy.

Women's bodies remain the terrain of political control, policed to signal morality, discipline populations, and enforce power. But women are fighting back with powerful, coordinated resistance, from legal advocacy to underground support networks.

Reproductive Justice: A Broader Vision

The term reproductive justice, coined by Black women activists in the 1990s, expanded the conversation beyond rights to real-world access and equity. It recognizes that reproductive freedom requires more than legality – it requires:

- Economic security
- Housing and education
- Freedom from violence
- Environmental safety
- The ability to raise children in safe, supportive communities

Reproductive justice connects abortion access to immigrant rights, anti-poverty efforts, LGBTQ+ equality, and disability justice. It demands a world in which *every person has the right to have children, not have children, and parent the children they have in safe and sustainable communities.*

Organizations like SisterSong, The Afiya Center, and Forward Together have led this movement – centering the voices of Black, Indigenous, and other marginalized women.

Autonomy Beyond Reproduction

Autonomy also includes the right to comprehensive sex education, consent-based relationships, gender-affirming care, and body sovereignty.

Feminists have fought to end:

- Forced sterilization of Indigenous, disabled, or incarcerated women
- Obstetric violence and coercion during childbirth
- Sexual abuse by health care providers
- Denial of care based on marital status, gender identity, or religion

They have also advocated for:

- LGBTQ+ inclusive reproductive care
- Transgender health equity
- Access to fertility treatments for all, regardless of marital or financial status

Autonomy is not just about reproduction – it's about dignity, knowledge, and control over one's life and body.

The Way Forward

The path to reproductive justice is long, but it is one of the most urgent frontiers of gender equality.

It requires:

- Investing in universal health care
- Protecting reproductive rights in law and practice
- Trusting women to know their needs
- Listening to the communities most affected
- Treating health as a public good, not a privilege or political tool

The struggle for reproductive rights is not just about policy – it's about humanity. It is about ensuring that every woman, girl, and gender-diverse person has the power to make decisions about their body, future, and family.

Without that power, freedom is incomplete.

This chapter highlights influential leaders, advocates, and organizations from around the world who have advanced reproductive rights, health equity, and bodily autonomy for women and marginalized communities.

Profiles in Action: Health, Reproductive Rights, and Autonomy

Control over one's body has always been at the heart of the feminist struggle. Access to healthcare, reproductive rights, and bodily autonomy not only affects personal well-being but also shapes women's social, political, and economic freedom. Across the globe, women have fought – and continue to fight – for the right to make decisions about their bodies, their families, and their futures.

This chapter highlights the women who transformed personal health into public advocacy and private struggle into global movements.

Margaret Sanger, a birth control activist and nurse, opened the first birth control clinic in the United States in 1916. Her advocacy led to the founding of Planned Parenthood and the eventual legalization of contraception. Though her legacy is complex – due to her associations with eugenics – her role in expanding reproductive choices remains pivotal to women's health history.

Dr. Helen Rodríguez-Trías, a pediatrician and women's health activist, was the first Latina president of the American Public Health Association. She fought against forced sterilization, advocated for maternal and child health, and worked globally to improve access to reproductive healthcare for marginalized communities. Her work bridged race, gender, and class justice in medicine.

Loretta Ross, a reproductive justice pioneer, helped coin and define the term "reproductive justice" – a framework that goes beyond the legal right to abortion and emphasizes the right to have children, not have children, and parent in safe environments. As a Black feminist and activist, Ross has connected reproductive rights with human rights, economic justice, and anti-racism.

Dr. Gita Sen, an Indian scholar and health policy expert, has been a leading voice in global debates on women's health and reproductive rights. She helped shape the 1994 International Conference on Population and Development, placing women's autonomy and consent at the center of global health policy.

Mónica Roa, a Colombian human rights lawyer, successfully led a legal strategy to liberalize abortion laws in

Colombia. Her efforts reframed the conversation from morality to human rights, making Latin America's deeply conservative legal systems more accountable to women's needs.

Rebecca Gomperts, a Dutch physician, founded Women on Waves, a nonprofit that sails to countries with restrictive abortion laws to provide reproductive healthcare on international waters. Her creative activism has brought medical access and international attention to abortion rights in some of the world's most restrictive regions.

Dr. Denis Mukwege and Nadia Murad, co-recipients of the 2018 Nobel Peace Prize, have spotlighted the use of sexual violence as a weapon of war. While Dr. Mukwege treats survivors in the Democratic Republic of Congo, Murad – a Yazidi survivor of ISIS captivity – has become a global advocate for justice, healing, and survivor-centered policy.

Cecile Richards, president of Planned Parenthood from 2006 to 2018, expanded access to reproductive health services across the United States while navigating intense political opposition. A gifted organizer and communicator, Richards emphasized that reproductive care is essential healthcare.

Marielle Franco, a Brazilian city councilwoman and human rights defender, was an outspoken advocate for LGBTQ+ rights, racial justice, and reproductive autonomy before her assassination in 2018. Her legacy continues to inspire feminist resistance movements in Brazil and beyond.

These women remind us that autonomy is not given – it is demanded, defended, and continuously redefined.

Health is political. Reproduction is not a side issue. And the right to control one's body is a prerequisite for freedom.

Their stories are blueprints for care that is just, inclusive, and life-affirming.

For a more complete list of Global Leaders and Advocates in Reproductive Health and Rights, see Appendix III.

Voices of Defiance

The fight for women's health and reproductive rights has never been just about medicine – it has always been about power, dignity, and freedom. Across time and continents, women have demanded the right to govern their bodies, challenge harmful taboos, and claim autonomy in a world that too often saw them as property, patients, or problems to be managed. These voices speak to defiance in the face of control, courage in the face of stigma, and the enduring belief that autonomy is not a luxury – it is a human right.

> *"No woman can call herself free who does not control her own body."*
>
> — Margaret Sanger,
> birth control advocate

Though her legacy is complex, Sanger's words ignited a century-long movement for reproductive access and sparked radical shifts in public health.

> *"Abortion is a personal decision. You can morally disagree with it and still believe it should be legal."*
>
> — Ruth Bader Ginsburg,
> U.S. Supreme Court Justice

Ginsburg's legal clarity continues to frame bodily autonomy as a constitutional and moral imperative.

> *"I am not your tragic heroine. I am a survivor. I am the author of my own health story."*
>
> — Padma Lakshmi,
> endometriosis advocate and TV host

Lakshmi brought national attention to reproductive health by sharing her own experience – breaking silence around pain, invisibility, and dismissal.

In conclusion, by reclaiming control over their bodies, women affirm that autonomy is not negotiable; it is the foundation of equality.

Reflection Prompts

1. Historical Perspective: What were some of the most significant turning points in the history of reproductive rights and healthcare access for women? What legacies from those moments are still felt today?
2. Global Landscape: In what ways do reproductive rights vary across the world today? What countries or regions are advancing, and which are regressing? What factors drive those changes?
3. Advocacy and Action: What role can individuals play in protecting reproductive rights and promoting healthcare equity in their communities? What organizations or causes do you feel called to support?
4. A Vision for the Future: Imagine a healthcare system designed with women's autonomy, dignity, and diversity at its center. What would it look like? How would care be delivered, and by whom?

CHAPTER 12:
THE ROAD AHEAD – LEADERSHIP, LEGACY, AND COLLECTIVE VISION

"The best way to predict the future is to create it."
— Eleanor Roosevelt

Women's hard-won progress offers both a legacy of courage and a blueprint for the future. Over the course of this book, we have traced the journeys of women who stepped into classrooms and parliaments, laboratories and living rooms, sports fields and boardrooms, community centers and global stages. From the pioneers of the 1950s to today's activists and innovators, women have reshaped society in ways once thought impossible. Yet the question that guided this book – how have women since 1950 reshaped society, and what remains to be done?

The chapters that came before reveal a mosaic of progress: the courage of activists who challenged colonialism and civil rights abuses, the determination of women who claimed access to education and health, the ingenuity of technologists and entrepreneurs, the creativity of artists, the resilience of mothers, workers, and community leaders. Together, their stories form a legacy. But legacy alone is not enough; it must be carried forward into collective vision and concrete action.

The future of gender equality isn't abstract; women are building it every day – leading, innovating, imagining differently. As we look ahead, the question is not only what has been achieved, but what remains possible when women's voices shape the agenda.

Jacinda Ardern and Compassionate Leadership. When Jacinda Ardern became Prime Minister of New Zealand in 2017, she embodied a new model of leadership: empathetic, transparent, and inclusive. Her response to the 2019 Christchurch mosque shootings – showing solidarity with Muslim communities and swiftly reforming gun laws – proved compassion is political strength. Ardern's style challenged traditional notions of power, offering a vision of governance rooted in care.

Greta Thunberg and Youth Climate Leadership

At just fifteen, Greta Thunberg began striking from school to demand climate action outside the Swedish parliament. Her solitary act grew into the *Fridays for Future* movement, mobilizing millions of young people worldwide. Thunberg's activism highlights the interconnection between gender, youth, and climate justice – demonstrating how the next generation is already reshaping global debates.

Grassroots Economic and Educational Initiatives

In Rwanda, women-led cooperatives have rebuilt communities in the wake of genocide, focusing on agriculture, microfinance, and literacy. These grassroots efforts show that leadership does not only reside in parliaments or boardrooms but also in villages, markets, and classrooms. By pooling resources and knowledge, women create models of sustainable development – models policymakers keep trying to copy.

These stories – of prime ministers, activists, and grassroots leaders – point toward a collective vision of the future: one in which power is shared, leadership is inclusive, and equity is non-negotiable. The road ahead is not without obstacles, from backlash politics to economic inequality. Yet the momentum of women's leadership shows that progress is not only possible but durable when vision is coupled with persistence. The legacy of women's progress is not what they have inherited but what they are building: a future where equality is the foundation, not the goal.

Concrete Steps for the Future

- Educate and Mentor: Invest in the next generation by mentoring young women and men alike in the values of equity. Support girls' education locally and globally.

- Challenge Stereotypes: In everyday conversations and choices – whether as parents, coworkers, or community members – reject limiting narratives of what women "should" or "should not" do.

- Vote and Advocate: Support policies that expand access to healthcare, childcare, reproductive rights, equal pay, and protection from violence. Use your civic voice to keep these issues at the forefront.

For Policymakers

- Strengthen Legal Frameworks: Enact and enforce laws on equal pay, workplace protections, and gender-based violence. Ensure reproductive rights are recognized as part of healthcare.

- Invest in Infrastructure of Care: Provide affordable childcare, parental leave, and elder care – recognizing that economic empowerment depends on redistributing care responsibilities.

- Support Inclusive Leadership Pipelines: Create quotas, incentives, or leadership programs that bring more women, especially from marginalized communities, into political and corporate leadership.

For Organizations and Institutions

- Audit and Act: Regularly assess gender pay gaps, promotion rates, and representation at all levels – and publish results transparently.

- Cultivate Inclusive Cultures: Move beyond token representation by embedding diversity and inclusion into organizational values, training, and accountability systems.

- Fund Women's Innovation: Channel venture capital, grants, and philanthropy toward women entrepreneurs, activists, and grassroots organizations worldwide.

Revisiting the Central Question

So – how have women reshaped society since 1950, and what remains to be done? The preceding chapters suggest three interwoven answers:

1. Women expanded boundaries – from classrooms and playing fields to parliaments and labs – redefining what was possible.
2. They revealed how struggles interlock, showing that gender justice is inseparable from racial, economic, and environmental justice.
3. And they built a solidarity that crosses borders, linking local fights into global movements that shift laws, norms, and power.

What remains: turn representation into durable rights and resources; close gaps in health, safety, and pay; and keep solidarity inclusive and accountable.

Legacy and Collective Vision

The road ahead belongs less to lone heroines than to collective vision. The legacy of women's progress is not only what has been won but the standing demand that justice, equity, and dignity be non-negotiable foundations of society. Advancing gender equality now calls for courage paired with strategy, durable policy, and patient persistence.

As we continue, the invitation is clear: see yourself as part of this unfinished story. Whether you are a student, a policymaker, a parent, a leader, or simply a citizen who believes in fairness, you have a role in carrying forward the legacy of women who have already reshaped our world. Their progress has opened the door; our collective vision must ensure it never closes again.

From mid-twentieth-century resistance to the digital rise of today's global movements, women have shattered barriers in art, politics, education, health, technology, and activism. And yet – despite all the gains – we are not done. The struggle for equality and dignity continues. And in that struggle, a new kind of leadership is emerging: collaborative, intergenerational, cross-cultural, and unapologetically structural.

In this chapter, we reflect on the legacy of those who came before, the lessons of the present, and the responsibilities that lie ahead.

Rewriting the Definition of Leadership

Leadership has too often been equated with dominance, charisma, or titles. But around the world, women are offering a different model – one rooted in service, empathy, resilience, and shared power.

They are:

- Elders mentoring the next generation of activists.
- Students mobilizing for climate justice.
- Midwives advocating for better maternal care in remote villages.
- Politicians challenging patriarchal systems in parliaments.
- Trans and nonbinary people redefining gender justice.

- Mothers, daughters, sisters, and friends building networks of survival, creativity, and hope.

These don't always make headlines, but they change history.

Legacy as a Living Force

The legacy of feminist progress is not a static archive – it is a living force, passed on through stories, actions, and memory. Every law changed, every door opened, and every silence broken is part of that inheritance.

But legacy also comes with questions:

- What kind of world are we leaving behind?
- How do we ensure that gains are not undone?
- Who are we lifting as we climb?

Today's feminists are inheritors – but also stewards. They must protect the progress made, deepen it, and adapt it to new challenges: climate collapse, digital authoritarianism, algorithmic bias, forced migration, and rising inequality.

As legacy builders, we must be willing to listen, to learn, and to reimagine what liberation looks like in a rapidly changing world.

The Role of Men and Boys

Feminism was never only for women. It calls on men and boys to reject toxic norms, to redefine what strength looks like, and to stand as partners – respectful, responsible, and fully engaged.

Movements like HeForShe, Promundo, and countless community-based programs are encouraging men to become allies, caregivers, and co-creators of change – not because women need rescuing, but because liberation benefits everyone.

Patriarchy limits not only women – it also harms men, trapping them in roles that silence emotion, discourage vulnerability, and equate power with control.

The road ahead demands *shared leadership* and a *shared vision* – not division, but partnership.

Intergenerational Power

A defining strength of today's feminist movement is its intergenerational power. Grandmothers march with teenagers. Elders bring wisdom. Youth bring urgency.

Rather than a single torch passed from one hand to the next, today's leadership is more like a bonfire – fed by many hands, many stories, and many flames.

But generational differences can also spark tension:

- Digital-native feminists may challenge older models of activism.

- Veteran organizers may feel dismissed or misunderstood.

- Language, tactics, and goals can differ.

The answer is not to divide – but to dialogue. To recognize that progress is strongest when it includes experience and innovation, history and hope.

Visions of the Future

A truly feminist future is clear.
It is a world where:

- Education, safety, and health care are rights, not luxuries.

- Work is valued not by profit alone but by its contribution to human well-being.

- Political power reflects the people it serves – diverse, representative, and just.

- Reproductive autonomy is universally protected.

- Technology is inclusive, ethical, and built by many hands.

- Art, culture, and sport reflect the full complexity of human experience.
- War, violence, and inequality are not inevitable, but preventable.

And most importantly: it is a world where every girl is born free – not only in law but in reality. If there is one thread that runs through the last seven decades of progress, it is this: change is possible – when we make it so.

We honor our foremothers not by imitation but by bold continuation. We do not need to be perfect to be powerful. We do not need permission to lead. And we do not need to wait for the right moment – it is already here.

Walk forward with vision and courage; carry each other; build not just a movement but a momentum that doesn't stop until every woman, everywhere, is free.

Beyond barriers lies a future still unwritten.

Let us write it – together.

The Road Ahead – Leadership, Legacy, and Collective Vision

As we look toward the future of feminism, the question is not whether progress will continue – it's how, by whom, and for whom. The road ahead is being shaped by women who blend legacy with innovation, leadership with collaboration, and advocacy with imagination. They are thinkers, organizers, creators, and bridge-builders crafting new blueprints for equity that are global, intersectional, and sustainable.

This chapter highlights women leading us into the next era – not by replicating old systems but by redefining what power, justice, and leadership can be.

Amanda Gorman, the youngest inaugural poet in U.S. history, uses the power of words to inspire unity, justice, and change. Her performance of "The Hill We Climb" at the 2021 presidential inauguration captivated a global audience and spotlighted how art can lead political dialogue. As a poet and public figure, Gorman embodies a generation that sees creativity as activism.

Greta Thunberg began a solo strike outside Sweden's parliament – at fifteen – sparking a global climate movement. Unafraid to speak truth to power, Thunberg has challenged world leaders with fierce moral clarity. She represents a youth-led push for environmental justice that centers intergenerational solidarity and urgent action.

Amanda Nguyen, a civil rights activist and the founder of Rise, transformed her experience as a sexual assault survivor into legislative change. Her advocacy led to the Sexual Assault Survivors' Bill of Rights, passed unanimously in the U.S. Congress and replicated globally. Nguyen demonstrates how personal trauma can be leveraged into systemic transformation.

Sviatlana Tsikhanouskaya, a Belarusian opposition leader, stepped into the political spotlight after her husband's imprisonment and became the symbolic face of democratic resistance against authoritarian rule. Though forced into exile, she continues to rally international support for free elections, civil liberties, and women's leadership in global diplomacy.

Ai-Jen Poo, already featured earlier for her work on labor rights, continues to expand her leadership through the Caring Across Generations campaign. Her coalition unites aging, disability, and labor justice – centering the care economy as essential infrastructure. Poo's model of coalition-based leadership is one of the most inclusive and impactful in modern policy work.

Sanna Marin, Finland's former Prime Minister, represented a new generation of young female leaders unafraid to challenge conservative norms. Her tenure focused on gender equity, education, and progressive social policy, proving that leadership can be both effective and empathetic.

Ngozi Okonjo-Iweala, the first woman and first African to lead the World Trade Organization, has long been a champion for economic justice and equitable development.

A former finance minister of Nigeria and a Harvard-trained economist, she brings expertise and integrity to one of the most powerful institutions in global trade.

Rana Ayyub, an Indian investigative journalist, risks her life to report on corruption, religious violence, and threats to democracy. Her fearless journalism holds power accountable and amplifies the voices of marginalized communities. Ayyub exemplifies the role of truth-telling in feminist leadership.

Reshma Saujani, already featured for founding Girls Who Code, has expanded her work to include the Marshall Plan for Moms – advocating for paid leave, childcare, and economic policies that center women's labor in the home and workplace. She is reframing motherhood as a policy priority, not just a personal experience.

These women are not just continuing a legacy – they are rewriting it. Their visions are bold, inclusive, and unapologetically future-focused.

They remind us that feminism is not only about dismantling systems – it's about building new ones rooted in care, courage, and collective action.

In their hands, the road ahead is not a continuation – it is a reimagination.

For a more complete list of Emerging Leaders: Voices Shaping the Future, see Appendix III.

Voices of Defiance

These voices aren't just echoes of resistance – they are blueprints for renewal. Each quote is a call to action, a refusal to surrender to fear, and a testament to the transformative power of women's leadership across every continent and cause.

> *"Empowerment is not a hashtag. It's the work you do every day to make the world safer and more just for those whose voices are silenced."*
> — Tarana Burke

Her words remind us that legacy is built through consistent, quiet acts of courage – far beyond trends or headlines.

*"Breaking ceilings is not enough. We must dismantle
the structure that made them necessary."*
— Ngozi Okonjo-Iweala

She challenges us not to settle for symbolic progress but to aim for systemic transformation that benefits all.

*"Change doesn't come from a single person or a single action. It comes
from mass mobilization, radical imagination, and relentless courage."*
— Alicia Garza

She calls us to collective action, where everyone contributes to building a freer, more just world.

A Global Call to Action

To readers of every age, background, and belief: your voice matters. Your actions matter. Feminism is not a closed chapter in history – it is a living movement, evolving with every generation.

Here's how you can join and contribute:

- Educate yourself and others. Read widely, listen deeply, and challenge stereotypes.
- Support women-led initiatives. Fund, mentor, promote, and elevate women's projects in your community or around the world.
- Vote and advocate. Use your civic power to support policies that promote equality, justice, and inclusion.
- Mentor and uplift. Help younger generations find their voice and path.
- Collaborate across differences. Solidarity grows stronger when built across race, class, nationality, age, and ability.

- Use your platform. Whether it's a classroom, a boardroom, or social media – use your voice to speak truth, advocate, and inspire.
- Rest and care. Sustainable change requires rest, healing, and community care. Feminist leadership includes self-preservation.

The legacy continues. The road is open. The pen is in our hands. Let's move beyond barriers – together.

In conclusion, the next chapter of progress will not be written by a few at the top but by the many who dare to lead, dream, and build together.

Reflection Prompts

1. Personal Legacy: What do you hope your personal or professional legacy will be? How does your life reflect the values of inclusion, justice, and leadership?
2. Defining Leadership: How do you define leadership in today's world? What qualities do you believe are most needed from women leaders in this moment in history?
3. Action Steps: After reading this book, what is one action you feel inspired to take? It could be personal, professional, creative, or political – big or small.
4. Continuing the Work: What commitments are you willing to make to support women's progress locally and globally? How can you help build a bridge between awareness and sustained action?

CHAPTER 13:
WOMEN IN CONFLICT
AND CRISIS ZONES

*"You don't make peace with your friends.
You make it with your enemies."*

— Leymah Gbowee

War and crisis heighten risks for women – and bring their leadership to the front. Across the globe, women in conflict and disaster zones organize, mediate, and rebuild, reshaping communities even in the bleakest conditions. This chapter examines both the costs of conflict, and the resilience and agency women bring to restoring peace and possibility.

Liberia: Women as Architects of Peace

In the early 2000s, Liberia was torn apart by a brutal civil war. Amid the violence, ordinary women – market traders, mothers, and church leaders – mobilized into a grassroots peace movement that would alter the nation's history.

Led by Leymah Gbowee, thousands of women in white held sit-ins and prayer vigils, forced the factions to negotiate, and helped secure the 2003 Accra Peace Accord, ending the war and paving the way for Ellen Johnson Sirleaf, Africa's first elected female head of state.

Their movement reflected a larger truth borne out by research: when women are included in peace processes, agreements are 35 percent more likely to last at least fifteen years (UN Women). The Liberian women's peace campaign stands as a model of how collective action can shift political outcomes.

Syria: Refugee Women as Entrepreneurs

Conflict in Syria displaced millions, creating one of the largest refugee crises of the twenty-first century. Women make up about 50 percent of the 6.8 million Syrian refugees registered by UNHCR, many of whom are heads of households due to conflict-related loss of male family members.

While many refugee women face heightened risks of exploitation and poverty, others have used ingenuity to rebuild lives in exile. In Jordan's refugee camps and host communities, Syrian women have launched small businesses – tailoring shops, catering services, and online platforms – to support their families. Organizations such as the International Rescue Committee and Womenpreneur Initiative have provided training and microloans, but the driving force has been women's determination to sustain households amid uncertainty.

These women not only generate income but also redefine the image of refugees: from dependent aid recipients to resilient entrepreneurs forging new paths in displacement.

Colombia: Women in Peacebuilding

In Colombia's decades-long conflict, women were often targeted with gender-based violence. Yet women's organizations also became central to peacebuilding. Groups such as the Ruta Pacífica de las Mujeres brought together rural and Indigenous women to demand an end to violence and inclusion in negotiations.

Their advocacy proved decisive. With more than 100 gender provisions – from women's political participation to sexual-violence reparations – the 2016 accord ranks among the most inclusive peace agreements.

Beyond Victimhood: Women's Agency in Crisis

Women in conflict zones are not passive victims;

despite disproportionate harm, they organize survival, lead negotiations, and rebuild communities. In South Sudan, women mediators have negotiated local ceasefires, often when male leaders failed.

- In Afghanistan, despite Taliban restrictions, underground networks of women continue to teach girls and organize healthcare access.
- In Ukraine, women represent nearly 60 percent of those displaced by the war and have mobilized humanitarian corridors, digital campaigns, and even military service.

The Dual Reality

Conflict zones illuminate a dual reality: women suffer acute vulnerabilities, but they also generate innovative responses that reshape societies. Recognizing women's roles in crisis as both survivors and leaders is essential for designing peace processes, humanitarian aid, and reconstruction programs that reflect lived realities rather than stereotypes.

The women of Liberia, Syria, Colombia, and beyond remind us that resilience is not passive endurance – it is active, strategic, and transformative. Their stories underscore a central theme of this book: that women's progress is measured not only in times of peace and prosperity but also in how they navigate, resist, and rebuild in the midst of crisis.

In times of war and humanitarian crisis, the stories that often dominate are those of soldiers, generals, and governments. But beneath the headlines, another story unfolds – of women as survivors, protectors, healers, and peacemakers. While conflict disproportionately harms women and girls, it also reveals their extraordinary resilience and leadership in the darkest of circumstances.

This chapter explores the gendered impact of war, the rise of women-led humanitarian responses, and how women have redefined peacebuilding from the ground up.

The Gendered Cost of War

Armed conflict devastates communities, but it does not affect all people equally. Women and girls often face unique risks:

- Sexual violence used as a weapon of war.
- Forced displacement and the loss of homes, families, and livelihoods.
- Early and forced marriage as a coping strategy in refugee settings.
- Increased domestic violence during and after conflict.
- Restricted access to health care, including maternal and reproductive services.
- Economic marginalization in post-war reconstruction.

From Bosnia to Syria and Sudan, armed groups have used rape to terrorize and fracture communities.

Despite these challenges, women in conflict zones are not just victims – they are architects of resilience.

Women Leading in Refugee Communities

When governments and international systems fail to respond adequately, women step in. In refugee camps, temporary shelters, and informal settlements, women organize:

- Childcare cooperatives.
- Literacy and vocational training.
- Safe spaces for survivors of violence.
- Community kitchens and micro-enterprises.
- Mental health circles and trauma recovery support.

In Uganda's Bidi Bidi camp, one of the world's largest refugee settlements, South Sudanese women have created peer support groups, taught each other tailoring, and established trauma healing centers. In Cox's Bazar, Bangladesh,

Rohingya women have become frontline responders, helping distribute aid and health supplies despite restrictive cultural norms.

These acts are not just practical – they are profoundly political. They assert that displaced women have agency, vision, and voice in shaping their futures.

Peacemakers and Negotiators: Women at the Table

Statistically, peace agreements are more durable and effective when women participate in negotiations. Yet women remain underrepresented in formal peace processes.

Still, history offers powerful examples of women changing the course of conflict:

- In Liberia, during the Second Civil War, Christian and Muslim women organized sit-ins and mass protests. Led by Leymah Gbowee, they forced warring factions to negotiate. Their organizing helped secure a peace deal and opened the path to electing Ellen Johnson Sirleaf, Africa's first elected female head of state.

- In Bosnia, survivors of wartime sexual violence broke decades of silence to demand accountability, leading to the first international tribunal prosecutions for rape as a war crime.

- In Colombia, women played a vital role in shaping the 2016 peace accord with the FARC, ensuring that gender-based violence was recognized in post-conflict justice.

Yet even when women are excluded from high-level negotiations, they continue building peace at the community level – healing divisions, rebuilding trust, and fostering reconciliation.

Healing the Body and the Spirit: Trauma Recovery

War leaves deep psychological scars – especially when violence targets the body. Women's trauma often goes unacknowledged or untreated. But across the globe, women are leading healing initiatives grounded in community, culture, and compassion.

In the Democratic Republic of Congo, Dr. Denis Mukwege and his all-women team at Panzi Hospital treat survivors of sexual violence with surgical, psychological, and legal care. Many survivors, once healed, become peer counselors or advocates.

In Iraq, Yazidi women who escaped ISIS captivity have created survivor networks to reclaim their voices and demand justice. Some have even run for office.

In post-genocide Rwanda, women came together to share their stories through *umuganda* (community gathering) and *gacaca* (traditional justice courts), helping to rebuild trust between neighbors.

Healing is not just about individual recovery – it is a collective act of resistance that defies the goal of war: to dehumanize and destroy.

Women Journalists, Documentarians, and Witnesses

In every crisis zone, courageous women bear witness – not only through humanitarian work but also through journalism, literature, and art. Their testimonies shape global understanding and push for accountability.

Syrian filmmaker Waad al-Kateab captured life under siege in Aleppo in her award-winning documentary *For Sama*, humanizing the war for international audiences.

Afghan photojournalist Fatimah Hossaini documented the beauty and resilience of Afghan women before being forced into exile by the Taliban's return.

Ukrainian women writers and reporters have become

vital sources of truth amid the fog of Russian disinformation and destruction.

Their work reminds us that to record suffering is also to resist it – to refuse erasure.

Redefining Security

Traditional security frameworks focus on borders, armies, and treaties. Feminist peacebuilders argue for a broader definition – one that includes:

- Economic opportunity
- Environmental safety
- Protection from gender-based violence
- Access to education and health
- Cultural belonging and dignity

In this view, security is measured by human well-being, not state power.

As the world faces climate-related disasters, resource conflict, and rising authoritarianism, women's leadership in peacebuilding will be more essential than ever.

Courage in the Ruins

In every conflict, women rise – often unseen, often unsupported, yet unshaken in their resolve. They hold communities together, demand justice, bury the dead, raise the living, and rebuild the future from rubble.

Theirs is a courage forged not in violence, but in care. Not in conquest, but in connection. They remind us that peace is not the absence of war – it is the presence of justice, dignity, and love.

Women in Conflict and Crisis Zones

Conflict exposes the fault lines of society – and in the shadows of war, displacement, and humanitarian crisis, women often bear the greatest burdens. Yet throughout history and across geographies, women have also been at the forefront of peacebuilding, survival, and resistance. In refugee camps, war-torn cities, and border crossings, women rise not only as victims but as leaders, healers, and defenders of human dignity.

This chapter honors those who have turned trauma into action and whose voices call for justice where silence once prevailed.

Zarifa Ghafari, one of Afghanistan's first female mayors, defied Taliban threats to lead her town of Maidan Shahr and advocate for women's rights. After multiple assassination attempts and the fall of Kabul in 2021, she continued her activism in exile, urging international support for Afghan women and the restoration of civil rights.

Yanar Mohammed, co-founder of the Organization of Women's Freedom in Iraq, shelters women facing gender-based violence and so-called "honor" killings in post-invasion Iraq. Despite threats to her life, she leads campaigns for legal reform, reproductive rights, and secular governance in one of the world's most volatile environments.

Hala Al-Dosari, a Saudi scholar and activist, has spoken out against the Saudi guardianship system and gender-based repression. Forced into exile for her safety, she remains a prominent voice for women's autonomy, academic freedom, and freedom of expression in the Gulf region.

Safa Al Ahmad, a Saudi journalist and filmmaker, has risked her life to document uprisings, human rights violations, and underground movements across the Arabian Peninsula. Her reporting reveals the often-hidden role of women in resistance movements under authoritarian regimes.

Khadija Ismayilova, an investigative journalist in Azerbaijan, exposed government corruption despite harassment, surveillance, and imprisonment. Her courage has earned global recognition and inspired other women to speak truth to power in deeply repressive states.

Dr. Alaa Murabit, a Libyan Canadian physician and advocate, founded the Voice of Libyan Women during the country's revolution. Her work bridges faith and feminism, advocating for peace through inclusive security and women's political participation in the MENA region and globally.

Binalakshmi Nepram, an Indigenous human rights activist from northeast India, supports women affected by armed conflict and ethnic violence. She founded the Manipur Women Gun Survivors Network and has worked to disarm militias, promote peace, and center women in post-conflict reconstruction.

Nadia Murad, a Yazidi survivor of ISIS enslavement and co-recipient of the Nobel Peace Prize, has turned personal tragedy into international advocacy. Through the Nadia Initiative, she campaigns for survivors of sexual violence in war, the prosecution of war crimes, and the reconstruction of Yazidi communities.

Loujain al-Hathloul, a Saudi women's rights activist, was imprisoned for defying the driving ban and challenging the male guardianship system. Her imprisonment and mistreatment drew global outcry. Since her release, she remains a symbol of nonviolent resistance and the costs of dissent.

In war zones, advocacy becomes survival, and survival becomes resistance.

Their leadership is not always celebrated. It is often punished. Yet they persist, rebuild, and reach out across borders to call for accountability and peace.

They are living proof that even in the bleakest corners of the world, justice has a voice – and often, that voice is a woman's.

For a more complete list of Women Peacebuilders and Grassroots Organizers in Conflict Zones, see Appendix III.

Voices of Defiance

In the world's most volatile regions – where war, displacement, and humanitarian crises fracture communities – women often stand at the crossroads of survival and leadership. They lead protests under threat of violence, negotiate peace across entrenched divides, and protect the vulnerable even when they themselves have lost everything. These women are not passive victims of circumstance; they are active shapers of history. Their courage isn't fear's absence; it's refusal.

"I want to be the last girl in the world with a story like mine."
— Nadia Murad, Iraq

Her words transform personal tragedy into a global mission to end sexual violence as a weapon of war.

"Silence is complicity, and I will not be complicit."
— Yevgenia Albats, Russia

Her defiance as a journalist under authoritarian rule shows that truth-telling is an act of survival.

"We will not bow to injustice, no matter how high the cost."
— Suu Kyi Khin, Myanmar

Her voice echoes the resilience of those who fight for democracy under oppressive regimes.

"You can kill the dreamer, but not the dream."
— Mursal Nabizada, Afghanistan

Her life and work stand as a testament to the enduring spirit of women's rights advocacy under siege.

Even in the darkest hours of war and displacement, women's resilience shows that peace is impossible without their leadership.

Reflection Prompts

1. Changing the Narrative: How have mainstream media shaped your perception of women in war or disaster zones? What narratives were challenged or expanded by this chapter?
2. Global Responsibility: What responsibility do those outside conflict zones have in supporting

women affected by war, political unrest, or humanitarian crises? What forms can that support take?

3. Your Role: How can you stay informed and take action on issues affecting women in conflict and crisis zones? Are there organizations, media outlets, or movements you can follow or support?

4. A More Peaceful Future: Imagine a world where women's leadership is prioritized in every stage of conflict response – from prevention to peace. What might that world look like, and what will it take to get there?

CHAPTER 14:
SHARED PROSPERITY: WOMEN AND COOPERATIVE ECONOMIC MODELS

"An economy that excludes women excludes prosperity."
— Michelle Bachelet

Beyond the Corporate Ladder

When we think about women's economic progress, it is tempting to measure success by the number of female executives in corner offices or the presence of women on corporate boards. We often tally women's progress by corner offices and board seats. But for millions worldwide, empowerment has taken shape outside corporate walls through collective and cooperative models. These alternatives to traditional capitalism – built on shared ownership, democratic decision-making, and mutual support – have enabled women to claim economic agency where conventional pathways were blocked.

For women excluded from capital markets, denied equal wages, or burdened with caregiving responsibilities, cooperatives and collective enterprises have offered something unique: an economy that values both productivity and community. The story of women's role in cooperative economics reveals how solidarity, rather than competition, has transformed lives across continents.

Historical Roots

The idea of collective economics is not new. These

initiatives tied directly to broader movements, as suffrage organizers in the U.S. and U.K. partnered with women's consumer co-ops to link voting rights with fair prices and community self-reliance.

During the Great Depression, women in both rural and urban America helped form credit unions and food co-ops to stabilize families and neighborhoods. In these spaces, women learned not only financial literacy but also governance – how to set bylaws, manage shared funds, and vote on collective decisions. These skills became a foundation for larger movements later in the century.

Consumer and Producer Cooperatives

By the mid-twentieth century, women were driving both consumer and producer cooperatives. In Europe and the United States, consumer co-ops grew around grocery and textile production, where women were primary decision-makers as both workers and buyers. Agricultural co-ops flourished across rural communities, often involving women in leadership roles, particularly in processing and marketing local goods.

In Latin America and Africa, women's producer cooperatives became lifelines for families. Through collective work in crafts, textiles, and agriculture, women reached markets otherwise closed to them – selling Peruvian alpaca weavings, Ghanaian shea butter, Rwandan coffee, and Oaxacan embroidered blouses. I am grateful to have served with the Virginia Gildersleeve International Fund (VGIF) in New York City. VGIF provides grants globally to fund and support locally led projects that advance women's and girls' rights and strengthen social justice worldwide. These cooperatives not only expanded market access and fairer prices but also preserved cultural traditions while raising household incomes.

Credit Unions and Microfinance

Few innovations show the power of cooperative

economics as clearly as credit unions and microfinance. In the United States, credit unions gave working-class women access to small loans and safe savings when commercial banks would not. Globally, the microfinance movement that began in the 1970s put women at the center.

In Bangladesh, Grameen Bank pioneered group lending to women. It started from a simple insight: women repaid more reliably and reinvested earnings in their families.

The basic unit was the five-member solidarity group; several groups formed a center that met weekly. Members guaranteed one another's loans and built a culture of mutual accountability.

Microfinance has real critiques – cycles of debt among them. Yet its core innovation – first access to credit, a path to enterprise, and public standing for women – proved transformative in many communities.

Worker Cooperatives

Worker-owned cooperatives have given women a direct role in shaping both their work environment and their income. These enterprises share profits among members and use democratic governance, with one member and one vote.

In Brooklyn, the Si Se Puede! Women's Cooperative was founded by immigrant women in 2006 to create safer, better-paying jobs in the cleaning industry. By setting their wages, negotiating collectively with clients, and providing mutual support, these women redefined the power dynamics of low-wage labor. Similar co-ops have sprung up in elder care, childcare, and domestic work – sectors often undervalued in traditional economies.

Internationally, the Self-Employed Women's Association (SEWA) in India stands as a remarkable example. Founded in 1972, SEWA is both a trade union and a federation of women-led cooperatives. It has empowered millions of women – street vendors, artisans, agricultural workers – by giving them access to healthcare, childcare, credit, and markets under a cooperative model.

Global Perspectives

The cooperative model has thrived across contexts. In Spain, the Mondragón Corporation became the world's largest cooperative, employing tens of thousands. Women's participation at Mondragón has grown, suggesting cooperative governance can open more equitable paths; likewise, across Africa, women's agricultural co-ops address food security while expanding access to tools, training, and markets.

What unites these diverse examples is not the scale but the principle: shared decision-making and shared prosperity. These models thrive where traditional markets fail, offering women both income and voice.

The Philosophy of Cooperation

At the heart of cooperative economics lies a philosophy that challenges traditional, patriarchal structures of ownership. Instead of wealth flowing upward to executives and shareholders, cooperatives distribute profits among members. Instead of exclusion, they prioritize inclusion. For women, this has meant not only income but also dignity and power within their communities.

Feminist economists have long argued that cooperative models align naturally with women's lived experiences of caregiving, collaboration, and resource-sharing. In this way, cooperatives are more than alternative businesses — they are vehicles for cultural transformation.

The Digital Age and New Collectives

The cooperative spirit has found fresh expression in the digital age. Platform cooperatives, for instance, offer alternatives to exploitative gig-economy models. Women-led tech collectives are building ridesharing, freelance, and e-commerce platforms owned by workers rather than venture capitalists.

Blockchain technology and decentralized autonomous

organizations (DAOs) hold further promise. But with caveats. Early pilots show how women across borders could pool remittances, co-own productive assets (e.g., a grain mill or cold storage), vote on budgets, and auto-split revenues via smart contracts – with transparent ledgers. Limits are real: price volatility and scams, clunky wallets and passwords, uneven internet/ID access, and unclear regulation. Think of the digital cooperative as a twenty-first-century successor to sewing circles and village credit unions – useful where safeguards and access exist, not a cure-all.

Redefining Success

The story of women in employment is incomplete if measured only by corporate promotions or executive salaries. Equally transformative are the collective and cooperative models that have empowered women to reshape economies from the ground up.

In these models, success is not about climbing the corporate ladder but about building ladders together – ensuring that when one rises, the community rises too. From microfinance groups in Bangladesh to cleaning cooperatives in Brooklyn, from agricultural co-ops in Africa to platform co-ops in the digital world, women have proven that shared prosperity is both possible and powerful.

As we look toward the future, the lesson is clear: women's economic progress cannot be confined to a single model. It is as diverse and innovative as women themselves, and cooperative economics will remain a vital force in the ongoing pursuit of equality and empowerment.

Collective Economic Models: Building Together

When formal systems excluded them, women built collective solutions. Cooperatives, microfinance groups, and solidarity economies have become alternative pathways to wealth and dignity.

Case Study: Grameen Bank – Microfinance and

Women's Credit

In 1976, economist Muhammad Yunus launched an experiment in Bangladesh: offering small loans to impoverished women who lacked collateral. The project grew into the Grameen Bank, pioneering the concept of microfinance. By focusing on women borrowers – who proved more reliable in repayment and more likely to reinvest in families – Grameen transformed access to credit in rural communities. Borrowers formed solidarity groups, guaranteeing one another's loans and fostering accountability. Outcomes vary by country; some borrowers face debt stress, yet many gained first-time access to credit, steady income, and local standing.

Case Study: Si Se Puede!: A Cooperative of Immigrant Women in New York

In 2006, a group of Latina immigrant women in Brooklyn founded the Si Se Puede! Women's Cooperative ("Yes We Can!"). Tired of exploitative conditions in the cleaning industry, they banded together to form a worker-owned cooperative. Members set fair wages, shared profits, and negotiated collectively with clients. The co-op not only provided better income but also offered training, safety protections, and mutual support. Today, it is one of the most visible examples of how immigrant women in the U.S. are using cooperative models to transform precarious work into stable livelihoods.

Wealth Equity, Labor Rights, Entrepreneurship

In every society, economic power shapes who has access to opportunity, who controls resources, and who makes decisions that affect daily life. For most of modern history, women have been excluded – first by law, then by practice – from owning property, opening bank accounts, holding jobs, or earning equal pay. As women entered the labor force, finance, and entrepreneurship, they improved their lives, transformed economies, and redefined prosperity.

The Informal Economy and Global South Leadership

In many parts of the Global South, the formal economy excludes women. Yet they lead vast informal economies:

- Street vendors in Latin America
- Market women in West Africa
- Waste recyclers in India
- Domestic workers across the Middle East

Together, these sectors generate household income, food security, and city services, yet operate with little legal protection, hence the turn to co-ops, unions, and advocacy.

Digital Access and the Gender Tech Gap

As the world economy becomes increasingly digital, access to technology has become a new frontier of inequality:

- Women are 20 percent less likely to use the internet globally.
- Girls are underrepresented in STEM fields, coding, and AI development.
- Rural and low-income women face barriers to mobile banking, digital skills, and online entrepreneurship.

But the digital economy also holds promise. Initiatives like SheTrades, Girls Who Code, and Women in Tech Africa are helping close the gap. E-commerce platforms enable women to reach global markets from their homes. Social media empowers entrepreneurs to market their services without intermediaries.

Toward Economic Justice

Women's economic power is not only about wages or profit – it's about freedom: the freedom to leave abusive relationships, educate children, access health care, and build generational wealth.

Achieving true economic justice requires:

- Equal pay and pay transparency.
- Childcare and family leave policies.
- Access to affordable credit and investment.
- Protection for domestic and informal workers.
- Land rights and inheritance reform.
- Financial literacy and inclusive innovation.

When women have money, they invest in others. They strengthen families, neighborhoods, and economies. They shift the values that drive our systems – from competition to care, from extraction to regeneration.

Wealth that Builds, Not Just Buys

As women continue to rise in economic influence, they are reimagining what wealth is for. It's not just about accumulation – but liberation. Not just about personal success – but collective uplift. And not just about breaking into existing systems – but building new ones that serve everyone better.

Women's economic power is more than a statistic – it's a revolution in progress.

Women Economic Leaders and Global Financial Changemakers

Economic empowerment is a foundation of equality. When women build wealth, start businesses, and move markets, they reshape their lives – and the systems around them.

From factory floors to corporate boardrooms, from street markets to investment firms, women are redefining what economic leadership looks like – and why it matters.

This chapter tells the stories of women who have broken financial barriers, built inclusive economies, and challenged centuries of gendered economic exclusion.

Esther Afua Ocloo, a Ghanaian entrepreneur and pioneer of microlending, co-founded Women's World Banking and advocated for women's access to capital. Starting her first business with less than a dollar, she championed financial inclusion before it became a global development strategy. Her legacy lives on in millions of women-led enterprises worldwide.

Women in rural India launched micro-enterprises using low-cost sanitary pad machines developed by Arunachalam Muruganantham; the design advanced menstrual health and income. Arunachalam transformed women's economic power in rural India by inventing low-cost sanitary pad machines. His innovation enabled thousands of women to launch micro-enterprises, promoting menstrual health and economic independence. His story is a powerful reminder of male allies who center women's dignity in development.

Jessica Jackley, co-founder of Kiva, revolutionized peer-to-peer microlending by connecting individual lenders with entrepreneurs in underserved regions. Kiva has facilitated over $1.7 billion in loans – largely to first-time women borrowers – expanding working capital for market stalls, farms, and home-based services.

Jackley's vision shows how tech can bridge financial gaps and unlock women's potential.

Victoria Kwakwa, a Ghanaian economist and regional vice president at the World Bank, advocates for gender-responsive economic policy, including gender-responsive budgeting; sex-disaggregated data and time-use surveys; childcare and paid family leave; equal-pay transparency and anti-harassment enforcement; land and inheritance rights; collateral and ID reforms to widen women's access to credit; public procurement targets for women-owned firms; and safe, affordable transport and digital payments that put cash in women's hands. Her aim is to ensure global financial decisions account for women's paid and unpaid labor and the structural barriers to participation.

These women – and a few essential allies – remind us that money is never just money. It is agency. It is access. It is possibility.

Whether they're reforming banks or selling haircare door-to-door, they challenge systems of exclusion with each invoice, loan, paycheck, and policy.

Their stories show that when women control capital, they direct it toward justice and shared prosperity.

For a more complete list of Women Economic Leaders and Global Financial Changemakers, see Appendix III.

Voices of Defiance

Economic power has long been wielded as a gatekeeping force – controlling access to opportunity, stability, and independence. Yet women across generations and geographies have defied economic exclusion, building enterprises, breaking glass ceilings, creating new markets, and rewriting the rules of ownership and wealth. Whether as CEOs, labor leaders, inventors, or social entrepreneurs, these women didn't wait to be invited into the economy – they took their place and opened the door wider for others.

"Poverty anywhere threatens prosperity everywhere."

— Ngozi Okonjo-Iweala (Nigeria)

Her work at the World Bank and WTO positioned women's economic participation as essential to global stability.

"Don't wait for permission to make
something meaningful. Just start."

— Jessica Jackley (United States)

Co-founder of Kiva, Jackley helped democratize micro-lending and empowered millions of women entrepreneurs globally.

*"We have to work at our own salvation.
No one will come and do it for us."*

— Esther Afua Ocloo (Ghana)

A pioneer in microfinance, she revolutionized women's access to capital in post-colonial Africa.

Movements and Platforms Also Worth Noting

- Women's World Banking – Financial inclusion for low-income women.

- FemTech Collective – Startups addressing women's health and financial wellness.

- UN Women's Empowerment Principles – Framework for businesses to advance gender equity in the workplace.

Prosperity grows strongest when it is built collectively, through cooperatives, unions, and shared wealth.

Reflection Prompts

1. Community versus Individual Success
   - How do you personally define success?
   - Does your definition lean more toward individual achievement or shared prosperity?

2. Cooperative Models in Your Life
   - Have you ever participated in a cooperative, union, or community-based economic initiative (e.g., credit union, food co-op, neighborhood association)?
   - What lessons from that experience could apply to other areas of your life or work?
   - How could collective models help address those barriers?

3. Leadership Reimagined

- How is leadership expressed differently in a cooperative setting compared to a corporate hierarchy?

- In what ways might you exercise "shared leadership" in your own family, workplace, or community?

4. Vision for the Future

- Imagine your community twenty years from now. What might it look like if cooperative and collective models were embraced more fully?

- hat role could you play in building that future?

CHAPTER 15:
SPIRITUAL ROOTS AND
PERSONAL PRACTICES

"Spiritual practice is the unseen ground beneath every journey of resilience — it steadies the heart when the road ahead is uncertain."

— Maria L. Ellis

The Inner Ground of Resilience

For centuries, women's spiritual traditions and communities have shaped identity and sustained their capacity to lead, nurture, and resist. Though institutional religion often excluded them, women forged their channels to the sacred — spaces of prayer, ritual, and reflection that built resilience.

Historical Roots of Women's Spirituality

Across many cultures, women have served as keepers of spiritual practice — midwives, healers, mystics, reformers — braiding faith into daily survival. From midwives and healers to mystics and reformers, they cultivated traditions that blended faith with daily survival. Figures like Hildegard of Bingen, Rabi'a al-Adawiyya, and Sojourner Truth revealed how women, often from the margins, spoke profound spiritual truths that challenged authority and inspired generations.

While formal religious hierarchies often denied women leadership, the home became a sanctuary where women preserved rituals, taught children's prayers, and nurtured communal bonds. In these intimate spaces, spirituality was not abstract theology but lived practice.

Everyday Practices Prayer circles at kitchen tables, quiet morning meditation, story-sharing after dinner, hymn-singing, and a few lines in a journal – sometimes by the light of a single candle – became ways to reach beyond material worry.

These practices, often dismissed as "private" or "domestic," in fact formed the foundation for resilience. They offered women clarity in the face of hardship, hope in times of loss, and renewal in moments of fatigue.

Spirituality as Healing

Spiritual practices have also served as pathways to healing – of body, mind, and spirit. Herbal remedies, contemplative prayer, and body-mind practices (breathwork, therapeutic touch) reflected a holistic view of wellness that anticipated today's integrative medicine.

For many women, spirituality provided not only solace but also agency over their health and wholeness.

The modern embrace of yoga, meditation, and mindfulness shows the continuity of this tradition: women as leaders in practices that bring balance to life in turbulent times.

Spiritual Lineages and Mentors

Many women trace their practices through lineages – mothers and grandmothers who hand down rituals, mentors and teachers who guide deeper awareness. These relationships reveal a simple truth: spirituality is rarely solitary; it is sustained by community and carried across generations.

The Ground Beneath the Journey

Chapter 15 is not about titles, institutions, or public power. It is about the quiet strength women cultivate through personal spiritual practices and the historical roots that continue to nourish them today. These inner practices form the ground beneath their journeys into leadership, activism, and social transformation.

As we will see later in Chapter 22, spirituality does not remain confined to the private sphere. It extends outward – shaping movements, inspiring communities, and transforming societies. But first, it must begin here: in the practices that give women strength, clarity, and resilience within their lives.

For generations, women have turned to faith and spirituality for strength, identity, and purpose. Religion has provided comfort during hardship, community in isolation, and meaning amid chaos. Yet across nearly all world religions, formal authority has long been denied to women – through exclusion from clergy roles, patriarchal interpretations of sacred texts, and institutional resistance to gender equality.

Religion has long been a paradox for women: a source of constraint, yet also a source of strength. While patriarchal traditions have often silenced women, faith has equally empowered them to resist oppression, reinterpret sacred texts, and lead communities toward justice.

Jarena Lee – The First Female Preacher in the African Methodist Episcopal Church

In 1819, Jarena Lee – a free Black woman in the United States – petitioned the AME Church to preach. Initially rejected, she kept preaching informally; after hearing her, Bishop Richard Allen authorized her call – cracking the barrier against women's preaching.

Buddhist Nuns in Nepal

In Nepal, the *bhikkhuni* movement – reviving the tradition of fully ordained Buddhist nuns – has gained traction. Nuns like Jetsunma Tenzin Palmo advocate for women's full ordination and equal access to education within Buddhism. Their movement is not just about ritual status but about ensuring that women's voices shape spiritual teaching and practice.

Women Rabbis in Judaism

Since the ordination of Sally Priesand in 1972 as the first female rabbi in the United States, women have steadily gained ground in Jewish leadership. Today, female rabbis serve across denominations and countries, often pioneering inclusive interpretations of Torah and Talmud. In Germany, Rabbi Regina Jonas, ordained secretly in 1935 before being killed in the Holocaust, has become a symbol of resistance and perseverance for Jewish feminists.

Interfaith Coalitions for Justice

Across the globe, women have formed interfaith networks to confront shared struggles. In Kenya, the Women of Faith Network – within the Inter-Religious Council of Kenya – unites Christian, Muslim, and traditional leaders to collect election early-warning data for national mediators, secure peace pledges from candidates, convene community dialogues, and survivor experience-sharing workshops; members have also submitted memoranda to government on reforms and services. Their cross-religious solidarity turns moral authority into political leverage.

From Jarena Lee's pulpit to Wadud's Qur'anic scholarship, from Nepalese nuns to Jewish rabbis, women are not only entering religious leadership – they are reshaping it. They show that belief systems are not static but living, evolving traditions that can be reinterpreted through the lens of justice and equality. Faith, once used to silence women, is now being wielded as a tool of liberation. Women of faith remind us that the sacred and the just are inseparable.

This chapter explores the evolving relationship between women and religion – from systems of exclusion to spaces of empowerment. It highlights how women are reinterpreting tradition, leading religious movements, and transforming spiritual practice around the world.

Faith as a Source of Strength and Resistance

Across many cultures, women draw power from spiritual life – kitchen-table prayer circles, courtyard zikr, sweatlodge ceremony. Prayer, meditation, ritual, and sacred storytelling have often been the only sanctioned spaces for women's voices in patriarchal societies. Spirituality has served as a private refuge and a public platform for protest.

Consider:

- Black women in the U.S. civil rights movement, who invoked Christian theology to demand justice and equality – from Sojourner Truth to Fannie Lou Hamer.

- Muslim women from Cairo to Jakarta lead women-led prayers and advance gender-aware tafsīr, reinterpreting the Qur'an.

- Indigenous women who preserve ancestral spiritual traditions that center nature, matrilineal lineage, and community healing.

In each case, faith is not passive acceptance – it is active resistance, a tool for liberation cloaked in sacred language.

Women as Religious Leaders: Breaking the Stained-Glass Ceiling

Women have long carried religious life – organizing, teaching, caring – yet were excluded from formal leadership.

But that's changing.

- In Judaism, women rabbis now serve in Reform, Conservative, and Reconstructionist branches. Rabbi Sally Priesand became the first female rabbi ordained in the U.S. in 1972.

- In Christianity, denominations like the Anglican Communion, United Methodist Church, and the Lutheran Church have opened leadership to women bishops and ministers.

- In Islam, women scholars and imams – such as Amina Wadud – are challenging male-dominated interpretations of scripture, leading prayers, and advocating for women's rights within Islamic law.

- In Buddhism, women monastics are reclaiming full ordination in traditions where it had been denied for centuries, including in Thailand, Korea, and Sri Lanka.

- In Hinduism, female gurus and sannyasin (ascetics) like Mata Amritanandamayi (Amma) have global followings and lead vast humanitarian networks.

These women are not just filling roles – they are reshaping religious life from within.

Feminist Theology and Sacred Reclamation

Feminist theology emerged as a critical discipline in the late twentieth century. Its central question: "Whose voice has shaped our understanding of the divine?"

Feminist theologians and scholars across traditions began to:

- Reinterpret sacred texts to challenge patriarchal bias.

- Unearth suppressed histories of women in scripture.

- Reclaim feminine imagery for God.

- Critique institutional hierarchies that marginalize women and LGBTQ+ people.

In Latin America, mujerista theology centered the spiritual experiences of working-class Latina women. In Africa, womanist theology addressed the intersection of faith, colonialism, and indigenous culture. In the U.S., feminist theologians like Phyllis Trible and Elizabeth Schüssler Fiorenza rewrote biblical narratives through a gender-justice lens.

Impact shows up in practice: women-led seminaries and formation programs; curricula that recover erased women's histories; trauma-informed chaplaincy and response protocols in congregations; and interfaith councils that negotiate directly with policymakers.

The Future of Women and Spirituality

As gender roles shift and younger generations question organized religion, many women are redefining spirituality on their terms:

- Some embrace eco-spirituality, connecting care for the Earth with divine purpose.
- Others turn to mindfulness, meditation, and wellness practices once separated from religious institutions.
- Many mix traditions – drawing from multiple faiths to create a personal and inclusive practice.

Others become interfaith leaders, building unity across divisions of doctrine.

The future of faith is not less spiritual; it is more expansive, more inclusive, and deeply aligned with justice.

Faith That Liberates

Religion has been used to justify exclusion – but also to fuel emancipation. Women are reclaiming its language, challenging its institutions, and forging new spiritual paths rooted in love, justice, and wholeness.

Faith – when wielded with compassion and courage – can become a liberating force, one that honors the divine in all people and centers the sacred in every act of care, creation, and community.

The Role of Faith and Spirituality

Faith has long played a dual role in the lives of women – sometimes a source of repression, sometimes a wellspring of liberation. For many women, spiritual belief is not separate from their activism but deeply entwined with it. This chapter explores how women of faith have reshaped religious narratives, redefined leadership, and built inclusive communities rooted in justice, compassion, and service.

Dorothy Day, co-founder of the Catholic Worker Movement, believed in radical hospitality and Christian anarchism. A devout Catholic and fierce advocate for the poor, she rejected capitalist materialism and committed her life to community building, nonviolence, and economic justice – all grounded in her unwavering faith.

Ruth Bader Ginsburg, while not typically framed as a religious figure, drew strength from her Jewish heritage and its values of justice (*tzedek*) and perseverance. Though not a religious leader, Ruth Bader Ginsburg drew on Jewish ethics – *tzedek* (justice) and perseverance – which informed her jurisprudence on dignity and equity.

Sister Simone Campbell, a Roman Catholic nun and lawyer, led the "Nuns on the Bus" movement, advocating for healthcare, immigration reform, and economic justice. Her activism reflects a deeply spiritual approach to politics – infused with love, justice, and public service.

Rabbi Regina Jonas, ordained in Germany in 1935, was the first woman rabbi in history. Though killed at Auschwitz, her pioneering work in religious leadership opened the door for generations of women in Judaism to serve as spiritual authorities, particularly in progressive movements.

Valerie Kaur, a Sikh civil rights lawyer and founder of the Revolutionary Love Project, turns her mantra – "love is a form of labor" – into practice: training congregations and classrooms in the "wonder–grieve–fight" ethic, building healing circles for survivors, and pairing storytelling with legal advocacy against hate and racism. After the 2012 Oak Creek gurdwara shooting, for example, she helped organize interfaith vigils, support affected families, and press with partners for stronger federal hate-crime tracking — love as sustained public work.

Wilma Mankiller, the first female Principal Chief of the Cherokee Nation, viewed leadership as a spiritual duty rooted in Indigenous traditions. Her vision of community health, education, and tribal sovereignty was grounded in a sacred respect for nature, ancestry, and collective well-being.

Beverly Lanzetta, a theologian and contemplative teacher, explores feminine mysticism and interfaith spirituality. She offers an inclusive vision of the divine that transcends religious borders, encouraging women to embrace spiritual empowerment through silence, service, and scholarship.

Phyllis Trible, a feminist biblical scholar, reexamined patriarchal texts through the lens of literary analysis and feminist theology. Her work challenged centuries of male-dominated interpretations of scripture, showing how sacred texts can also be sources of liberation.

These women turn ritual into resistance, devotion into dialogue, and belief into action.

They challenge us to see that faith can be more than dogma. It can be a radical force for equity. It can be a sanctuary and a spark.

Their stories are a reminder that spirit and struggle are not separate paths — they are parallel roads converging toward justice.

For a more complete list of Global Faith Leaders and Feminist Theologians, see Appendix IV.

Voices of Defiance

Faith and spirituality have often been used to justify women's exclusion — but they have also been powerful tools for resistance, renewal, and social change. Across cultures and religions, women have reinterpreted sacred texts, led communities in prayer and protest, and rooted their activism in spiritual conviction. Their defiance lies not in rejecting faith but in reclaiming it – challenging patriarchal interpretations and illuminating paths of justice, compassion, and collective healing.

"If you can't feed a hundred people, then feed just one."
— Mother Teresa (Albania/India)

Her global work with the poor revealed a spirituality of service that transcended dogma.

"We were not only praying for peace – we were demanding it."
— Leymah Gbowee (Liberia)

Through faith-based organizing, Gbowee helped end a civil war, showing that prayer can be a political force.

"The extremists are afraid of books and pens. The power of education frightens them. They are also afraid of women."
— Malala Yousafzai (Pakistan)

Her spiritual resilience against violence is rooted in belief – not just in religion, but in humanity's higher purpose.

In conclusion, women of faith have long walked the line between silence and song, and each step toward equality transforms tradition into liberation.

Reflection Prompts

1. Personal Practices
    - What daily or weekly practices help you feel grounded and connected to something larger than yourself?
    - How do these practices nourish your sense of resilience?
2. Ancestral Influences

- What spiritual traditions or rituals have been passed down to you through family or community?
- How have you adapted or reinterpreted those practices in your own life?

3. Spirituality and Healing

- Have you ever turned to spiritual practices – prayer, meditation, journaling, ritual – for healing during times of loss or difficulty?
- What role did these practices play in your recovery or growth?

4. Passing It On

- If you could pass one spiritual habit, ritual, or practice to the next generation, what would it be – and why?

CHAPTER 16:
GLOBAL CULTURAL SHIFTS.
WOMEN IN SPORTS

"Sport has the power to change the world."
— Nelson Mandela

For much of modern history, sport was framed as male terrain – speed, strength, and stamina cast as incompatible with femininity. Women were excluded or relegated to "graceful" events. Across the twentieth and twenty-first centuries, they claimed the field, the court, and the track, turning athletic victories into social revolutions.

Kathrine Switzer and the Boston Marathon

In 1967, Kathrine Switzer registered for the Boston Marathon as K.V. Switzer. When officials tried to pull her off the course, she kept running and finished. Her run forced a reckoning and helped secure women's official inclusion five years later (1972).

The 1999 U.S. Women's World Cup Victory

On July 10, 1999, the U.S. Women's National Soccer Team won the FIFA World Cup before a record crowd of 90,000 in the Rose Bowl. Brandi Chastain's iconic celebration – ripping off her jersey after scoring the winning penalty – became a global image of joy, power, and liberation. The win supercharged women's soccer and reset cultural attitudes about women's strength and visibility.

Caster Semenya and the Fight for Fairness

South African middle-distance runner Caster Semenya, a two-time Olympic champion, underwent gender verification testing and later challenged regulations targeting athletes with naturally higher testosterone levels. Her case became a flashpoint over eligibility rules, bodily autonomy, and the definition of fairness in women's sport.

Indigenous Women and Cultural Pride Through Sport

In Canada, Indigenous women athletes like Waneek Horn-Miller, a Mohawk water polo Olympian, turned sport into a platform for cultural pride and reconciliation. Having survived being stabbed during the Oka Crisis as a teenager, Horn-Miller used her Olympic journey to speak about resilience, Indigenous rights, and the healing power of sport. Her story illustrates how women athletes can carry not only personal but collective identities into the global arena.

From Switzer's marathon run to Chastain's penalty kick, from Semenya's legal battles to Horn-Miller's cultural advocacy, women in sports have proven that athletic competition is never just about the game. It is about visibility, fairness, and dignity. These athletes show that when women enter arenas once closed to them, they do more than play – they change the rules, the narratives, and the future. Every medal won by women is more than a victory – it is a statement that strength, endurance, and leadership belong to all of humanity.

This chapter explores the global cultural shifts that moved women from the margins to the center of sporting life – breaking stereotypes, demanding equity, and redefining what it means to be an athlete.

The Long Road to the Starting Line

Women's entry into competitive sports was fraught with resistance. For decades, critics claimed they were too fragile, too unfeminine, or even biologically unfit for exertion. The Olympic Games excluded women from many track and field events until the late twentieth century. Yet pioneers defied these boundaries:

- In 1928, women were first allowed to compete in Olympic track and field, sparking both triumph and outrage.

- Suzanne Lenglen, the electric French star of the 1920s, shocked crowds with short skirts and attacking play – and won six Wimbledons.

- Althea Gibson, breaking racial and gender barriers in the 1950s, became the first Black woman to win Wimbledon and the U.S. Open.

- In 1967, Kathrine Switzer became the first woman to officially run the Boston Marathon, despite officials trying to pull her off the course mid-race.

These acts were not only athletic feats; they were political statements that redefined who belonged on the playing field.

Global Icons and Cultural Shifts

Across the globe, women athletes have risen not only as champions but as cultural *leaders – as the following examples demonstrate:*

- Nadia Comăneci (Romania) stunned the world with the first perfect ten in Olympic gymnastics (1976).

- Serena Williams dominated tennis while challenging racial and gender stereotypes, becoming one of the most influential athletes of all time.

- Megan Rapinoe and the U.S. Women's Soccer Team turned their fight for equal pay into a global rallying cry.

- Caster Semenya (South Africa) has become a symbol of the fight for bodily autonomy amid gender verification rules.

- Ibtihaj Muhammad, the first U.S. Olympian to compete in hijab, redefined visibility and representation in fencing.

- Chloe Kim (U.S.), an Olympic snowboarder, opened new doors for Asian American athletes in winter sports.

- Marta Vieira da Silva (Brazil), often called the greatest female footballer in history, put women's soccer at the center of Latin American pride.

- Naomi Osaka (Japan/Haiti) sparked global conversations about mental health and racial equity in elite sports.

These figures show that medals are not the only measure of victory – visibility, voice, and advocacy matter too.

Cultural Struggles and Inclusion Battles

This section maps the battlegrounds where sport mirrors wider culture wars – eligibility and classification, pay equity, maternity and health protections, trans inclusion, protest and speech, racial justice, religious expression, and safe sport.

- Transgender athletes face eligibility rules and, in some regions, outright bans, especially in school and amateur leagues.

- Muslim women athletes challenge restrictive uniform codes to compete while wearing hijab, changing international rules in sports like basketball and weightlifting.

- Women with disabilities, such as Paralympians Tatyana McFadden and Beatrice Hess, have demanded recognition equal to their able-bodied peers.

- Indigenous women athletes in Canada, Australia, and New Zealand use sport to reclaim identity, culture, and voice.

These struggles reveal that the battle for equity is not only about access but about who gets to define what is "natural," "elite," or "acceptable" in sport.

Media, Money, and Representation

Even at the pinnacle of success, women athletes face systemic inequities:

- The U.S. Women's National Soccer Team fought a years-long battle to secure equal pay despite outperforming their male counterparts. Salary differentials map to institutional design: divergent revenue pools, broadcasting valuations, season length, and collective-bargaining caps – alongside rising WNBA ratings and sponsorship momentum.
- Women's sports receive less than 10 percent of global sports media coverage, perpetuating cycles of invisibility.

Change is accelerating, as sponsorships, standalone broadcast deals, and sellout crowds multiply. In 2024, the WNBA recorded its highest attendance in 22 years – 2,353,735 fans and 154 sellouts.

- Major brands (Nike, Adidas, Visa) are investing heavily in women's sports campaigns.
- Streaming platforms broadcast women's leagues independently of men's programming.
- Social media allows women athletes to bypass traditional gatekeepers, building direct connections with fans and sponsors.

Cultural representation is no longer a gift – it is a demand, and women are creating new ecosystems to ensure their voices are heard.

Leadership and Legacy

Women remain underrepresented in coaching and sports administration, but trailblazers are paving the way:

- Pat Summitt and Dawn Staley built powerhouse basketball programs and fought for equal resources.
- Becky Hammon broke barriers by coaching in the NBA.
- Women athletic directors, sports scientists, and agents are steadily reshaping the culture from within.

Mentorship programs and grassroots initiatives are preparing a new generation of women leaders who will carry the fight forward.

Sports are more than games – they are cultural battlegrounds where questions of gender, race, body, and belonging are fought openly. Women athletes, through resilience and advocacy, have transformed arenas into platforms for justice.

Their victories are measured not only in medals but in the dismantling of stereotypes, the rewriting of policies, and the inspiration of generations. From Wilma Rudolph to Simone Biles, from Billie Jean King to Megan Rapinoe, women's progress in sports reflects a global truth: when barriers fall, excellence rises.

Global Icons and Game Changers

From grassroots athletes to global superstars, women have redefined what excellence looks like in sport:

- Serena Williams shattered records and racial expectations in tennis, becoming one of the greatest athletes of all time.

- Megan Rapinoe and the U.S. Women's Soccer Team sued for equal pay and used their global platform to speak out on racism, LGBTQ+ rights, and gender justice.

- Simone Biles redefined gymnastics by prioritizing mental health as part of peak performance, withdrawing from Olympic events to protect her well-being.

- Caster Semenya, a South African runner, became a lightning rod for debates over gender verification, human rights, and bodily autonomy.

- Naomi Osaka has challenged media norms and racial bias in tennis while also sparking global conversations about mental health and athlete advocacy.

- Ibtihaj Muhammad, the first hijabi U.S. Olympian, broke barriers in fencing and spoke out for Muslim representation in sport.

These women are not just champions on the field — they are advocates for justice, wellness, and equity off it.

Cultural Shifts and Inclusion Battles

Sport has become a frontline for wider social struggles. Across federations and school leagues, eligibility fights over transgender participation intensifies; uniform rules are revised and resisted as Muslim women insist on competing in hijab or modest dress; Paralympians — among them Tatyana McFadden and Beatrice Hess — press for equal recognition of achievement; and Indigenous women use competition to reclaim land, language, and identity. These are not side stories but tests of who belongs on the field.

Feminist sport scholars return to a few core questions: Who is allowed to play? Who is visible? Whose body is treated as natural – or elite? The answers shape classification and eligibility rules, uniform codes and safety standards, contract terms and maternity protections, and even how media narrates "greatness." In this terrain, athletic performance doubles as cultural argument, and policy becomes the scorecard of inclusion.

Equity in Media and Money

Even at the highest levels, women athletes face structural economic disparities. The U.S. Women's National Soccer Team – despite outsized success – waged a multi-year legal fight to secure equal pay with their male counterparts. In professional basketball, WNBA salaries remain a fraction of NBA pay because the leagues operate on different revenue bases, media-rights valuations, season lengths, and salary-cap designs, even as WNBA audiences and cultural influence climb. Sponsorship and endorsement dollars have long skewed toward men, reinforcing gaps in visibility and income.

That balance is starting to shift. Major brands such as Nike, Adidas, and Visa are committing larger, longer-term investments in women's sport. Streaming and broadcast partners now carry women's leagues and tournaments as standalone products, creating appointment viewing and new rights markets. And social platforms let athletes speak directly to fans, grow their audiences, and negotiate with sponsors and federations on stronger terms.

Women are not just demanding space in sports – they are creating new ecosystems to support one another.

But the tide is turning.

Leadership, Coaching, and Future Champions

Women remain underrepresented in coaching and athletic administration – even in women's leagues – but trailblazers are rebuilding the pipeline. Becky Hammon broke through by coaching an NBA team in live game action as the San Antonio Spurs' interim head coach; Dawn Staley and the late Pat Summitt built powerhouse programs while pressing for equal resources and respect; and growing numbers of women now serve as athletic directors, sports scientists, and agents, reshaping sports culture from the inside. Mentorship networks, pipeline fellowships, and grassroots training camps are widening entry points so the next generation can rise on merit, not exception.

Sport is more than competition; it is a mirror and a lever for change. When women break records, they break stereotypes; when they demand fairness, the whole system gets fairer. Strength arrives in many forms – speed, stamina, strategy, and solidarity – and when the whistle blows, the message can matter as much as the score.

Trailblazing Women Athletes and Advocates for Gender Equity in Sports – athletes whose achievements and advocacy reshaped the game.

Women in Sports – From Margins to Medals

Women's sports have long been a battlefield for visibility, respect, and equity. Despite systemic barriers, female athletes have not only broken records but also shattered stereotypes, redefined excellence, and turned competition into activism. This chapter highlights women who transformed the sporting world – on the field, track, court, and beyond – claiming space, power, and purpose.

Wilma Rudolph, the first American woman to win three gold medals in a single Olympics (1960), overcame polio as a child and emerged as a global icon of athleticism and resilience. Her victories became a symbol of Black excellence and civil rights momentum during a segregated era in U.S. history.

Billie Jean King, a tennis legend and activist, won thirty-nine Grand Slam titles and famously defeated Bobby Riggs in the 1973 "Battle of the Sexes." Off the court, she fought for equal prize money and founded the Women's

Tennis Association and the Women's Sports Foundation, championing gender equity in sports.

Nadia Comăneci, a Romanian gymnast, earned the first perfect ten in Olympic history at the 1976 Montreal Games. Her grace and precision captivated the world and redefined what was possible in women's gymnastics.

Mia Hamm, a two-time FIFA Women's World Cup champion and two-time Olympic gold medalist, brought global attention to women's soccer and inspired a generation of female athletes. As a founding member of the Women's United Soccer Association (WUSA), she helped create pathways for others.

Flo Hyman, an American volleyball player and vocal advocate for gender equity, used her platform to promote Title IX and fight for better conditions for female athletes. She died tragically young, but her legacy lives on in continued efforts to support women in sports.

Simone Biles, widely considered the greatest gymnast of all time, has revolutionized gymnastics with her unparalleled skill. She has also bravely used her voice to speak about mental health, abuse, and athlete autonomy, transforming how we define strength.

Serena Williams, with twenty-three Grand Slam titles, redefined power, endurance, and dominance in tennis. As a Black woman in a historically white sport, she fought for pay equity, maternal rights, and representation – changing not only the game but the conversation around it.

Naomi Osaka, a four-time Grand Slam champion, became a new face of sports activism when she withdrew from major tournaments to prioritize her mental health. Her actions sparked global dialogue about athlete well-being and the pressures placed on women of color in elite sports.

Caster Semenya, a South African middle-distance runner and Olympic gold medalist, has faced invasive gender testing and discriminatory regulations. Her courage to challenge the system has made her a global symbol for the rights of intersex and gender-diverse athletes.

Chloe Kim, an Olympic snowboarder, broke records and barriers for Asian American athletes. With grace and grit, she has inspired new generations to see themselves in winter sports, an arena often lacking diversity.

These women prove that sports are not just games – they are platforms for advocacy, visibility, and transformation. They've turned their victories into opportunities for others and shown that the pursuit of excellence is inseparable from the pursuit of justice.

They remind us that medals are earned not just with talent, but with tenacity, vision, and courage.

For a more complete list of Trailblazing Women Athletes and Advocates for Gender Equity in Sports, see Appendix IV.

Organizations and Movements

- Women's Sports Foundation (founded by Billie Jean King) – Advocates for girls' participation and equity in sports

- Athletes for Impact – Coalition of athletes using sport to advocate for social justice

- Equal Pay for Equal Play – Ongoing campaigns for salary equity in professional and national team sports

- She's Independent – Mentorship programs for women in sports leadership and sports tech

- Athlete Ally – Advocates for LGBTQ+ inclusion in sports across all levels

Voices of Defiance

For decades, women in sports were told to stay quiet, sit still, or smile more. They were barred from competition, denied equal pay, and dismissed as unfit for greatness. And yet, they ran, jumped, swam, fought, lifted, skated, and soared – turning every restriction into a record. Their defiance lives not only in medals and victories but in the barriers they broke just by showing up. These women didn't just play to win – they played to change the rules for everyone who came after them.

"I don't run away from a challenge because I am afraid. Instead, I run toward it because the only way to escape fear is to trample it beneath your feet."

— Nadia Comăneci (Romania, Gymnastics)

Her perfect ten shattered expectations of what was possible for young women in sport and life.

"I've never been the right kind of woman. Too strong, too black, too confident, too muscular, too outspoken. And I wouldn't have it any other way."

— Serena Williams (United States, Tennis)

Serena redefined power, femininity, and excellence – on her own terms.

"When you have lost everything, you realize the power of your own body to keep going."

— Yusra Mardini (Syria/Germany, Swimming)

As a refugee Olympic swimmer, her journey shows that survival and strength are not separate; they are synchronized.

In conclusion, every medal won is more than a victory in competition – it is proof that women's bodies, voices, and ambitions belong on the world stage.

Reflection Prompts

1. Historical Gaps and Modern Triumphs: What surprised you most about the early limitations placed on women in sports? How have those restrictions changed – or persisted – over time?
2. Equity versus Equality: What is the difference between equality and equity in sports (e.g.,

equal pay versus equitable resources and support)? Why does this distinction matter?

3. Global Reach: How does access to sports and athletic resources differ for girls and women in different parts of the world? What are the barriers, and what's being done to overcome them?

CHAPTER 17:
WOMEN AND ENVIRONMENTAL ACTIVISM – FROM SACRED LANDS TO GLOBAL CLIMATE POLICY

"Those who contemplate the beauty of the earth find reserves of strength that will endure as long as life lasts."
— Rachel Carson

At the Sacred Stone and Oceti Sakowin camps outside Cannon Ball, North Dakota – where the Cannonball meets the Missouri – Lakota and Dakota women such as LaDonna Brave Bull Allard, Phyllis Young, and elder activists like Madonna Thunder Hawk, alongside youth leaders including Jasilyn Charger, linked arms to resist the Dakota Access Pipeline. They defended not only the water but also cultural heritage, future generations, and a worldview in which the Earth is a relative to be honored, not a resource to be consumed.

From the Amazon to Africa to the Paris negotiating table, women have driven change: in the Amazon, Nemonte Nenquimo (Waorani) and Patricia Gualinga (Kichwa of Sarayaku) helped halt new oil expansion and defend Indigenous territory; across Africa, Wangari Maathai (Green Belt Movement) and Cécile Ndjebet (REFACOF) mobilized women-led reforestation that restores land and livelihoods; and at COP21, Christiana Figueres and Laurence Tubiana – working with small-island negotiators – pressed climate equity into the Paris Agreement. Together, they connect land, water, and climate to family well-being and rights, treating environmental health as inseparable from human rights.

Wangari Maathai and the Green Belt Movement

In 1977, Kenyan environmentalist Wangari Maathai launched the Green Belt Movement to mobilize women against deforestation. They organized nursery co-ops, paid stipends tied to seedling survival, and linked tree planting to local democracy and rights education – work that helped plant over 50 million trees and culminated in Maathai's 2004 Nobel Peace Prize.

Standing Rock and the Water Protectors

In 2016, Indigenous women in North Dakota helped lead the protests against the Dakota Access Pipeline at Standing Rock. Women like LaDonna Brave Bull Allard framed the struggle not only as environmental but also as sacred, defending water as "life itself." Through human chains, prayer circles, and global solidarity, the Standing Rock water protectors reminded the world that environmental battles are also cultural and spiritual struggles.

Christiana Figueres and the Paris Agreement

Costa Rican diplomat Christiana Figueres became one of the central architects of the *2015 Paris Agreement*, the landmark global accord to combat climate change. As Executive Secretary of the UN Framework Convention on Climate Change, she orchestrated years of difficult negotiations, emphasizing collaboration, transparency, and inclusion. Figueres' leadership showed how women at the highest levels of diplomacy could shape policy frameworks that affect the fate of the planet. Her coalition-building helped secure Article 2's "pursue efforts to limit global warming to 1.5°C" goal and preambular language urging respect for human rights and gender equality – proof of what inclusive diplomacy can deliver.

Berta Cáceres and Indigenous Resistance in Honduras

Honduran activist Berta Cáceres, co-founder of the Council of Popular and Indigenous Organizations of Honduras (COPINH), led campaigns against destructive dam projects threatening Indigenous Lenca lands. Despite threats, she successfully halted the Agua Zarca Dam, drawing international recognition with the Goldman Environmental Prize in 2015. She was assassinated in 2016, but her legacy continues as a symbol of courage in the face of environmental injustice.

From Maathai's tree planting to Standing Rock's prayer chains, from Figueres' diplomacy to Cáceres' resistance, women's environmental activism demonstrates that ecological survival is intertwined with cultural sovereignty, gender justice, and global solidarity. In every corner of the world, women have shown that to defend the Earth is to defend life – and that sustainability, at its core, is about justice across generations.

This chapter explores how women have stood at the frontlines of ecological defense, pioneered ecofeminist thought linking patriarchy with environmental exploitation, and shaped policy from the grassroots to global summits. Their voices remind us that environmental justice is not only about protecting ecosystems but also about reimagining our relationship with the planet – and with one another.

For much of modern history, the environmental movement was dominated by male scientists, policymakers, and industrial narratives. Yet women – especially Indigenous leaders, grassroots organizers, and ecofeminist thinkers – have reframed the struggle for the planet as inseparable from struggles against patriarchy, colonialism, and inequality.

Ecofeminism: Linking the Earth and Women's Liberation

Ecofeminism is a philosophy and social movement that emerged in the 1970s and 1980s, arguing that the domination of women and the exploitation of nature are interconnected systems of oppression. Early ecofeminist thinkers such as Françoise d'Eaubonne and Vandana Shiva pointed out how patriarchal societies often view both women and the Earth as objects for extraction and control. Across rural regions, women farm without title as extraction and enclosure push them off land and deny compensation; deforestation and water scarcity lengthen daily treks for fuel and water, deepening time poverty and risk while "free" care labor subsidizes households and polluters; their ecological knowledge – seed saving, soil and water stewardship – is sidelined by top-down "expert" schemes, leaving them to absorb the fallout without voice when decisions fail; and yet resistance – from India's Chipko movement to Kenya's Green Belt Movement – shows that when women organize to protect forests and watersheds, they defend community survival and political rights together, challenging the twinned domination of women and nature.

Ecofeminism emphasizes that sustainability requires dismantling hierarchies – between men and women, humans and nature, North and South. It is not just an environmental ethic but also a social critique and a call for holistic justice.

Indigenous Leadership and Climate Justice

Women at the frontlines of Indigenous movements have been among the most effective environmental defenders.

- North America: Leaders like Winona LaDuke and the women of Standing Rock highlight how Indigenous sovereignty and environmental justice are intertwined.

- Amazon Basin: Indigenous women such as Nemonte Nenquimo of the Waorani people have led campaigns against oil drilling, winning historic court victories to protect rainforests.

- Africa: Women in the Green Belt Movement, founded by Wangari Maathai in Kenya, planted over 50 million trees while linking reforestation to women's empowerment, democracy, and peace.

These movements are not symbolic; they reshape policy, force corporate accountability, and inspire global solidarity.

From Grassroots to Global Policy

Paris Agreement (2015): Women negotiators from island and developing states pressed for equity and rights; the accord set a global framework for nationally determined contributions, transparency, and a ratchet to increase ambition.

The Paris Agreement, adopted in December 2015 at the United Nations Climate Change Conference (COP21), is the world's most ambitious and comprehensive climate accord to date. Signed by 196 parties, it represents a global consensus to confront climate change collaboratively.

Key Elements of the Agreement

- Global Temperature Goals: Limit global warming to well below 2°C, with efforts to cap it at 1.5°C above pre-industrial levels.

- National Commitments: Countries submit Nationally Determined Contributions (NDCs) and strengthen them on a five-year cycle under a common transparency framework. Adaptation and Finance: Wealthier nations committed to mobilizing $100 billion per year by 2020 and through 2025 to support developing countries in mitigation and adaptation.

- Equity and Justice: Recognized the principle of "common but differentiated responsibilities," acknowledging different nations' historical contributions to emissions and capacities to act.

Gender and Women's Role in the Paris Agreement

The Paris Agreement is notable for explicitly referencing gender equality and human rights in its framing, signaling that gender is integral to effective climate action.

- Women Negotiators: Female delegates, particularly from small island states and the Global South, played crucial roles in embedding language about gender, human rights, and intergenerational equity in the final text.

- Climate Justice Lens: Women leaders argued that climate policies cannot succeed without addressing social inequalities – including how women, especially in vulnerable communities, disproportionately face the impacts of droughts, floods, and food insecurity.

- Institutional Change: Following Paris, the UNFCCC expanded its Gender Action Plan, which strengthens women's participation in climate governance and ensures that adaptation and mitigation policies account for gender dynamics.

Why the Paris Agreement (2015) Remains Important Today

- Global Commitment: It set the stage for a common framework – all nations, rich or poor, pledged to act.

- Accountability Mechanism: While targets are nationally determined, reporting, transparency, and the global stock take are mandatory, creating peer pressure and upward ambition every five years.

- Catalyst for Local Action: Cities, businesses, and grassroots organizations worldwide now align with Paris goals, giving it influence beyond government policy.

- Intersectional Justice: For women activists, Paris was a watershed moment in showing that climate justice is inseparable from gender justice, Indigenous rights, and economic equity.

The integration of women's perspectives has shifted climate policy away from narrow carbon metrics toward broader ideas of resilience, community survival, and intergenerational justice.

Sustainability and Everyday Action

Women are also at the center of practical sustainability:

- **Lead household energy transitions** to solar and clean cooking – for example, **Solar Sister** entrepreneurs in Nigeria, Tanzania, and Uganda distributing solar kits and efficient stoves, and women's groups in Nepal running village biogas digesters and pay-as-you-go fuel swaps.

- Run recycling and upcycling cooperatives – from Brazil's catadora co-ops in São Paulo and Belo Horizonte to Bogotá's Asociación de Recicladores led by Nohra Padilla – turning waste into income and municipal contracts.

- Drive circular-economy design and green finance – with Kenyan women policymakers advancing the 2017 single-use plastic-bag ban,

Ellen MacArthur Foundation leaders pressing brand commitments on materials, and women executives structuring sustainability-linked loans **that reward emissions** and waste cuts.

Here, sustainability is not abstract – it is embedded in food security, health, and family survival.

Women's environmental activism – from ecofeminist theory to Indigenous land defense, from grassroots mobilization to international negotiation – redefines what climate justice means. It insists that protecting the Earth cannot be separated from dismantling systems of patriarchy, racism, and economic exploitation.

When women gain a seat – or take it – policy shifts, communities strengthen, and sustainability deepens. Climate justice becomes not only a scientific necessity but a moral and cultural imperative.

The survival of the planet depends on many forces, but among the strongest are the voices of women who remind us that defending the Earth is inseparable from defending life itself.

Women Environmental Leaders and Changemakers

Wangari Maathai (Kenya)

- Founder of the Green Belt Movement, which planted over 50 million trees.
- First African woman to win the Nobel Peace Prize (2004) for linking environmental conservation, democracy, and women's rights.

Vandana Shiva (India)

- Ecofeminist thinker and activist who critiques industrial agriculture and promotes biodiversity and seed sovereignty.

- Author of *Staying Alive* and *Earth Democracy*, shaping global ecofeminist discourse.

Nemonte Nenquimo (Ecuador)

- Waorani Indigenous leader who won a landmark 2019 court case to block oil drilling in the Amazon.
- Named to the TIME 100 list for her role in protecting the rainforest.

Greta Thunberg (Sweden)

- Climate activist who began the Fridays for Future movement in 2018.
- Her speeches at the UN Climate Summit and COP meetings galvanized global youth activism.

Winona LaDuke (United States, Anishinaabe)

- Advocate for Indigenous sovereignty, food justice, and renewable energy.
- Co-founder of Honor the Earth, linking cultural survival with climate justice.

Christiana Figueres (Costa Rica)

- Former Executive Secretary of the UNFCCC, she played a pivotal role in brokering the Paris Agreement (2015).
- Advocates for collaborative, inclusive climate diplomacy.

Marina Silva (Brazil)

- Championed Amazon protections as Brazil's environment minister (2003 to 2008).
- Helped steer the 2004 Action Plan for the Prevention and Control of Deforestation in the

Legal Amazon (PPCDAm), under which Amazon deforestation fell roughly 59 percent from 2004 to 2007.

Sheila Watt-Cloutier (Canada, Inuit)

- Inuit leader and environmental activist who brought climate change impacts on Arctic communities to global attention.

Environmental degradation is one of the defining crises of our time – threatening ecosystems, livelihoods, and the survival of future generations. And yet, women – often among the most affected by climate change – have emerged as some of the strongest voices in the global environmental movement. Their leadership is grounded in lived experience, community stewardship, and a vision of sustainability that connects the health of the planet to the dignity of its people.

This chapter explores how women are leading environmental activism across cultures and continents, linking ecological protection with gender justice.

Why Women Lead in Environmental Justice

In many communities, women are primary caregivers, water gatherers, food producers, and healers – roles that put them on the front lines of environmental change, from longer dry-season walks for water in Sahelian villages to shifting planting calendars in the Himalayan foothills and saltwater intrusion on Pacific atolls.

When land is degraded, forests are cut down, or water is polluted, women often feel the impact first:

- Increased time spent collecting fuel and water
- Reduced crop yields and food insecurity
- Greater vulnerability to climate-related displacement

- Increased exposure to environmental health hazards

These realities have turned women into frontline defenders of the Earth – not just out of ideology, but out of necessity.

Ecofeminism: Linking Nature and Gender

Ecofeminism emerged in the 1970s and '80s as a movement and philosophy that connects the exploitation of women with the exploitation of nature. It argues that both are products of patriarchal, extractive systems that prioritize domination over harmony.

Key ideas include:

- Interconnectedness: The health of human communities depends on the health of the natural world.

- Decentralization: Local, community-based governance is essential for sustainability.

- Valuing care work: Environmental protection requires nurturing and long-term thinking – traits often devalued in male-dominated economies.

Ecofeminism has been expressed through activism, literature, and policy advocacy – and women leaders worldwide have embodied its principles in action.

Indigenous Women: Guardians of the Earth

Indigenous women have played a unique role in environmental activism, combining traditional ecological knowledge with modern advocacy.

- Berta Cáceres (Honduras): Lenca environmental activist who led a grassroots movement against a hydroelectric dam on Indigenous land. She was assassinated in 2016, but her legacy continues to inspire global environmental defenders.

- Nemonte Nenquimo (Ecuador): Co-founder of the Ceibo Alliance, she won a 2019 court ruling protecting approximately 500,000 acres of Waorani territory from oil concessions, setting a precedent for Indigenous consent.

- Winona LaDuke (USA): Ojibwe leader and economist advocating for food sovereignty, renewable energy, and Indigenous rights in North America.

These women's activism is rooted in the belief that the Earth is not a resource to exploit, but a living relative to protect.

Women in Global Climate Movements

Women have been pivotal in shaping the international climate justice agenda:

- Gro Harlem Brundtland (Norway): Former Norwegian Prime Minister Gro Harlem Brundtland chaired the World Commission on Environment and Development, whose 1987 report Our Common Future defined "sustainable development" and tied poverty alleviation to environmental protection.

- Christiana Figueres (Costa Rica) played a central role in negotiating the 2015 Paris Climate Agreement.

- Youth activists like Greta Thunberg (Sweden) and Vanessa Nakate (Uganda) have mobilized millions to demand urgent climate action.

- Sunita Narain (India) has been a global leader in advocating for equity in climate policy, stressing that developing countries need fair solutions that don't replicate exploitation.

Grassroots and Local Movements

While international summits attract headlines, some of the most effective environmental activism is happening at the local level:

- In Kenya, the Green Belt Movement, founded by Nobel laureate Wangari Maathai, mobilized thousands of women to plant over 50 million trees, restoring ecosystems and empowering rural communities.

- In the Philippines, women-led fisherfolk associations are reviving coral reefs and protecting coastal waters from destructive fishing practices.

- Across the Sahel region of Africa, women farmers are reviving degraded land through community-driven agroforestry techniques.

These efforts demonstrate that environmental justice is inseparable from economic justice.

Environmental Health and Gender

Women are also leading campaigns around environmental health – exposing the dangers of toxic chemicals, pollution, and unsafe industrial practices.

For example:

- Erin Brockovich in the United States became a household name for her role in exposing water contamination in Hinkley, California.

- Lois Gibbs organized residents of Love Canal, New York, to fight against toxic waste buried beneath their homes – leading to the creation of the U.S. Superfund program.

These cases show that environmental harm is not abstract – it affects homes, bodies, and communities.

Barriers and Risks

Women environmental defenders face significant risks:

- Criminalization of protest
- Gender-based violence
- Threats to family safety
- Limited access to funding and media platforms

Despite these dangers, they persist – often drawing strength from community solidarity and international support networks.

The Earth as Common Ground

Women's environmental leadership offers a vision that goes beyond "sustainability" as a policy buzzword. It calls for a fundamental rethinking of how we live, produce, and consume – placing care for the planet and its people at the center of decision-making.

Their work reminds us that the fight for gender justice and environmental justice are not separate battles – they are the same fight, rooted in the same commitment to life, dignity, and the future.

Women Environmental Leaders and Movements for Climate Justice, created to accompany Chapter 17 of *Beyond Barriers: Women's Progress from Mid-twentieth Century to Today*, highlights women who have made substantial contributions to environmental justice through advocacy, leadership, science, and grassroots organizing.

Women and Environmental Activism

Environmental justice is feminist justice because, in many communities, women shoulder unequal burdens and frontline responsibilities for land, water, food, and health – from long water treks in the Sahel to saltwater intrusion on Pacific atolls to caregiving amid urban pollution – while remaining underrepresented where those decisions are made.

Wangari Maathai, the Kenyan environmentalist who founded the Green Belt Movement and became the first African woman to win the Nobel Peace Prize, scaled impact through women-run nurseries, stipends tied to seedling survival, and local councils that turned planting days into civic education – a model that planted more than 50 million trees and linked reforestation to women's income and civic power, binding ecology, democracy, and women's rights.

Greta Thunberg, a Swedish teenager who sparked the global Fridays for Future movement, embodies youth-led environmental resistance. With a cardboard sign and unwavering moral clarity, she challenged world leaders to act on climate change. She launched school strikes in 2018 that grew into Fridays for Future, mobilizing about 7.6 million people across more than 150 countries during the September 2019 global climate strikes.

Berta Cáceres, a Lenca Indigenous leader from Honduras, defended land and water rights against powerful hydroelectric projects. Her assassination in 2016 exposed the deadly risks environmental defenders face. Her legacy lives on in grassroots resistance across Latin America, especially among Indigenous women protecting sacred lands.

Sunita Narain, an Indian environmentalist and director of the Centre for Science and Environment, has been a fierce advocate for climate justice in the Global South. She helped draft India's first climate plan and exposed water contamination and environmental inequities through policy reform and citizen engagement.

Rachel Carson, author of *Silent Spring*, catalyzed the modern environmental movement by exposing the dangers of pesticides. A marine biologist and writer, she challenged powerful chemical industries and inspired the formation of the U.S. Environmental Protection Agency. Her work laid the groundwork for environmental science as a public concern.

Marina Silva, a former rubber tapper from Brazil's Amazon region and former Minister of the Environment, led efforts to reduce deforestation and preserve biodiversity. Her leadership as an Afro-Indigenous woman in Brazilian politics demonstrated how conservation can be driven by those closest to the land.

Isatou Ceesay, known as "The Queen of Recycling" in The Gambia, founded the Women's Initiative for Sustainable Environment. She organized women to collect and repurpose plastic waste, transforming environmental cleanup into income-generating work and community empowerment.

Hindou Oumarou Ibrahim, an Mbororo pastoralist and coordinator of AFPAT, turns traditional knowledge into policy tools, leading participatory 3D mapping with Chadian communities (2012, 2016 to 2017) to chart grazing routes, water points, and conflict zones that now guide adaptation plans and reduce resource conflicts around Lake Chad. On the global stage, she has co-chaired the UNFCCC's Local Communities and Indigenous Peoples Platform (LCIPP) Facilitative Working Group and earlier the Indigenous Peoples' Caucus at COP21, helping open negotiating space for Indigenous knowledge and rights. Her leadership has been recognized with the 2019 UCLA Pritzker Emerging Environmental Genius Award and roles such as UN SDG Advocate and 2021 Rolex Awards laureate.

Leah Thomas, founder of Intersectional Environmentalist, created a platform that links environmentalism with racial and social justice. As a millennial leader in the U.S., she is reshaping the environmental conversation to be inclusive, accessible, and justice centered.

Vandana Shiva, an Indian scholar and ecofeminist, has long criticized industrial agriculture and global trade systems that harm small farmers, particularly women. She advocates for seed sovereignty and organic farming, reminding the world that care for the Earth is care for communities. She founded Navdanya in 1991, building more than 120 community seed banks across twenty-two Indian states and training hundreds of thousands of mostly women farmers in agroecology, while helping overturn patents on neem and basmati and mobilizing campaigns that contributed to India's 2010 moratorium on Bt brinjal – showing how seed sovereignty ties women's livelihoods to care for the Earth.

These women have planted seeds of resistance and regeneration, challenging extractive models and lifting up the life-sustaining practices explored next.

Their movements remind us that the fight for the planet is inseparable from the fight for justice – economic, racial, gendered, and ecological.

From forests to cities, their voices echo with clarity: the Earth is not a commodity. It is a shared home. And women are among its fiercest defenders.

For a more complete list of Women Environmental Leaders and Movements for Climate Justice, see Appendix IV.

Voices of Defiance

At Standing Rock, women linked arms in winter cold; in the Amazon, Waorani leaders faced down oil roads. Across the planet, women defend land and water at great personal risk – and reimagine our relationship with the Earth.

These women are not only protesting pollution or climate inaction; they are reimagining our relationship with the Earth. Their defiance is rooted in reverence, justice, and urgency. Whether through science, Indigenous wisdom, or grassroots organizing, they show that caring for the planet is inseparable from protecting human rights, economic justice, and future generations.

"I have learned you are never too small to make a difference."

— Greta Thunberg (Sweden)

Her school strike sparked a global climate movement, proving that moral clarity has no age.

*"We must shake the world into awareness.
Our rivers are not for sale."*

— Berta Cáceres (Honduras)

Assassinated for defending Indigenous lands, she became a martyr for environmental and human rights.

*"Our rainforest is not empty land. It is full
of life, stories, and resistance."*

— Nemonte Nenquimo (Ecuador, Waorani Nation)

As an Indigenous leader, she defends the Amazon with ancestral knowledge and global strategy.

In conclusion, in defending the Earth, women defend the future, showing that sustainability is as much about justice as it is about survival.

Reflection Prompts

1. Women on the Front Lines: Were there any specific women environmental activists in this chapter who inspired you? What risks have they taken, and how have they made an impact?
2. The Global Perspective: How do environmental challenges differ between high-income and low-income countries, and how are women responding uniquely within those contexts?
3. Barriers to Participation: What prevents women from being fully included in environmental policymaking, science, or green technology sectors? What actions can be taken to ensure their inclusion?
4. Future Vision: Imagine a world where women-led environmental movements have shaped climate policy globally. What policies, values, or practices would define that world?

CHAPTER 18:
TECHNOLOGY, SOCIAL MEDIA, AND DIGITAL FEMINISM

"A single voice online can be drowned out, but when women speak together, the digital echo becomes a movement no power can ignore."
— Maria L. Ellis

In the twenty-first century, feminism found a new arena of struggle and solidarity in the digital world, where hashtags become movements, smartphones become tools of resistance, and a single post can spark global change.

The digital revolution has given women unprecedented tools to connect, mobilize, and resist. Where traditional media once silenced or distorted their voices, social media platforms have amplified them, allowing women to shape narratives, spark movements, and hold institutions accountable.

"Digital activism isn't just a protest tool; it defines what many call feminism's fourth wave. Since the 2010s, social platforms have exposed harassment, amplified survivors, and powered global campaigns like #MeToo and #TimesUp. Fast, viral, and insistent on accountability in public and private life, this wave shows feminism adapting – and advancing."

Women in the Arab Spring During the Arab Spring (2010 to 2011), women activists used Facebook, Twitter, and YouTube to mobilize protests, document abuses, and demand reform. In January 2011, Egyptian activist Asmaa Mahfouz posted a YouTube video urging citizens to gather in Tahrir Square – a clip that spread across Facebook and satellite TV – helping to catalyze mass demonstrations. Though outcomes varied across the region, women's digital voices were central to challenging authoritarian rule.

India's "Pinjra Tod" (Break the Cage) Movement

In India, young women students launched the *Pinjra Tod* campaign online to protest discriminatory hostel curfews and restrictions that treated women as liabilities rather than adults. Using Facebook and Twitter, the movement quickly gained national attention, forcing universities to reconsider paternalistic rules. The campaign demonstrated how digital activism could dismantle everyday sexism in institutions.

#NiUnaMenos in Latin America

In 2015, Argentine feminists launched *#NiUnaMenos* ("Not One [Woman] Less") on social media to protest femicide and gender-based violence. The campaign spread across Latin America, leading to massive street protests in Mexico, Peru, and Chile. Online hashtags became offline marches, showing how digital platforms could transform private pain into collective outrage and policy demands. #NiUnaMenos drew hundreds of thousands to the streets within weeks and spread across the region.

Feminist Hackers and Cyber Collectives

Beyond hashtags, women have also built alternative digital spaces. Groups like Deep Lab and Latin America's Coding Rights collective challenge surveillance, misogyny, and exclusion in tech. By blending coding with activism, these cyber feminists ensure that digital tools themselves are not only used by women but also shaped by them.

From Burke's solidarity hashtag to Mahfouz's viral call, from Pinjra Tod's university protests to NiUnaMenos' continent-wide marches, women have turned technology into a megaphone for justice. Digital feminism is not just about visibility – it is about rewriting who controls information, who tells the story, and whose voices are amplified. In the age of algorithms, women remind us that technology is never neutral; it is a battleground where silence can be broken, power contested, and justice demanded.

In October 2017, the hashtag #MeToo swept across the internet. First coined by activist Tarana Burke, it exploded globally when women shared their stories of harassment and assault on Twitter, Instagram, and Facebook. What might once have been whispered privately was now shouted collectively. Within days, the hashtag had appeared in more than eighty countries, forcing governments, corporations, and cultural institutions to confront uncomfortable truths.

This viral moment revealed the transformative potential of digital feminism. No longer confined to marches, newsletters, or conferences, feminist voices now travel instantly, mobilizing millions across borders. The smartphone has become both witness and weapon, turning personal testimony into public reckoning.

Defining Digital Feminism

Digital feminism is feminist activism that uses online platforms and digital tools to challenge sexism, amplify marginalized voices, and organize collective action. Emerging in the early 2000s, it builds on earlier waves of cyberfeminism, which imagined the internet as a space to disrupt patriarchal norms.

What makes digital feminism distinctive is its speed, reach, and inclusivity. A survivor in Lagos, an activist in Buenos Aires, and a student in Seoul can all participate in the same conversation. This decentralized structure has made digital feminism one of the most democratic and global forms of activism to date.

Hashtags as New Protest Banners

Digital platforms have given rise to hashtag

movements that act as both rallying cries and archives of testimony:

- #MeToo (2017): A global reckoning on sexual harassment that reshaped workplace policies and spurred legal reforms.
- #NiUnaMenos (Argentina, 2015): "Not One Less," a campaign against femicide that began in Argentina and spread across Latin America.
- #BringBackOurGirls (Nigeria, 2014): Mobilized international pressure after Boko Haram kidnapped 276 schoolgirls.
- #MosqueMeToo (2018): Gave Muslim women space to speak about harassment during pilgrimages, breaking taboos in religious spaces.
- #FridaysForFuture (2018): Initiated by Greta Thunberg, the campaign linked youth climate strikes with feminist and intergenerational justice.

These campaigns show how digital storytelling fuels real-world protest – hashtags becoming marches, tweets becoming policy debates, and viral posts becoming global solidarity.

Digital Tools for Justice

Beyond hashtags, activists use technology strategically:

- Documentation: Smartphones record abuses – from protests in Iran to femicide reporting in Mexico – creating verifiable evidence for courts, journalists, and watchdogs.
- Resource Apps: Platforms connect survivors of gender-based violence with shelters, legal aid, and medical care.

- Online Campaigns: Petitions and coordinated digital strikes target corporations and governments.

- Education and Outreach: TikTok explainers, feminist podcasts, and Instagram campaigns bring theory and solidarity to younger audiences.

Digital feminism blurs the boundary between personal diary and political manifesto: a single post can spark outrage, community, and action.

Barriers and Backlash

Digital feminism is powerful but contested:

- Harassment: Women activists face trolling, doxxing, and threats, often aimed at silencing their voices.

- Digital Divide: In many low- and middle-income countries – especially rural areas – women have less access to affordable devices, data, and reliable connectivity, limiting their ability to organize, document abuse, and reach services. Women in rural or low-income regions remain 20 percent less likely to have internet access.

- Surveillance: Authoritarian regimes monitor feminist activity, censor dissent, and criminalize online organizing.

- Commodification: Feminist messaging is sometimes co-opted as "femvertising," diluting radical critique into marketable slogans. These challenges reveal that technology is not neutral; it can reproduce inequality even as it offers tools to resist it.

From Outrage to Reform

The true measure of digital feminism is not the volume of tweets but the depth of change they inspire:

- #MeToo sparked investigations, resignations, and legal reforms worldwide.

- #NiUnaMenos helped spur concrete reforms: the Micaela Law (Law 27.499) mandating gender-violence training for all public officials, and the Brisa Law (Law 27.452) providing monthly compensation and health coverage to children of femicide victims.

- #BringBackOurGirls forced international leaders to act on gendered violence in conflict.

- Digital campaigns now shape debates at the UN, in parliaments, and in boardrooms – bridging online protest with institutional change.

Glossary of Digital Feminism

- Cyberfeminism: A 1990s movement that saw the internet as a tool to challenge patriarchy and create feminist digital spaces.

- Digital Feminism: Contemporary activism using online platforms to fight gender inequality and mobilize global solidarity.

- Slacktivism: A critique suggesting online actions (likes, shares, petitions) lack depth – though large-scale campaigns show they can lead to reform.

- Femvertising: The commercial use of feminist messaging in advertising, often criticized for watering down activist goals.

Feminism in the Digital Age

Technology has redefined feminist activism. It

amplifies voices, connects struggles across continents, and forces institutions to reckon with inequality. Yet it also exposes activists to harassment, surveillance, and commodification.

Still, digital feminism has proven that when women raise their voices collectively online, they can alter culture, influence law, and expand solidarity. In this digital age, the feminist maxim "the personal is political" takes on new resonance: now, the personal is also viral, global, and far harder to ignore.

Case Studies in Digital Feminism

#MeToo (Global, 2017): Sparked by Tarana Burke's earlier work, the movement reshaped workplace policies and created global accountability structures for sexual harassment.

#NiUnaMenos (Argentina, 2015): Mobilized millions against femicide and gender violence, pushing Argentina and other Latin American countries to adopt stronger legal protections.

#BringBackOurGirls (Nigeria, 2014): Global online pressure forced world leaders to respond to the kidnapping of schoolgirls by Boko Haram, spotlighting the intersection of terrorism and gendered violence.

#MosqueMeToo (Global, 2018): Muslim women publicly shared experiences of harassment in sacred spaces, expanding feminist conversations into religious contexts long considered untouchable.

#FridaysForFuture (Sweden/Global, 2018): Started by Greta Thunberg's solitary strike, it became a worldwide youth movement for climate justice, explicitly connecting environmental and gender equity. Within a year, coordinated strikes spread to more than 100 countries, drawing millions of students into the streets.

#SayHerName (United States, 2015): Highlighted police violence against Black women, ensuring their stories were not erased from the broader racial justice movement.

As the twenty-first century unfolded, a new frontier of feminist activism emerged – not in the streets or halls of power, but across screens and servers. Social media and digital technology opened up vast new possibilities for expression, organizing, and visibility. Women, particularly younger generations and marginalized communities, harnessed these tools to challenge oppression, build solidarity, and tell their stories in their voices.

This chapter explores the intersection of gender and technology – how digital platforms have empowered feminist movements and how they have also amplified new threats.

The Rise of Digital Feminism

Digital feminism refers to the use of online platforms and technologies to advance gender justice. It is fast, global, accessible – and deeply personal.

From hashtags to livestreams, viral videos to encrypted organizing, the digital age has:

- Amplified women's voices beyond mainstream media.

- Enabled intersectional activism across geography, race, ability, and class.

- Democratized storytelling, allowing survivors and activists to lead their narratives.

Movements once sidelined by traditional media gained visibility through digital tools.

Hashtag Movements That Shaped the Decade

- #MeToo – Originally coined by Tarana Burke in 2006, this movement exploded globally in 2017, exposing the scale of sexual harassment and abuse in workplaces, industries, and institutions. From Hollywood to hospitality, women demanded accountability.

- #BringBackOurGirls – Sparked international outrage over the 2014 abduction of Nigerian schoolgirls by Boko Haram. Led by women in Nigeria and supported by figures like Michelle Obama, it highlighted gendered violence in conflict zones.

- #NiUnaMenos – A Latin American movement against femicide and gender-based violence. Originated in Argentina and spread across the region, uniting women against impunity and silence.

- #SayHerName – Amplified the stories of Black women and girls killed by police or experiencing state violence, often overlooked in broader racial justice movements.

- #FreePeriods – Led by teens and young women in the UK and globally, this campaign broke the stigma around menstruation and fought for free period products in schools.

These movements used social media to do what traditional systems couldn't: elevate the urgent, the invisible, and the deeply personal.

Platforms of Empowerment – and Exploitation

While social media has been a powerful tool, it has also become a space of risk – especially for women.

Opportunities

- Online communities for LGBTQ+ youth, disabled activists, and BIPOC feminists to find solidarity.

- Crowdfunding campaigns for reproductive health, legal support, or crisis aid.

- Entrepreneurial tools for women in business to market, network, and grow globally.

- Education and advocacy, from virtual webinars to TikTok explainer videos on systemic sexism.

Risks

- Online harassment, including doxxing, stalking, and deepfake abuse, disproportionately targets women, especially women of color and public figures.

- Censorship and algorithm bias, where feminist content is flagged while hate speech flourishes.

- Digital divides, which limit access for women in rural, poor, or under connected regions.

- Surveillance capitalism, which commodifies women's data and behavior without consent.

Tech Industry Gender Gaps

Despite tech's image as progressive, the industry remains male-dominated:

- Women hold fewer than 30 percent of tech jobs globally.

- Leadership and funding gaps are stark: only 2 percent of VC funding goes to female-founded startups.

- Sexual harassment and workplace discrimination are common in major tech firms.

- Technologies such as facial recognition and AI exhibit racial and gender bias – reflecting the lack of diversity in design.

Initiatives like Girls Who Code, Black Girls Code, and AnitaB.org are building new pipelines for inclusion – but systemic change remains slow.

Intersectionality in Digital Spaces

Digital feminism is not one-size-fits-all. Online

movements have made space for:

- Queer and trans voices in feminist conversations.

- Disability justice advocates creating accessible activism.

- Global South organizers mobilizing around labor, migration, and health.

- Youth climate leaders, especially Indigenous and Afro descendant girls, leading viral campaigns. What unites them is a shared conviction that liberation must be intersectional – accounting for race, class, disability, sexuality, migration, and place, not gender alone.

New Frontiers: AI, Virtual Worlds, and Feminist Futures

As we move deeper into an era of artificial intelligence, the metaverse, and biotechnology, feminist voices are shaping ethical debates:

- Who designs AI, whose values it encodes, and how those choices shape hiring, policing, health care, and credit?

- How will reproductive technologies evolve – and who will access them?

- Can virtual spaces be made safe, inclusive, and liberating?

- What digital rights should protect bodies, privacy, and consent?

"Women are working not only to use technology but to govern it, question it, and redesign it around justice, care, and shared power."

Coding a More Just World

The digital age has not solved patriarchy – but it has

cracked it open. Through hashtags, hacking, coding, and connection, women have used technology to make power visible, make pain heard, and make resistance viral.

Translate symbols into systems, turn privileges into rights, and build structures so the next generation inherits equality, not just legacy.

The revolution may not be televised. But it is most certainly live-streamed.

Technology, Social Media, and Digital Feminism

Digital spaces have become battlegrounds for justice and platforms for revolution. As the internet reshaped communication, women harnessed it to amplify voices, expose injustices, organize globally, and imagine new modes of activism. This chapter celebrates women who've wielded technology not just as users – but as builders, storytellers, and disruptors of old power structures.

Tarana Burke, founder of the original #MeToo movement in 2006, created a space for Black women and girls to speak about sexual violence. When survivors worldwide drove the hashtag viral in 2017, years of grassroots work gained global visibility and helped catalyze policy reviews, workplace reforms, and legal action.

Shafiqa Ahmadi, an Afghan-American legal scholar and advocate, uses digital platforms to challenge Islamophobia and promote gender equity in education. Through academic writing and social media, she bridges research and activism, modeling how tech can democratize knowledge.

Roxane Gay, a writer and cultural critic, transformed Twitter into a literary and feminist forum. Through essays, threads, and real-time responses, she brings nuance to complex topics – race, gender, trauma – with wit and honesty, helping reframe what intellectual discourse can look like in digital form.

Alicia Garza, co-founder of Black Lives Matter, understands the internet as both a tool and a terrain of struggle. With a viral hashtag and a powerful vision, she helped catalyze a decentralized global movement. Her digital organizing models how hashtags can evolve into tangible systemic change.

Zainab Al-Khawaja, a Bahraini human rights activist, used Twitter to document state repression during the Arab Spring. Despite multiple arrests, she continued to broadcast the truth, making social media a lifeline for those silenced by authoritarian regimes.

Imani Barbarin, also known as @Imani_Barbarin, is a Black disabled activist who uses TikTok, Twitter, and her blog to challenge ableism and highlight the intersections of race, gender, and disability. Her bold, informative content has brought disability justice into mainstream digital conversations.

Kimberlé Crenshaw, while known for coining "intersectionality," has leveraged podcasting and online education to bring legal and social justice concepts to broader audiences. Her platform *Intersectionality Matters!* bridges academic theory and popular discourse in a digital era.

Joy Buolamwini, founder of the Algorithmic Justice League, exposed racial and gender bias in AI facial recognition systems. Her viral TED Talk and MIT research prompted global tech reforms, proving how digital feminism also includes dismantling bias in the very code that shapes our lives.

Raquel Willis, a transgender rights activist and writer, utilizes digital media to center Black trans voices. As former editor of *Out* magazine and a leading voice on Twitter, she merges journalism, storytelling, and advocacy into a vision of justice grounded in visibility.

Nadya Okamoto, founder of PERIOD., built a global menstrual equity movement by leveraging Instagram and YouTube. Her content destigmatizes menstruation while mobilizing youth to fight period poverty, showing how Gen Z feminism flourishes through clicks and campaigns.

These women didn't just go viral – they went vital.

They show us that hashtags can become history,

algorithms can be interrogated, and the internet – far from neutral – can be reclaimed as a tool for feminist transformation.

They remind us that in the digital world, every click can be a spark, every share a signal of resistance, and every story a strategy.

For a more complete list of Notable Digital Feminist Leaders, see Appendix IV.

Voices of Defiance

The digital world has become one of the most powerful battlegrounds for gender justice. Women have used the internet to disrupt narratives, challenge oppression, mobilize movements, and build global solidarity. But they have also faced unprecedented harassment, censorship, and surveillance. In the face of such challenges, these women have refused to log off. Instead, they have coded, created, campaigned, and connected – reshaping the tech space as a tool for feminist expression and resistance.

> *"Technology is not neutral. It reflects the power structures of the society that creates it."*
> — Gina Neff (United Kingdom)

Her scholarship reminds us that digital equity demands deeper systemic change – not just better gadgets.

> *"The norms of yesterday will not serve the visions of tomorrow."*
> — Amanda Gorman (United States)

Though known for poetry, her use of digital platforms made her voice a force that mobilized millions toward hope and activism.

> *"If you're not included in the data, you're not seen. If you're not seen, you don't exist."*
> — Joy Buolamwini (Ghana/United States)

Her work on algorithmic bias exposed how AI can reproduce racial and gender discrimination – and sparked global reform. "In the end, hashtags organized marches, posts triggered investigations, and networks rewrote policies – proof that digital spaces can be as revolutionary as the streets."

Reflection Prompts

1. Digital Tools as a Force for Change: How has technology – particularly social media – amplified feminist voices and movements? Have you seen or participated in digital activism that made a real-world impact?

2. Global Digital Solidarity: How has social media created new forms of global feminist connection? What are the benefits and challenges of building solidarity across cultural and geographic lines?

3. Your Digital Voice: In what ways do you use – or could you use – your digital presence to support feminist values or causes? What stories, issues, or communities would you want to amplify?

4. The Future of Digital Feminism: As AI, virtual reality, and new technologies continue to emerge, what opportunities or concerns do you see for the future of feminist organizing in digital spaces?

CHAPTER 19:
POWER IN TRANSITION:
WOMEN'S POLITICS IN THE
TWENTY-FIRST CENTURY

"Women belong in all places where decisions are being made."
— Ruth Bader Ginsburg

A New Century, Familiar Questions

The twenty-first century opened with momentum for women in politics – women in top office, more diverse legislatures, and gender equality on the global agenda – yet gains proved fragile as backlash and barriers showed empowerment is neither linear nor guaranteed.

Representation Gains

Across the globe, women's representation in parliaments and congresses increased steadily during the first two decades of the new century. In 2005, Ellen Johnson Sirleaf became Africa's first elected female head of state, winning the presidency of Liberia. In Latin America, leaders like Michelle Bachelet of Chile and Dilma Rousseff of Brazil reshaped expectations of women's leadership in historically patriarchal societies.

By 2020, gender quotas across Latin America, Africa, and Europe helped lift women to roughly one-quarter of parliamentary seats worldwide; Rwanda was the outlier, with women holding over 60 percent – the highest share globally.

In the United States, the 2018 "Year of the Woman"

elections sent a record number of women to Congress, including the most racially and ethnically diverse cohort in history. Figures like Nancy Pelosi, the first woman to serve as Speaker of the House, demonstrated the durability of female leadership at the highest levels of American politics.

Persistent Barriers and Backlash

Even with these gains, obstacles remain formidable. Women continue to face online harassment and disinformation campaigns at higher rates than men, discouraging political participation. Gendered double standards persist: women are judged more harshly for leadership style, family choices, and appearance, and coverage often frames them through personality rather than policy.

Moreover, women's gains in politics have often sparked backlash. In some countries, quotas have been met with tokenism or deliberate manipulation, with parties placing women in unwinnable districts. In others, progress has stalled as populist movements have reinforced traditional gender roles. The twenty-first century has shown that progress is never secure; it requires constant defense.

Intersectionality and Representation

Another defining feature of this century has been the growing recognition that representation is not only about gender but also about race, ethnicity, class, and sexuality. The election of women like Kamala Harris, the first woman and woman of color to serve as Vice President of the United States, reflects the concrete dimensions of representation in a diverse democracy. Similarly, Indigenous and minority women leaders across Canada, New Zealand, and Latin America have broadened the meaning of political inclusion.

Global Movements and Digital Activism

The digital age has amplified women's political voices in unprecedented ways. Hashtags like #MeToo and #TimesUp have pushed issues of harassment and workplace inequality into legislative debates around the world. Grassroots women's movements have harnessed social media to mobilize protests, influence policy, and demand accountability.

At the same time, the digital sphere has become a battlefield of harassment and disinformation. Women politicians, particularly young and outspoken figures, face coordinated online abuse that threatens both personal safety and democratic participation.

Leadership in Crisis

The COVID-19 pandemic highlighted women's leadership with specific moves: Jacinda Ardern closed borders early, pursued an elimination strategy, paired strict lockdowns with wage subsidies, and held plain-English daily briefings; Angela Merkel led science-forward national addresses, coordinated state-level testing and ICU expansion, and explained the reproduction rate to the public; Tsai Ingwen in Taiwan scaled mask production and implemented a name-based rationing system while deploying targeted digital contact tracing; Katrín Jakobsdóttir backed Iceland's population-wide testing with deCODE; Erna Solberg in Norway even held children-only press conferences to address anxiety. These concrete choices – early containment, mass testing, transparent data, targeted supports, and citizen-centered communication – show how diverse leadership styles can deliver in a crisis.

Yet the pandemic also exposed vulnerabilities: women leaders often bore disproportionate criticism, and the economic downturn hit women harder, threatening to roll back decades of progress.

The Road Ahead

The twenty-first century has already rewritten the story of women in politics. Women now occupy presidencies, parliaments, and cabinets on every continent. Their presence has shifted policy priorities, amplified new voices, and challenged stereotypes about leadership. But the path forward is far from secure. Structural barriers, cultural biases, and digital-age challenges continue to slow progress.

The challenge of this century is not only to elect women but to ensure that their participation is sustainable, impactful, and protected. The promise of representation lies not just in the number of women holding office but in the ability of those women to transform institutions, policies, and possibilities for the generations that follow.

For much of modern history, political power was a male preserve. Women were relegated to the sidelines – seen but rarely heard, and certainly not elected. Yet across the globe, from the mid-twentieth century onward, women began to chip away at the walls of political exclusion. In parliaments, courts, cabinets, and grassroots assemblies, they fought not just to be present but to lead.

For much of modern history, political decision-making was a male preserve, with women relegated to the margins. Yet across continents, women have forced open the doors of parliaments, cabinets, and grassroots assemblies. Their leadership has not only changed who sits at the table but also how decisions are made, what policies are prioritized, and whose voices are heard.

Jacinda Ardern and Crisis Leadership in New Zealand

When a gunman attacked two mosques in Christchurch in 2019, New Zealand Prime Minister Jacinda Ardern responded with compassion and resolve. Wearing a headscarf in solidarity, she comforted grieving families and swiftly enacted gun reform. Her empathetic leadership style became a global model, showing that political strength is not incompatible with care and that femininity can coexist with decisive governance.

Indigenous Women in Bolivia and Grassroots Politics

In Bolivia, Indigenous women have risen from grassroots activism to national politics. Leaders such as Silvia Lazarte, a Quechua activist, helped draft Bolivia's 2009 constitution, embedding Indigenous rights and gender equality. Their participation reshaped national identity and policy, demonstrating that marginalized women can become central to political transformation. In Bolivia, Indigenous women in office wore polleras, shawls, and bowler hats, making cultural identity part of authority and pushing land rights and communal sovereignty onto the national agenda.

Combating Political Violence Against Women

While progress is real, women leaders face gendered attacks, harassment, and even violence. In Mexico, scores of women candidates have been targeted during elections. Online abuse campaigns in the U.S., U.K., and India attempt to silence women leaders through intimidation. In response, women's movements and NGOs are pushing for stronger legal protections and digital safety measures, ensuring that participation in politics does not come at the cost of personal security.

From Sirleaf's post-war governance to Ardern's empathetic crisis leadership, from Rwanda's parliamentary majority to Bolivia's constitutional reformers, women are not only participating in politics – they are reshaping its culture. Their presence often correlates with lower corruption, more investment in social services, and broader public trust. The rise of women in politics is not simply about representation; it is about transformation. When women lead, nations see new possibilities for justice, peace, and inclusive prosperity.

This chapter explores the struggle for women's political power as both a story of barriers broken and institutions transformed – revealing how women's leadership has shifted politics from a tool of exclusion into a platform for change.

Barriers to Entry: The Long Fight for a Seat at the Table

The barriers to women's political participation were – and often still are – steep:

- **Legal exclusions from voting and candidacy**
- **Patriarchal party systems and gatekeepers**
- **Violence, harassment, and disinformation targeting women candidates**
- **Cultural expectations about family roles and femininity**
- **Lack of campaign** financing and media support

Women's Movements and Legislative Shifts

In many countries, feminist activism played a central role in:

- Passing gender quotas to increase women's representation
- Legalizing reproductive rights, equal pay, and anti-violence legislation
- Establishing ministries for women's affairs or gender equality

Women's political power has rarely come from invitation – it has been fought for, from the grassroots to the global stage.

Modern Leadership and Intersectional Power

In recent decades, a new wave of women leaders has emerged – often more diverse, vocal, and unapologetically feminist:

- Jacinda Ardern (New Zealand) – Led with empathy and action during the Christchurch massacre and COVID-19; championed inclusive politics.
- Michelle Bachelet (Chile) – First female president and later UN High Commissioner for Human Rights.
- Ellen Johnson Sirleaf (Liberia) – Africa's first elected female head of state and a Nobel Peace Prize recipient.
- Sanna Marin (Finland) – Became Prime Minister at age thirty-four, leading an all-female coalition cabinet.
- Kamala Harris (United States) – First woman, Black, and South Asian Vice President of the United States.
- Ilhan Omar and Alexandria Ocasio-Cortez (United States) – Progressive congresswomen reshaping U.S. political discourse with an intersectional lens.

These leaders stand on the shoulders of generations – but they also represent a new generation, committed to justice, climate action, and inclusive policy.

Resistance and Retaliation

With power has come backlash. Women in politics face:

- Online and in-person harassment, including threats of rape and murder
- Media scrutiny focusing on looks, tone, or family choices rather than policy
- Political smear campaigns and disinformation
- Gendered expectations to "soften" or "humanize" male-dominated institutions

Despite these challenges, women are not stepping back – they're stepping forward, reshaping politics from a transactional to a transformational space.

The Power of Representation

When women lead, policy changes:

- Greater investments in education, health, and social services
- More attention to domestic violence, childcare, and gender equity
- Transparent governance and anti-corruption measures
- Inclusive peace negotiations and post-conflict recovery plans

Representation is the starting point, not the finish line; presence must be paired with power – coalitions, enforceable rules, and accountability – to change systems. As feminist scholars remind us, the presence of women does not guarantee the power to change systems. It must be paired with accountability, alliances, and a vision for justice.

Toward Transformative Politics

Women in politics are not just "filling seats." They are:

- Rewriting laws
- Changing narratives
- Building coalitions across differences
- Bringing lived experience into decision-making rooms long closed to them

The future of political power is not simply more women – it is more vision, more courage, and more equity. It is a world where leadership is not judged by strength alone, but by the capacity to listen, include, and uplift.

Female Political Leaders, Movements, and Milestones

in Global Politics was created to accompany Chapter 19 of *Beyond Barriers: Women's Progress from Mid-twentieth Century to Today*. It highlights groundbreaking women in politics, landmark policies, and pivotal movements that have shaped global gender equity in governance.

For centuries, political arenas were fortified strongholds built to exclude women. But through persistence, strategy, and courage, women have surged from the margins to the main stage, reshaping policy, challenging patriarchy, and leading nations. This chapter features women who have broken barriers, written legislation, and inspired movements that extend well beyond their constituencies.

Shirley Chisholm, the first Black woman elected to the United States Congress and the first to seek a major party nomination for president, ran under the slogan "Unbought and Unbossed." She challenged racial and gender norms with unapologetic boldness and left a legislative legacy that championed education, labor, and minority rights.

Benazir Bhutto, Pakistan's first female prime minister and the first woman to lead a Muslim-majority country, brought global visibility to Muslim women in politics. Despite political upheaval and personal tragedy, she advocated for women's education and healthcare in a volatile environment.

Alexandria Ocasio-Cortez, elected at age twenty-nine to the U.S. Congress, became a digital-age political force. Her candidness, social media fluency, and policy boldness on issues like climate justice and economic equity marked a shift in political leadership toward younger, more diverse representation.

Sanna Marin, Prime Minister of Finland, became the world's youngest serving government leader when elected in 2019. Her all-female-led coalition government prioritized climate action, gender equity, and transparency in governance – illustrating what inclusive politics can look like in action.

Jacinda Ardern, former prime minister of New

Zealand, exemplified empathetic leadership, especially in crisis – be it the Christchurch mosque shootings or the COVID-19 pandemic. Her ability to balance strength with compassion reshaped global expectations of political leadership.

Michelle Bachelet, twice elected president of Chile and former UN High Commissioner for Human Rights, combined medical training and political acumen to advocate for democratic accountability and gender justice across Latin America and beyond.

Ilhan Omar, a Somali-American refugee and one of the first Muslim women in the U.S. Congress, uses her platform to speak boldly on immigration, anti-racism, and foreign policy. Her election represents a profound shift in American politics toward pluralism and inclusion.

Cristina Fernández de Kirchner, former president and current vice president of Argentina, expanded social programs and gender parity during her terms. Though controversial, her legacy includes elevating women's role in Latin American politics.

Ngozi Okonjo-Iweala, Nigeria's former finance minister and the first woman and first African to lead the World Trade Organization, brings an economist's lens to global trade and development. Her ascent marks a breakthrough in international leadership for women of the Global South.

These women stand at the helm of global transformation – not by replicating patriarchal politics but by reimagining what leadership can look like.

They show us that power, when fused with purpose, can rebuild nations, heal divides, and shape the world anew.

For a more complete list of female political leaders, movements, and milestones in global politics, see Appendix IV.

Voices of Defiance

For much of history, women were barred from political life – not only excluded from leadership but discouraged from imagining themselves as decision-makers. But women did not wait for permission. They organized, protested, legislated, and led. From local councils to heads of state, they redefined what governance looks like and who it must serve. Their rise to political power has not come without resistance – but with every step onto the main stage, they've proven that the future of democracy depends on their full and fearless participation.

"If they don't give you a seat at the table, bring a folding chair."
— Shirley Chisholm (United States)

As the first Black woman elected to Congress, she made space where none existed, paving the way for generations of diverse leadership.

"If your dreams do not scare you, they are not big enough."
— Ellen Johnson Sirleaf (Liberia)

As Africa's first elected female head of state, she turned hope into political transformation in a post-conflict nation.

*"You can't have development without democracy,
and you can't have democracy without women."*
— Michelle Bachelet (Chile)

From exile to the presidency to the UN, her career is a testament to resilience, inclusion, and global impact.

In conclusion, each woman elected is not just a seat filled but a system transformed, signaling that democracy cannot thrive without women's voices.

Reflection Prompts

1. Progress and Setbacks
   - Where do you see the most meaningful progress for women in politics in the twenty-first century?

- Where do you notice setbacks or areas where progress has stalled?

2. Digital Activism and Risk

   - How have social media and digital platforms amplified women's political voices?

   - What dangers do these same platforms pose for women in public life?

3. Leadership Styles

   - Do you think women leaders bring distinct qualities to governance?

   - How have leaders like Jacinda Ardern or Angela Merkel shaped your understanding of effective leadership?

4. Sustaining Change

   - What steps can individuals and communities take to ensure women's political gains are not temporary but lasting?

   - What role might you play – directly or indirectly – in supporting women's leadership where you live?

CHAPTER 20:
POWER AND POISE – RECLAIMING FEMININITY IN A SHIFTING WORLD

"Feminism is not about making women strong. Women are already strong. It's about changing the way the world perceives that strength."

— G.D. Anderson

For centuries, power was measured by masculine ideals of toughness, aggression, and dominance, and women were told to mute visible femininity to be taken seriously. Today, women are proving that femininity on their terms is a source of authority and transformation, using poise, care, and cultural identity as instruments of power that shift policy, heal societies, and redefine governance.

Leadership Outcomes: When Femininity Becomes Power

Research consistently shows that women in politics alter institutional outcomes – corruption decreases, welfare spending increases, and peace agreements last longer. Yet numbers tell only part of the story. What matters equally is how women lead and how their self-presentation reshapes the very meaning of power. In local government, electing women often shifts budgets toward clean water, clinics, and schools; at peace tables, women's participation correlates with agreements that embed community provisions and endure longer.

New Zealand: Jacinda Ardern and Empathetic Authority

Ardern's leadership broke from convention by embracing empathy and visible motherhood. Her choice to wear a headscarf while comforting mourners after the Christchurch mosque attacks symbolized inclusion and respect across cultural lines. She governed with openness, even bringing her infant daughter to the United Nations. Ardern showed that self-presentation rooted in care and compassion could be wielded as a form of authority that strengthened national unity. Ardern demonstrated that care can carry authority, pairing symbolic inclusion – her headscarf at Christchurch vigils – with swift firearms law reform and consistent, plain-spoken crisis briefings that reinforced social cohesion.

Bolivia: Indigenous Women and Visible Identity

In Bolivia, Indigenous women entering politics refused to abandon their polleras (skirts), shawls, and bowler hats. By maintaining traditional dress, they asserted femininity and cultural identity as inseparable from authority. Their visibility brought issues of land rights and cultural sovereignty to national debate, showing that power could be rooted in authenticity rather than assimilation. Femininity became a visible statement of defiance and belonging.

For a more complete list of Data Snapshot – Women in Politics Today, see Appendix IV.

The Backlash: Gendered Attacks and Political Violence

Yet this reclamation of femininity has also provoked backlash. Women leaders face attacks that rarely target their policies and instead weaponize gender, family roles, or appearance. When Ardern was criticized for "smiling too much" or Johnson Sirleaf was dismissed as "too motherly," the underlying message was clear: femininity is still policed in politics.

Across the globe, online harassment disproportionately targets female politicians with gendered insults. In Latin America and South Asia, women activists face not only slander but also physical violence and assassination. Their very presence – often accompanied by unapologetic femininity – threatens entrenched patriarchal systems.

Backlash in Numbers

Indicator	Finding	Source
Female politicians experiencing online abuse	73 percent report harassment, mostly gendered	Amnesty International
Women MPs facing physical violence or threats	44 percent	Inter-Parliamentary Union
Assassinations of women human rights defenders (2023)	Over 400 worldwide	Front Line Defenders
Nature of attacks	Majority target appearance, sexuality, or family roles, not policy positions	UN Women

Reclaiming Femininity as Strength

Despite the backlash, women leaders are redefining the terms of political participation. They show that femininity – once used as a reason to exclude them – can be reframed as a tool for inclusion, legitimacy, and reform. Their self-presentation is not superficial; it is strategic. Whether through dress, rhetoric, or public gestures, they wield femininity to challenge old hierarchies and model new ones.

This shift has broader implications for governance

itself. When femininity becomes a political language, leadership is no longer tied to domination but to collaboration. Authority becomes less about commanding and more about connecting. And power becomes not a performance of masculinity but a reimagining of what leadership can look like for everyone.

By explicitly reclaiming femininity as strength, women leaders are not only reshaping institutions but also redefining how power is perceived and practiced. Their stories remind us that self-presentation is not cosmetic – it is political. In the twenty-first century, femininity is no longer the opposite of authority; it is its transformation.

Power and poise together reveal a new truth: when women lead authentically, they change not only policies but the very definition of leadership itself.

Combating the Challenges

In response, women leaders and allies are mobilizing. National caucuses, international bodies, and NGOs are creating legal protections and security frameworks. The Inter-Parliamentary Union has launched initiatives to address sexism in politics, while UN Women supports programs to safeguard female candidates during elections.

At the grassroots level, women are building solidarity networks across borders. Social media – though often a platform for harassment – is also being reclaimed as a tool for empowerment, allowing women politicians to bypass traditional media filters and connect directly with voters.

The New Face of Power

The twenty-first century has proven that women's leadership is not only viable but often more effective. During global crises – from pandemics to climate disasters – female leaders have demonstrated that resilience, inclusivity, and empathy are critical tools of governance. Their styles have redefined what authority looks like, creating models of power rooted in collaboration rather than domination.

This new face of power rejects the false choice between femininity and leadership: poise can coexist with decisiveness, and grace can sharpen authority.

By reclaiming femininity as strength, women leaders are reshaping governance and redefining the possibilities of power in the twenty-first century. Their presence correlates with stronger democracies, better welfare outcomes, and more durable peace. Yet they remain on the front lines of backlash, harassment, and political violence that threaten not just individuals but democratic systems themselves.

Power and poise together remind us that true leadership is not about mirroring the past but about creating new possibilities for the future – where authenticity, resilience, and grace stand at the center of decision-making.

In a world where power has often been defined by masculine ideals, a new generation of women is reclaiming femininity – not as weakness or frivolity – but as a source of strength, identity, and expression. This chapter honors women who have challenged restrictive gender norms and embraced their femininity as a vital part of leadership, creativity, and resilience.

Audre Lorde, a Black lesbian feminist poet and activist, redefined femininity through her exploration of erotic power, identity, and the body. Her writing, including *Uses of the Erotic*, emphasized the power of self-expression and emotional depth as radical tools for transformation.

Frida Kahlo, the Mexican painter known for her deeply personal and surreal self-portraits, used fashion, floral motifs, and symbolic imagery to assert her femininity amid physical pain and political turmoil. She became an icon of feminist resistance and cultural pride.

Princess Diana, often dubbed the "People's Princess," combined grace and vulnerability with an unshakable humanitarian spirit. She reshaped the image of royal femininity, bringing warmth, empathy, and authenticity into a space traditionally defined by restraint.

Marsha P. Johnson, a Black transgender woman and

drag performer, fought for LGBTQ+ rights with radiant joy and radical courage. Her floral crowns, bold style, and unrelenting activism redefined feminine expression as a tool for liberation during the Stonewall era and beyond.

Adele, the Grammy-winning British singer, brings an unapologetically emotional presence to her music and public persona. Her vocal strength is matched by her openness about heartbreak, motherhood, and body image, making her a symbol of empowered vulnerability.

Zendaya, actress, singer, and fashion icon, fluidly navigates between traditionally masculine and feminine aesthetics, reshaping how femininity is represented in media. She uses her platform to challenge racial stereotypes and redefine what it means to be a young woman in Hollywood. On-screen in *Euphoria*, she centers a complex Black teen and refuses stereotype. On red carpets, she swings from razor suiting to fluid gowns – expanding what young Black femininity can look like in Hollywood.

Tracee Ellis Ross, an actress and entrepreneur, openly celebrates aging, sensuality, and self-love. As the founder of Pattern Beauty and a champion of natural Black hair, she inspires women to embrace every aspect of themselves – glamorous, bold, and complex.

Dita Von Teese, a burlesque artist and entrepreneur, reclaimed vintage glamour and sensuality as feminist performance. She challenges assumptions about sexuality, performance, and empowerment, celebrating femininity on her own terms.

Meghan Markle, the Duchess of Sussex, broke from royal convention by speaking openly about mental health, racism, and gender roles. Her style and advocacy have sparked global conversations about modern femininity, autonomy, and tradition.

Megan Rapinoe, soccer champion and activist, expresses femininity with strength and confidence, challenging expectations within the sports world. Her short hair, bold lipstick, and political voice embody a new kind of athlete-leader.

These women have taught us that femininity is not a performance for others – it is an evolving expression of self.

Through art, activism, fashion, and leadership, they've redefined what it means to be feminine in a world still learning to embrace its full spectrum.

Power and poise are not opposites. In their stories, they are beautifully and fiercely intertwined.

The Misunderstanding of Femininity

For generations, society reduced femininity to looks – dresses, makeup, gentleness – and treated it as a lack of seriousness. Women who embraced softness were labeled weak; those who led with grace were overlooked in favor of masculine mimicry.

What it actually is: not appearance but a set of capacities and practices that shape how we work, relate, and lead:

- Emotional attunement and regulation
- Empathic listening and responsiveness
- Discernment and sound judgment
- Creative problem-solving and collaboration
- Care work and healing

None of these are liabilities. In fact, they are the very qualities that leaders, families, companies, and societies increasingly need.

Femininity as a Choice, Not a Cage

The danger lies not in femininity itself but in its enforcement. When women are told they must be feminine in a particular way – or punished for not being feminine enough – they are trapped. Likewise, when women are told that embracing their femininity makes them less serious, less capable, or less revolutionary, they are robbed of part of their humanity.

True empowerment means having the freedom to

define femininity for yourself:

- A woman can be ambitious and tender.
- She can wear heels or boots – or neither.
- She can be loud, or quiet, or both at once.
- She can mother children, companies, or communities.

Femininity is not about conforming to outdated scripts. It's about honoring the parts of yourself that feel most alive, expressive, and whole.

The Risk of Losing Ourselves

As more women enter historically male-dominated fields – business, law, science, politics – there's a temptation to "toughen up," to neutralize, to fit in. Sometimes it's a necessary survival strategy. But if we're not careful, we can lose the very essence that makes our contributions unique.

If power requires that we dull our intuition, suppress our warmth, or bury our joy – we must ask: Is that really power? Or just another form of pressure?

We must model leadership that includes, rather than excludes, the fullness of who we are.

Redefining Strength

Let us expand what we call strength:

- Strength is standing in your values even when it's unpopular.
- Strength is raising children with love and discipline.
- Strength is holding space for another's pain without needing to fix it.
- Strength is asking for help, setting boundaries, and trusting your gut.

The women who have shaped the world – artists,

activists, mothers, teachers, peacemakers – have done so not by abandoning their femininity, but by integrating it into their work and wisdom.

Passing It On

To the next generation of girls and women: Do not be ashamed of your softness. Do not apologize for your sparkle. You do not need to be louder to be stronger, harder to be braver, or more masculine to be taken seriously.

Your femininity is not a distraction – it's a gift.

Honor it. Own it. Let it evolve. And let it shine through your leadership, your art, your decisions, and your life.

Voices of Defiance

Femininity has too often been defined by others – confined to narrow standards of beauty, behavior, and worth. But across cultures and generations, women have reclaimed femininity as a force – not of fragility, but of authenticity, duality, and power. These women challenge the idea that strength must come at the expense of softness or that grace cannot exist beside grit. Their defiance lies in embracing the fullness of womanhood, unapologetically and on their terms.

"I'm not bossy – I'm the boss."

— Beyoncé Knowles-Carter (United States)

She reclaimed power, sexuality, and motherhood as dimensions of feminine strength in the spotlight of global fame.

"Women's rights are human rights. There is no excuse
for denying equality to half the population."

— Amal Clooney (Lebanon/United Kingdom)

Her elegance, intellect, and global advocacy prove that poise is not weakness – it's precision.

"I'm feminine, I'm confident, and I'm in charge."

— Rihanna (Barbados)

She turned fashion, beauty, and music into tools of feminine entrepreneurship and cultural disruption.

"Caring for myself is not self-indulgence, it is self-preservation, and that is an act of political warfare."

— Audre Lorde (United States)

Lorde's voice redefined the feminine as a site of resistance, wholeness, and unapologetic self-love.

In conclusion, by reclaiming femininity as power, women prove that leadership is strongest when it is authentic, unapologetic, and their own.

Reflection Prompts

1. Reclaiming the Narrative: How has your understanding of femininity evolved over time? Were there moments when you felt pressured to suppress or perform it in a certain way?

2. Cultural Influences: How do different cultures shape and define femininity? Have you experienced or witnessed conflicts – or harmonies – between cultural expectations and personal identity?

3. Media and Femininity: How is femininity portrayed in the media today? Are there portrayals you find empowering or problematic? Why?

4. Future of Integration: Imagine a society where femininity is fully valued in all its forms. What does that world look like? How would relationships, leadership, and creativity be different?

CHAPTER 21:
REDEFINING FEMININITY – ICONS, THINKERS, AND CULTURAL VOICES

"Femininity is not about fitting into a mold – it's about breaking it, reshaping it, and owning it on our own terms."

— Chimamanda Ngozi Adichie

This chapter highlights modern women who have redefined femininity through action, art, and leadership. Across cultures and generations, they've expanded its meaning – merging intellect, creativity, courage, and care – and shattered narrow ideals of softness and passivity, revealing a living spectrum that is fluid, strong, complex, and deeply personal.

Femininity is no longer confined to a narrow script. Across cultures and generations, women have expanded and reimagined its meaning – merging intellect, creativity, and courage. This chapter honors icons, thinkers, and cultural voices who've questioned the status quo and redefined what it means to be feminine.

Chimamanda Ngozi Adichie and Feminist Storytelling

Nigerian author Chimamanda Ngozi Adichie has challenged stereotypes of femininity through literature and cultural commentary. In We Should All Be Feminists, she argued that femininity is not incompatible with ambition or leadership, calling for women's right to define themselves beyond rigid gender roles. Her essay and TED Talk, We

Should All Be Feminists, sampled in Beyoncé's "Flawless" and taught worldwide, helped move feminist language from lecture halls to pop culture.

Frida Kahlo and the Aesthetic of Pain and Power

Mexican painter Frida Kahlo used her art to redefine femininity not as perfection, but as authenticity. With self-portraits that displayed disability, pain, and sexuality, she rejected beauty norms and embraced the full complexity of female identity. Kahlo's work remains a global symbol of how femininity can carry suffering and power in equal measure. In self-portraits like The Broken Column and The Two Fridas, she made disability, pain, and sexuality visible, rejecting perfection and insisting on truthful beauty.

Leymah Gbowee and Peace as a Feminine Force

Liberian peace activist Leymah Gbowee mobilized thousands of women in nonviolent protest to help end Liberia's brutal civil war. Wearing white to symbolize peace, she reframed femininity as a force for political transformation. Awarded the Nobel Peace Prize, her story demonstrates that collective feminine solidarity can stop wars and rebuild nations.

Rihanna and Entrepreneurial Femininity

Global icon Rihanna redefined femininity through entrepreneurship. With her Fenty Beauty brand, she disrupted the cosmetics industry by centering inclusivity – offering shades for all skin tones and rejecting narrow beauty ideals. Her brand became both a business success and a cultural shift, proving that femininity, when reimagined, can democratize industries. With Fenty Beauty, she disrupted cosmetics by launching more than forty foundation shades at debut, centering inclusivity and rejecting narrow beauty ideals. The brand's success turned entrepreneurial femininity into a cultural reset.

From Adichie's storytelling to Malala's activism, from

Kahlo's paintings to Gbowee's peace movement, from Rihanna's entrepreneurship to countless unnamed women worldwide, femininity is no longer confined to fragility. It is intellect, resilience, artistry, leadership, and care.

By reclaiming femininity, women are not asking permission to exist – they are redefining existence itself. Their voices, images, and actions insist that femininity is not weakness but one of the most powerful cultural forces shaping the twenty-first century.

Simone de Beauvoir, the French existentialist philosopher and author of The Second Sex, laid the intellectual foundation for modern feminism. Her provocative declaration – "One is not born, but rather becomes, a woman" – challenged biological determinism and invited women to define themselves outside patriarchal norms.

Maya Angelou, the American poet, memoirist, and civil rights activist, gave voice to Black womanhood with unmatched grace and strength. Her works, such as I Know Why the Caged Bird Sings, blend resilience, sensuality, and empowerment, making her a global symbol of dignified femininity.

Gloria Steinem, journalist and organizer, became the face of second-wave feminism in the U.S. With her signature aviator glasses and unwavering clarity, she fought for reproductive rights, equal pay, and media representation, proving that intellect and activism are pillars of feminine identity.

Toni Morrison, Nobel Prize-winning novelist, wrote richly layered stories about the inner lives of Black women. Her prose, unapologetically lyrical and fierce, redefined beauty, power, and pain in the feminine experience.

Chimamanda Ngozi Adichie, Nigerian author of We Should All Be Feminists, blends cultural critique with storytelling. Her TED Talk-turned-manifesto reached millions, challenging stereotypes and promoting global feminism rooted in dignity and inclusivity.

Laverne Cox, Emmy-nominated actress and

LGBTQ+ advocate, was the first transgender woman to appear on the cover of TIME magazine. Her activism and visibility have redefined femininity through a lens of identity, pride, and possibility.

Lady Gaga, pop icon and philanthropist, has used performance art to push boundaries around gender, fame, and vulnerability. Her fashion, advocacy, and raw emotion have made her a cultural shapeshifter – transforming what power in femininity can look like.

Michelle Obama, former First Lady of the United States, redefined grace under scrutiny. Through initiatives on girls' education, healthy living, and leadership, she merged intellect, empathy, and style into a powerful modern image of womanhood.

Sofia Coppola, filmmaker and director, brought quiet introspection to female coming-of-age stories. Her aesthetics of softness and detachment challenged the hypersexualized portrayals of women in Hollywood, creating space for subtle emotional landscapes.

Zanele Muholi, South African visual activist and photographer, documents Black queer life through haunting, intimate portraits. Their work challenges both racial and gender invisibility, insisting on the full recognition of every feminine identity.

These women don't fit into a single definition – they forge their own.

They teach us that femininity can be cerebral or sensual, loud or silent, universal or radically personal. It is not a cage, but a canvas.

Through pen, lens, microphone, and stage, they've painted new possibilities for all who seek to live fully and freely as themselves.

For a more complete list of Cultural Icons Embracing Feminine Power, see Appendix IV.

Voices of Defiance

Femininity is not a fixed ideal – it is fluid, plural, and

deeply personal. For too long, it has been defined through the lens of patriarchy, confined to beauty, obedience, or domesticity. But artists, philosophers, fashion icons, and everyday women have challenged and expanded those definitions. Through their voices, femininity becomes not a limitation but a language – one of resilience, creativity, contradiction, and truth. These women didn't just reflect their cultures – they reimagined them.

> *"Imperfection is beauty, madness is genius, and it's better to be absolutely ridiculous than absolutely boring."*
>
> — Marilyn Monroe (United States)

Behind the glamour, Monroe redefined vulnerability and complexity as central to feminine power.

> *"Elegance is the only beauty that never fades."*
>
> — Audrey Hepburn (United Kingdom)

Her grace and humanitarian work made quiet strength and compassion the heart of her iconic feminine legacy.

> *"You are your best thing."*
>
> — Toni Morrison (United States)

Her literary voice gave Black women space to see themselves as whole, beautiful, and beyond any imposed definition.

> *"I don't follow fashion – I follow my own rules."*
>
> — Vivienne Westwood (United Kingdom)

She made femininity punk, political, and powerfully rebellious in an industry known for conformity.

In conclusion, icons and voices of modern femininity remind us that identity is not conformity but a spectrum of strength, beauty, and defiance.

Reflection Questions: Reclaiming Your Own Feminine Power

1. How do you personally define femininity?
2. Does your definition come from family, culture, religion, media – or your own lived experience?

   In what ways do you express your femininity creatively – through fashion, writing, movement, relationships, or spiritual practice?
3. Is there a part of you that longs for more expression?
4. How might embracing your femininity – on your own terms – help others around you do the same?
5. How can you model freedom for others?
6. What is one thing you want to teach the next generation about femininity?
7. What message do you want your daughter, niece, student, or mentee to carry forward?

CHAPTER 22:
SPIRIT IN ACTION: WOMEN'S SPIRITUALITY AS COLLECTIVE POWER

*"What begins in the quiet of the soul can, when shared,
ignite the transformation of a people."*
— Maria L. Ellis

From the Private to the Public

Spirituality has always sustained women privately, but in the twenty-first century, it has also emerged as a public force, shaping communities, movements, and institutions. Women have carried their inner practices into the social sphere, transforming prayer into protest, ritual into resilience, and belief into activism. This outward-facing spirituality does not replace personal practice – it amplifies it, creating ripples that extend far beyond the individual.

Historical Foundations of Collective Spiritual Power

Women have long gathered in spiritual communities that transcended personal faith. From the convents of medieval Europe to the circles of abolitionist women in the nineteenth-century United States, spirituality gave women both language and legitimacy to act publicly. Sojourner Truth's declaration, "Ain't I a Woman?" was at once spiritual testimony and political demand. Sojourner Truth's 1851 address at the Women's Rights Convention in Akron, Ohio – remembered as "Ain't I a Woman?" – was at once spiritual testimony and political demand.

These legacies remind us that spirituality has often been the doorway through which women entered public life, especially in societies that denied them secular authority.

Spirituality and Social Movements

Throughout the twentieth and twenty-first centuries, women's spirituality has fueled movements for justice:

- Civil Rights Movement (U.S.) – Black church-women turned faith into organizing power, running voter clinics and freedom kitchens from church basements while freedom hymns kept march lines steady.

- Liberation Theology (Latin America) – Women in base communities mobilized scripture into action, holding kitchen-table Bible circles, parish-hall literacy classes, and seed exchanges tied to land claims.

- Peace and Anti-War Movements – From Greenham Common to Buenos Aires, women made ritual into resistance: candlelit encirclements and ribboned fences at the U.K. base; white-scarf Thursday marches in the Plaza de Mayo.

These examples reveal that spirituality, when collective, becomes a resource not only for resilience but for resistance.

Women Clergy and Faith Leadership

The late twentieth and early twenty-first centuries witnessed breakthroughs in women's formal religious leadership. Protestant denominations ordained women in growing numbers, while Catholic women created parallel communities of faith leadership despite institutional barriers. Female rabbis, imams, priests, and spiritual leaders across traditions have challenged patriarchal hierarchies and opened new possibilities for inclusive worship.

Exemplars across traditions include: Anglican/Episcopal – Barbara Harris (first woman bishop, 1989), Katharine Jefferts Schori (first female Presiding Bishop, 2006), Libby Lane (first CoE woman bishop, 2015); Lutheran (ELCA) – Elizabeth Eaton (Presiding Bishop); United Methodist – Leontine T. C. Kelly (first Black woman bishop, 1984); Judaism – Regina Jonas (first woman rabbi, 1935), Sally Priesand (first in the U.S., 1972), Amy Eilberg (first Conservative woman rabbi, 1985), Rabba Sara Hurwitz (Orthodox women's clergy title, 2009); Islam – Amina Wadud (led mixed-gender Friday prayer, 2005), Sherin Khankan (founder, women-led Mariam Mosque, 2016); Buddhism – Bhikkhunī Dhammananda (re-established full ordination for women in Thailand, 2003), Pema Chödrön (teacher/abbess); Hinduism – Mata Amritanandamayi ("Amma"), a global guru and humanitarian; Catholic (parallel/lay-led) – women religious leaders (e.g., Sister Joan Chittister, Sister Simone Campbell) and movements such as Roman Catholic Women priests and the Women's Ordination Conference. These leaders expand the public face of spirituality, showing that faith leadership is not confined to men, nor is spiritual authority tied to rigid tradition.

Global and Interfaith Dimensions

In India, women leaders in Hindu, Muslim, and Sikh communities have used religious festivals and gurudwara platforms for education and peace initiatives, notably joint campaigns after 2008 to 2010 communal tensions.

Women's spirituality as collective power has also flourished across faiths and borders. In India, women leaders in Hindu, Muslim, and Sikh communities have used spiritual platforms to promote education and peace. In Africa, women spiritual leaders have blended indigenous and Christian traditions to support reconciliation in post-conflict societies.

Interfaith women's groups have emerged as powerful

voices for peacebuilding, environmental stewardship, and gender equality. Spirituality has proven to be a language that transcends political divides, allowing women to create coalitions across faith lines.

Spirituality and Contemporary Activism

In today's world, spirituality is woven into movements for climate justice, gender equality, and human rights. Many women activists speak of their work as a "calling," rooted in a sense of moral responsibility beyond politics. Rituals – chanting, drumming, silent vigils – remain central, providing collective energy and visibility.

Spiritual frameworks also inform women's approaches to leadership, emphasizing compassion, interconnectedness, and healing. These qualities challenge traditional models of power and propose new forms of collective governance.

Challenges and Critiques

Spiritual power, like any form of power, is not free of contradictions. Women leaders often face resistance from conservative institutions that view them as transgressors. Moreover, spirituality can be co-opted to reinforce traditional gender roles rather than liberate them. Recognizing these tensions is essential to understanding the complexity of spirituality as a collective force.

Spirit as Catalyst for Change

From prayer circles to parliaments, women have proven that spirituality can be both personal sanctuary and public catalyst. When women channel their spiritual lives into collective action, they create movements that transform societies.

Where Chapter 15 explored the inner ground of resilience, this chapter shows how those roots blossom outward – into communities, into institutions, into global change. Women's spirituality is not only about surviving the world as it is but about imagining and building the world as it should be.

Religion has long been a paradox in the story of women's progress. It has been a source of oppression – limiting women's autonomy, confining them to silence, and reinforcing patriarchal norms. Yet it has also been a source of resilience and renewal, providing the moral foundation, spiritual authority, and community networks through which women have mobilized for justice. Today, the story is not simply about exclusion or inclusion within individual faith traditions. It is about women reimagining the role of belief itself in the pursuit of equality – across interfaith coalitions, modern reform movements, and twenty-first-century feminist theologies.

For centuries, religion has been both a site of restriction and a wellspring of empowerment. While patriarchal institutions often barred women from leadership, many women reinterpreted sacred texts, reclaimed spiritual spaces, and used belief as a foundation for resistance. Today, interfaith coalitions and feminist theology are reshaping what spiritual authority looks like in the twenty-first century.

Sister Joan Chittister and Catholic Feminism

Benedictine nun Joan Chittister has long challenged the Catholic Church's exclusion of women from the priesthood and decision-making. Through her books, speeches, and activism, she reframed obedience not as silence but as prophetic resistance. For women across the Catholic world, Chittister became a voice of courage, insisting that faith could be both devout and disruptive.

Hindu Women Priests in India

In Maharashtra, India, women like Shradha Ghule have broken into priesthood roles traditionally reserved for men. By performing marriages, funerals, and religious ceremonies, they disrupted entrenched hierarchies and demonstrated that spiritual authority is not bound by gender. Their presence in sacred rituals reframed femininity not as impurity but as divine agency.

Interfaith Coalitions for Justice

Around the world, women of different faiths are working together to fight gender violence, poverty, and environmental destruction. The Women of Faith Network has brought together Christian, Muslim, Hindu, and Jewish leaders to advocate for peace in conflict zones, while Indigenous women at climate summits highlight how spirituality, land, and sustainability are intertwined. These coalitions show that belief can transcend doctrine and become a unifying force for justice.

Feminist Theology in the Twenty-First Century

From womanist theology in the U.S. – which centers the spiritual experiences of Black women – to liberation theology in Latin America, women are creating intellectual traditions that link faith to freedom. They argue that patriarchy is not divine but human-made and that reclaiming scripture is a necessary step in dismantling oppression.

Across traditions, women are not abandoning faith but redefining it. They lead prayers, write new theologies, and build interfaith alliances that connect spirituality with activism.

By reclaiming belief, women close the circle of this book's journey: art, politics, education, economics, environment, technology, and spirituality are not separate spheres but deeply connected struggles for dignity. Faith – once a justification for exclusion – has become, in their hands, a source of liberation.

Interfaith Coalitions: Shared Values, Shared Struggles

In today's interconnected world, women of faith increasingly work across traditions to advance common causes. Whether confronting gender-based violence, defending human rights, or tackling climate change, they argue that justice is a spiritual imperative transcending creed.

- In Nigeria, Christian and Muslim women mediate during sectarian clashes, showing that women's voices can bridge divides where politics has failed.

- At Jerusalem's Western Wall, Jewish women demanding equal prayer rights have been supported by Christian and Muslim allies, underscoring how sacred spaces can unite rather than divide.

- Global networks like Religions for Peace elevate women leaders, placing gender equality at the heart of interfaith dialogue.

These movements prove that when women redefine belief as a commitment to shared humanity, faith becomes a force of solidarity rather than separation.

Feminist Theology in the Twenty-First Century

If twentieth-century feminist theology sought recognition within patriarchal traditions, the twenty-first century has expanded the scope:

- Feminist theology insists that the divine cannot be confined to male imagery, reinterpreting scripture through the lens of equality.

- Womanist theology, rooted in Black women's experiences, centers survival, resilience, and liberation at the intersections of race, gender, and faith.

- Liberation theology, with its origins in Latin America, ties spiritual practice to struggles against poverty and inequality, inspiring women to link belief with economic justice.

Across Islam, Buddhism, Hinduism, and Indigenous

traditions, women are reclaiming authority: Muslim scholars challenge patriarchal readings of the Qur'an, Buddhist nuns in Thailand push for full ordination, and Indigenous women reassert spiritual stewardship of land and water. Collectively, these movements redefine religion not as static doctrine but as a living practice of justice.

Across traditions, women are reclaiming authority: Muslim scholars such as Asma Barlas and Amina Wadud challenge patriarchal readings of the Qur'an; bhikkhuni movements in Thailand and Sri Lanka press for full ordination; Hindu women priests in Maharashtra conduct weddings and funerals; and Indigenous leaders from the Waorani and Anishinaabe nations assert spiritual stewardship of land and water.

Reform Movements: From Sacred to Secular Policy

Women have also leveraged faith as a tool for public reform.

- In Morocco, murshidat – female religious guides – preach equality within Islam while influencing policy on education and family law. In Morocco, murshidat – state-trained female religious guides – have operated since 2006; through mosque-based literacy and counseling they preach equity and help socialize reforms such as the 2004 Moudawana family code and the 2018 violence-against-women law. Human Rights Watch+3The New Arab+3Morocco World News+3

- In the United States, faith-based women's coalitions have fought for protections against gender-based violence and workplace discrimination.

- In Latin America, Catholic and Protestant women may diverge on reproductive rights, but many unite in campaigns to end femicide and domestic abuse.

By anchoring reforms in spiritual language, women challenge not only secular institutions but the very moral frameworks that underpin them.

Synthesis: Belief as the Thread of Progress

Throughout this book, we have explored women's impact in every domain: art and representation, education and opportunity, politics and leadership, economics and entrepreneurship, technology and digital activism, environmental stewardship and global solidarity. What ties all these arenas together is belief – belief in equality, in dignity, in justice, and in the sacredness of human life. Across this book, we traced women's impact in culture, education, politics, economics, technology, the environment, and faith. The common thread is belief: in equality, dignity, justice, and the sacredness of life.

Faith traditions – whether religious, cultural, or secular – shape the values that guide societies. To transform belief is to transform possibility. Women of faith are not simply asking to be included in old systems; they are rewriting the moral compass of the twenty-first century.

Faith remains one of the most powerful forces in human life. For too long, it has been used to silence women. But today, women are using faith to speak louder than ever. They are reinterpreting sacred texts, reclaiming sacred spaces, and building interfaith coalitions that redefine what it means to live with justice.

Just as women artists reshaped culture, activists redefined politics, educators expanded access, entrepreneurs built wealth, and leaders reclaimed femininity as power, women of faith now illuminate the spiritual dimension of liberation. Together, these struggles form one truth: progress is never linear, but it is unstoppable when rooted in conviction.

The Tension: Religion as Restriction and Refuge

In many cultures, women have been taught to see faith and feminism as incompatible. This false dichotomy arises from:

- Male-dominated religious hierarchies
- Literalist interpretations of sacred texts
- Control over female sexuality, dress, and roles
- Social sanctions for questioning religious traditions

And yet, women across faiths have long been active in spiritual life – as mystics, healers, reformers, and moral leaders – even when denied formal authority. They have carved out power in private devotion, community leadership, and activist theology.

Feminist Theology and Religious Reform

Beginning in the 1960s and '70s, women scholars and spiritual leaders began re-examining religious texts and traditions through feminist lenses:

- Christian feminist theologians challenged male imagery of God and called for inclusive language in liturgy.
- Jewish feminists demanded access to Torah study and the rabbinate, redefining ritual practices for women.
- Muslim feminists emphasized gender equality inherent in the Qur'an, pushing back against patriarchal interpretations.
- Buddhist nuns and practitioners revived female monasticism and emphasized mindfulness as liberation from gendered suffering.

These thinkers not only critique religious patriarchy – they reimagine sacredness itself, expanding it to embrace the feminine and the marginalized.

Women Leading Within Their Faiths

Women have increasingly claimed leadership roles in religious communities worldwide:

- Pope Francis's advisory appointments of women to Vatican councils marked a shift, though women still cannot be ordained in Catholicism.

- Sally Priesand became the first woman ordained as a rabbi in the United States in 1972; today women serve widely across Reform, Reconstructionist, and Conservative movements, with Orthodox inclusion still contested.

- Amina Wadud, an African American Islamic scholar, led mixed-gender prayer services, challenging gender norms in Muslim spaces.

- Pema Chödrön, an American Buddhist nun, popularized Buddhist teachings of compassion and resilience among global audiences.

- Desmond Tutu's daughter, Mpho Tutu van Furth, a lesbian priest, was forced to renounce her Anglican license – highlighting tensions between doctrine and identity.

These leaders prove that one can be deeply faithful and fiercely feminist – and that change often comes from within.

Faith-Based Feminist Movements

In the Global South, women-led faith-based activism is transforming communities:

- In India, Hindu and Muslim women led Shaheen Bagh protests against discriminatory citizenship laws, invoking scripture and secular values alike.

- In Latin America, Catholic women formed Las Católicas por el Derecho a Decidir ("Catholics for the Right to Decide") – demanding reproductive justice.

- In Nigeria, interfaith women's groups mobilize against terrorism and sectarian violence through prayer, peacebuilding, and public dialogue.

- In Iran, underground religious feminist networks reinterpret the Qur'an to advocate for legal reform and women's rights.

These movements offer a model of spiritual resistance – challenging injustice not despite faith, but because of it.

Spirituality Beyond Religion

For many women, the search for meaning goes beyond organized religion. Feminist spirituality has emerged in forms such as:

- Goddess worship and Earth-based traditions that honor feminine divine imagery.

- Contemplative practices, including meditation, yoga, and ancestral rituals.

- Decolonial spiritual reclamation, reviving Indigenous knowledge systems erased by colonial religion.

- Wellness and mindfulness movements, often led by women of color seeking healing from intergenerational trauma.

These practices prioritize wholeness over hierarchy, intuition over dogma, and liberation over obedience – redefining sacredness as inclusive, embodied, and relational.

The Politics of Belief

Faith is never neutral – it shapes laws, policies, and

social norms. Women's voices in religious spaces affect:

- Debates over abortion, LGBTQ+ rights, and family law.
- Access to education and leadership in faith institutions.
- Human rights work in conflict zones and humanitarian settings.
- Global interfaith dialogue and peacebuilding.

When women interpret faith for justice, they challenge both political and spiritual gatekeepers – and bring moral authority to movements for change.

A Faith Worth Fighting For

Faith and feminism are not enemies. They are, for many women, interwoven pathways to dignity, courage, and compassion.

In every faith tradition, there are stories of resistance – of women who, like prophets and poets, refused to remain silent. Their belief was not blind – it was bold. Not passive – it was prophetic.

Their legacy invites us to ask: What would our spiritual traditions look like if they were shaped by all of us – so what now?

Female Religious Reformers, Spiritual Thinkers, and Faith-Based Movements

Spiritual traditions have long shaped women's lives – sometimes as instruments of restriction, and other times as foundations for liberation. This chapter explores women who embraced their faith not as contradiction, but as inspiration for feminist thought, activism, and cultural change. These leaders show how belief, when paired with courage, can move mountains.

Sister Joan Chittister, a Benedictine nun and theologian, challenges patriarchal structures within the Catholic Church. With powerful writing and public speaking, she calls for gender equality, social justice, and a return to the inclusive roots of Christian compassion.

Rev. Dr. Pauli Murray, the first Black woman ordained as an Episcopal priest and a civil rights pioneer, fused theology, law, and activism. She helped shape the legal framework for gender equality and viewed her priesthood as part of her mission for justice.

Leymah Gbowee, a Liberian peace activist, mobilized Christian and Muslim women to end civil war in her country through nonviolent protest and prayer. Awarded the Nobel Peace Prize, she continues to show how interfaith solidarity can be a force for peace and gender equity.

Asma Lamrabet, a Moroccan doctor and Islamic feminist, writes extensively about gender and the Qur'an. Her research reframes Islamic texts to highlight women's agency, dignity, and equality, offering a counter-narrative to patriarchal interpretations.

Sarah Bessey, a Christian writer and co-founder of the Evolving Faith conference, reimagines evangelical Christianity through a feminist and inclusive lens. Her work speaks to women seeking to hold onto faith while rejecting harmful doctrines.

Bhakti Sharma, an open-water swimmer from India and devout Hindu, blends physical endurance with spiritual devotion. She credits her beliefs with the strength and focus to achieve historic swims, including across the Antarctic Ocean.

Rabbanit Dr. Avital Hochstein, a Jewish scholar and educator, works to expand women's participation in Torah study and Halakha (Jewish law). She challenges traditional gender boundaries in Orthodox Judaism through inclusive interpretation and education. She co-founded Jerusalem's Kehillat Shira Hadasha, a partnership minyan that expanded women's public ritual roles within Orthodox practice.

Rigoberta Menchú Tum, a K'iche' Maya woman from Guatemala and Nobel laureate, blends Indigenous spirituality with activism. Her work elevates Indigenous women's voices in human rights, linking cultural heritage with resistance. In 1999, she helped file a universal-jurisdiction case in Spain that led to 2006 arrest warrants for former Guatemalan officials on genocide charges.

These women remind us that faith and feminism are not mutually exclusive.

They use belief as a bridge – between tradition and transformation, between the sacred and the just.

Their lives offer proof that conviction – whether religious or spiritual – can be a mighty tool for dismantling injustice and elevating women's place in the world.

For a more complete list of notable female religious leaders and reformers, see Appendix IV.

The Continuing Legacy

These women and movements remind us that faith is not fixed – it is alive, contested, and evolving. They reclaim sacred authority, affirm spiritual agency, and open doors for generations to encounter the divine on their terms.

They teach us that belief can be both reverent and revolutionary – a tool for survival, solidarity, and systemic change.

Beyond Barriers, Toward Possibility

From art studios to courtrooms, sports fields to refugee camps, classrooms to parliaments, and pulpits to protest lines – women have moved beyond barriers. Not in a straight line, and not without resistance. But always with determination, courage, and vision.

This book has traced the arc of women's progress from the mid-twentieth century to the present day, capturing the complexity and richness of their journeys. Across regions, cultures, and generations, women have challenged what was, reimagined what could be, and demanded a more just, inclusive world.

Themes That Emerged Across Chapters

- Resistance and resilience: Whether facing war, poverty, systemic racism, or personal loss, women have refused to be silenced or sidelined.

- Leadership in unlikely places: Women have often led not from positions of official power, but from the margins – organizing, healing, creating, and mobilizing in grassroots and global spaces alike.

Intersectionality: True progress is not achieved by advancing the most privileged women alone, but by centering the experiences of Black, Indigenous, disabled, LGBTQ+, migrant, and working-class women.

- Solidarity over sameness: Women's movements have succeeded not by erasing difference, but by embracing it – building alliances across identities and ideologies.

- Imagination as activism: Artists, educators, athletes, spiritual leaders, and digital feminists remind us that creating something new is itself a radical act.

From Inspiration to Action

This story isn't finished – it's a living movement. Barriers remain: political backlash, rising authoritarianism and fundamentalism, digital harassment and disinformation, economic inequality, reproductive injustice, and climate breakdown. The legacy in these pages offers a blueprint: ordinary people doing extraordinary things with courage, community, and clarity.

Name the barrier. Find your lane. Move with others.

- Speak truth to power.
- Mentor and uplift others.
- Create new systems, not just critique old ones.

- Use your platforms, privileges, and passions to open doors.

You are part of this story. Your choices ripple outward. This book honors real, unfinished struggle – and invites continued work together.

Barrier by barrier. Voice by voice. Generation by generation. Let's keep going.

Voices of Defiance

For many women, faith has never been a contradiction to feminism – it has been the root of it. In sacred texts, in community rituals, and in inner convictions, women have found the strength to challenge injustice, call out exclusion, and lead with moral clarity. Their defiance is not in denying the divine but in expanding how it is understood – fighting for a spirituality that uplifts rather than oppresses, includes rather than erases. These women speak with the authority of belief – and use it to transform the world.

> *"If the man may preach, because the Savior died for him, why not the woman?"*
>
> — Jarena Lee (United States)

As the first authorized female preacher in the African Methodist Episcopal Church, she broke barriers with unapologetic spiritual force.

> *"The secret of our strength as a people is that we never, ever gave up. Our spiritual traditions kept us whole."*
>
> — Wilma Mankiller (United States, Cherokee Nation)

Her Indigenous leadership wove together tribal identity, feminine power, and sacred land stewardship.

> *"Empowered women of faith are not the exception. They are the future."*
>
> — Dr. Nelly van Doorn-Harder (Netherlands/Indonesia)

As a Christian scholar working with Muslim feminists,

she bridges belief systems to advocate for mutual respect and religious reform.

In conclusion, in reimagining faith, women are not only transforming religion – they are shaping the moral compass of the world beyond barriers.

Belief as Foundation and Frontier

Throughout this book, we have traced women's progress from the margins to the center of modern history – through art and culture, where women reshaped representation; through activism and politics, where they forced open doors of power; through education and economics, where they redefined access and prosperity; through environmental stewardship and technology, where they fought for sustainability and innovation; and through the intimate battles of body, identity, and representation, where they reclaimed dignity on their terms.

At each turn, belief – whether religious, cultural, or personal – has been the ground on which these struggles unfolded. Belief systems have often been used to justify exclusion: that women should be silent in classrooms, subordinate in households, invisible in boardrooms, or absent from pulpits. Yet, at the same time, belief has provided women with language, courage, and community – the tools to demand justice, reimagine possibility, and sustain resistance across generations.

When women reinterpreted scripture, they also reinterpreted society. When they challenged cultural myths, they dismantled hierarchies. When they built new spiritual movements, they linked faith with freedom, showing that liberation is as much about inner transformation as it is about outer change.

The stories in these chapters remind us that the struggle for equality is not confined to one sector – it is a web of interconnections: the artist painting truth, the activist marching for justice, the student demanding access, the politician passing reform, the entrepreneur funding change, the climate defender protecting the Earth, the technologist designing futures, and the spiritual leader reframing belief.

Together, they demonstrate a profound truth: women's progress is not simply about entering existing systems but about transforming the values on which those systems are built.

And so, as this book closes, the question remains: What kind of future will we believe in? Will we cling to beliefs that divide and diminish, or will we embrace those that empower and unite?

The legacy of the women in these pages suggests the answer. Their lives testify that belief – rooted in justice, dignity, and equality – is not just a private conviction but a public force. It underpins art, activism, education, politics, economics, environmental action, technology, and spirituality. It is the thread that weaves struggle into progress and progress into hope.

To believe in women is to believe in the possibility of a world remade.

Final Call to Action

The stories in this book are not meant to be admired from a distance – they are meant to be a spark.

You don't have to be famous or fearless to make a difference. You only need to start.

Here's how you can act:

- Learn more about women's history where you live – who are the pioneers in your own community?

- Support women-led organizations and movements – especially those working at the grassroots level.

- Mentor someone younger. Share your story, listen to theirs.

- Speak up when others can't. Use your voice and your platform, no matter how small.

- Vote for leaders who advocate gender equity. Run for office if you're called to.

- Challenge norms in your workplace, school, or faith community. Don't wait for permission.

- Honor intersectionality – recognize that gender justice must include racial, economic, LGBTQ+, and disability justice.

- Create something – write, paint, teach, build, organize. Culture is changed by creators.

The world we want isn't far off – it's being made every day in choices like these.

You are part of this movement. Keep going.

Reflection Prompts

1. Spirituality in Action
   - Have you ever witnessed or participated in a moment where spirituality fueled collective action (e.g., a vigil, a march, a prayer gathering)?
   - How did it shape your understanding of community power?

2. Building Bridges
   - How can spirituality create common ground across different cultures, traditions, or beliefs?
   - Where might interfaith or intercultural cooperation strengthen your community today?

3. Challenges and Contradictions
   - In what ways can spirituality both empower and restrict women's roles in society?
   - How do you reconcile those tensions in your own experience or observations?

4. Your Call to Action

- If you could channel your spiritual values into a cause or movement, what would it be?

- What first step could you take to bring that vision into reality?

BONUS NOTE:
FEMINISM, GENDER,
AND EMERGING DEBATES

One of the most pressing and polarizing debates shaping the Fourth Wave of Feminism is the question of how feminism engages with transgender and non-binary identities. Public discourse often frames this tension as a sharp divide. On one side, some feminists – prominently J.K. Rowling and others – argue that including trans women in women's spaces risks undermining hard-won rights and protections. On the other side, many activists see trans inclusion as inseparable from the pursuit of gender justice, framing exclusion itself as a form of discrimination.

The reality, however, is far more nuanced. Many feminists and allies are actively wrestling with how to balance legitimate concerns about safety, fairness, and identity with the principles of inclusion, dignity, and equality. These discussions take place in classrooms, courtrooms, legislatures, and online platforms, often with passion but also with deep complexity. These debates play out in high school athletic associations (eligibility rules), Title IX rulemaking (teams, facilities), courts and legislatures (anti-discrimination and privacy laws), prisons and shelters (placement and safety protocols), health care boards and insurers (what care is covered), and ID/passport offices (legal recognition). The stakes are immediate: who can play, where people are housed, what care is accessible, which documents are valid, how privacy and safety are protected, and whether dignity and equal participation are real.

This book does not attempt to resolve these debates. Instead, it acknowledges their importance as a defining feature of contemporary feminism. How this conversation evolves will inevitably shape the trajectory of the Fourth Wave, and perhaps a Fifth. The task for all who care about gender justice is to approach these issues with humility, openness, and a willingness to engage perspectives that may challenge their own. This book doesn't resolve these debates; it treats them as central to contemporary feminism and to the shape of the Fourth Wave – and whatever comes next – offering a practical lens for engaging them with care.

Useful questions include:

- What harm are we preventing, and for whom?
- Whose risk is being weighed, and on what evidence?
- Which solutions protect dignity and safety for all users of a space?
- What data gaps remain, and who is missing from the table?

Epilogue: Carrying the Torch

The journey of this book has moved across decades, continents, and disciplines, but its core message is simple: when women rise, societies rise with them. From the canvas to the courtroom, from classrooms to boardrooms, from climate summits to sacred spaces, women have reshaped what is possible – not only for themselves but for everyone. Across decades, continents, and disciplines, the message is simple: when women rise, societies rise. From art and law to education and enterprise – and from climate governance to spiritual life – women have widened what is possible for all.

Their victories did not come easily. Each step forward was met with resistance, backlash, and doubt. Yet in art, they painted new visions; in activism, they marched toward justice; in education, they demanded access; in politics, they claimed the right to lead; in economics, they built prosperity; in environmental movements, they defended the Earth; in technology, they shaped digital futures; and in faith, they reclaimed the power of belief.

These stories remind us that women's progress is not a single narrative but a global chorus – multi-voiced, diverse, and interconnected. They show us that liberation is never only about the individual; it is about communities, systems, and the reimagining of values that shape us all.

But the work is not finished. Inequalities persist in wages, representation, safety, and dignity. Crises – whether environmental, political, or technological – continue to test our shared humanity. The question that remains is not whether women can lead us forward, but whether societies will allow themselves to be transformed by their leadership.

The women of the past century have taught us that progress is not inevitable – it is made. It is painted in bold colors, marched into the streets, written into law, woven into cooperative economies, coded into algorithms, and prayed into being. Now the torch passes to us. To believe in women is to invest in a future where dignity, equality, and justice become daily practice. The story is still being written. Write your line.

APPENDIX I:
PIONEERS AND TRAILBLAZERS
(CHAPTERS 1 TO 4)

This appendix provides detailed catalogs of early women artists, activists, and reformers whose work laid the foundations for later breakthroughs. While the chapters highlight their stories in narrative form, the tables here offer a consolidated reference of names, contributions, and defining moments from the early to mid-twentieth century.

Chapter 1: Pioneers of Modernism – Women Artists Who Resisted and Reimagined

Artist Name	Country	Medium	Key Themes	Suggested Visual Work
Hannah Höch	Germany	Photomontage	Gender roles, Dadaism	*Cut with the Kitchen Knife Dada through the Last Weimar Beer-Belly Cultural Epoch of Germany*
Maria Lassnig	Austria	Painting	Body awareness, internal perception	*You or Me*
Sonia Delaunay	France (born Ukraine)	Painting, Textile Design	Orphism, abstraction, color theory	*Prismes électriques*
Anni Albers	Germany/ USA	Textile Art	Bauhaus, abstraction, pattern	*Wall Hanging (1926)*
Frida Kahlo	Mexico	Painting	Identity, pain, female experience	*The Two Fridas*
Sophie Taeuber-	Switzer-land	Painting, Textile,	Dada, abstraction,	*Vertical-Horizontal Composition*

Arp		Architecture	geometric form	
Toyen (Marie Čermínová)	Czech Republic	Painting	Surrealism, gender fluidity, eroticism	*The Myth of Light*
Gabriele Münter	Germany	Expressionist Painting	Landscape, emotion, color	*Portrait of Marianne von Werefkin*
Lyubov Popova	Russia	Constructivism, Collage	Movement, revolution, geometry	*Painterly Architectonic*

Chapter 2: Voices of Change – Notable Female Activists of the Post-War Era (1945 to 1979)

Name	Country	Role	Focus Areas	Notable Contribution
Simone de Beauvoir	France	Philosopher, Author	Existential feminism, gender theory	Author of *The Second Sex* (1949), a foundational feminist text
Betty Friedan	USA	Writer, Organizer	Feminism, education, women's rights	Author of *The Feminine Mystique* (1963); Co-founder of NOW
Rosa Parks	USA	Civil Rights Activist	Racial justice, transportation equality	Sparked Montgomery Bus Boycott in 1955
Dolores Huerta	USA	Labor Leader	Farmworkers' rights, Chicana activism	Co-founder of the United Farm Workers union
Aileen Hernandez	USA	Labor Organizer, Commissioner	Employment equity, intersectionality	First African American president of NOW
Angela Davis	USA	Scholar, Activist	Prison abolition, racial	Influential in civil rights

			and gender justice	and feminist thought; author of *Women, Race and Class*
Rigoberta Menchú	Guatemala	Indigenous Rights Advocate	Anti-colonial resistance, education	Nobel Peace Prize recipient for activism in Indigenous and women's rights
Malangatana Ngwenya (honorary mention for intersectional movements)	Mozambique	Artist, Political Figure	Anti-colonial activism	Used art to express resistance under colonial rule; supported women's participation in liberation
Wangari Maathai	Kenya	Environmentalist, Political Leader	Women's empowerment, sustainability	Founded the Green Belt Movement; later Nobel Peace Prize winner
Ulrike Meinhof	Germany	Journalist, Radical Activist	Anti-imperialism, state violence critique	Controversial figure in post-war Germany's protest movements

Chapter 3: Educating for Equality – Female Pioneers in Access and Reform (Post-WWII Era)

Name	Country/ Region	Role	Focus Areas	Notable Contribution
Shirley Chisholm	USA	Educator, Politician	Equal access, early childhood	First Black woman elected to U.S. Congress;

			education	championed public education reform and Title IX
Malala Yousafzai	Pakistan	Student, Activist	Girls' education, human rights	Survived Taliban attack; Nobel Peace Prize winner advocating for girls' education globally
Wangari Maathai	Kenya	Environmentalist, Educator	Literacy, sustainability, women's empowerment	Founded Green Belt Movement, integrating education with environmental activism
Sylvia Méndez	USA (Mexican–Puerto Rican descent)	Civil Rights Pioneer	School desegregation	Center of *Méndez v. Westminster*, a landmark 1947 court case that ended segregation in California schools
Kamla Bhasin	India	Feminist Educator, Author	Gender equity, rural education	Developed accessible feminist education tools for marginalized women in South Asia
Ellen Johnson Sirleaf	Liberia	Educator, Economist, President	Post-conflict education, gender parity	First female head of state in Africa; prioritized girls' education and rebuilding schools
Frances Oldham Kelsey	Canada/ USA	Pharmacologist, University Professor	Ethics in medical education	Prevented the approval of thalidomide in the U.S.; advocated for higher scientific standards in education
Dora Akunyili	Nigeria	Pharmacist, Educator	Public health, female academic leadership	Former Director General of NAFDAC; advanced education for women in medicine and

Name	Country	Role	Focus Areas	Notable Contribution
				science
Fatima Jinnah	Pakistan	Dentist, Educator, Political Leader	Women's literacy, education for Muslim girls	Advocated for girls' education in the early years of Pakistan's independence
Ellen Swallow Richards *(Honorary legacy figure)*	USA	Chemist, Educator	Women's access to science education	First woman admitted to MIT; pioneered domestic science as a formal discipline in education reform

Chapter 4: Trailblazers on the Field – Women Who Changed Sports and Equity Through Title IX

Name	Country	Role	Focus Areas	Notable Contribution
Bernice Sandler	USA	Educator, Advocate	Title IX policy and enforcement	Known as the "Godmother of Title IX"; worked to expose systemic discrimination in academia
Donna de Varona	USA	Olympic Swimmer, Activist	Gender equity in athletics, media rights	Co-founded the Women's Sports Foundation; major advocate for Title IX in sports broadcasting
Billie Jean King	USA	Tennis Champion, Activist	Pay equity, gender equality	Beat Bobby Riggs in 1973's "Battle of the Sexes"; founded Women's Tennis Association
Mia Hamm	USA	Soccer	Youth	Helped lead

		Player	sports, women's visibility	U.S. to multiple World Cups and Olympic medals; inspired girls' soccer boom
Wilma Rudolph	USA	Track and Field Olympian	Overcoming barriers, racial and gender equity	First American woman to win three gold medals in a single Olympics (1960)
Pat Summitt	USA	Basketball Coach	Women's college basketball, mentorship	Legendary University of Tennessee coach with eight national titles; mentor to many athletes and coaches
Simone Biles	USA	Gymnast	Athlete advocacy, mental health	Widely considered the greatest gymnast of all time; spoke out about athlete safety and well-being
Cheryl Miller	USA	Basketball Star, Broadcaster	Women's sports excellence, representation	One of the most dominant players in college basketball; pivotal in popularizing women's hoops
Nancy Hogshead-Makar	USA	Olympic Swimmer, Lawyer	Legal defense of Title IX	Founder of Champion Women; legal advocate for equity in college athletics

| Julie Foudy | USA | Soccer Player, Activist | Equal pay, athlete leadership | Former U.S. team captain; helped push for stronger protections under Title IX |

APPENDIX II:
POLITICAL AND SOCIAL LEADERS
(CHAPTERS 5 TO 10)

Appendix II gathers key tables charting women's rise in politics, government, and social leadership from the mid-twentieth century onward. It includes early parliamentary breakthroughs, executive appointments, and the expansion of feminist movements across the globe. These lists complement the narratives of Chapters 5 to 10 by offering a broader overview of milestones and leaders

Chapter 5: Opening Doors: Early Political Breakthroughs

Women in Political Leadership – Pioneers and Changemakers (1980s to 2000s)

Name	Country	Role	Focus Areas	Notable Contribution
Margaret Thatcher	United Kingdom	Prime Minister (1979 to 1990)	Conservative policy, Cold War diplomacy	First female Prime Minister of the UK; known as the "Iron Lady"
Benazir Bhutto	Pakistan	Prime Minister (1988 to 1990, 1993 to 1996)	Education, women's rights, democracy	First woman to lead a Muslim-majority nation
Corazon Aquino	Philippines	President (1986 to 1992)	Democratic reform, anti-corruption	Led the People Power Revolution; restored democracy post-dictatorship
Gro Harlem	Norway	Prime Minister (1981, 1986 to	Health policy, sustainable	Chaired the World Commission on

Brund-tland		1989, 1990 to 1996)	development	Environment and Development (Brundtland Report)
Geraldine Ferraro	United States	U.S. Congresswoman, VP Candidate (1984)	Women's rights, economic equity	First woman nominated for U.S. Vice President by a major party
Carol Moseley Braun	United States	U.S. Senator (1993 to 1999)	Civil rights, education, environmental justice	First Black woman elected to the U.S. Senate
Ellen Johnson Sirleaf	Liberia	President (2006 to 2018)	Post-war recovery, gender equity	First female elected head of state in Africa; Nobel Peace Prize co-laureate
Angela Merkel	Germany	Chancellor (2005 to 2021)	Economic stability, EU diplomacy	Known for pragmatic leadership; first woman to lead Germany
Michelle Bachelet	Chile	President (2006 to 2010, 2014 to 2018)	Social protection, gender equality	First female president of Chile; later served as UN High Commissioner for Human Rights
Vigdís Finnbogadóttir	Iceland	President (1980 to 1996)	Cultural preservation, education	First democratically elected female head of state in the world

Chapter 6: Economic Changemakers – Women Who Redefined Work and Leadership (1980s to 2000s)

Name	Country	Role	Focus Areas	Notable Contribution
Indra Nooyi	India/ USA	CEO of PepsiCo	Corporate leadership, global strategy	One of the first women of color to lead a Fortune 50 company;

Name	Country	Role	Focus	Contribution
				prioritized sustainable growth
Oprah Winfrey	USA	Entrepreneur, Media Mogul	Entertainment, self-made wealth	First Black woman billionaire; built a multimedia empire and uplifted women entrepreneurs
Sheryl Sandberg	USA	COO of Facebook, Author	Women in tech, workplace equity	Authored *Lean In*; helped normalize women's leadership in Silicon Valley
Anne Mulcahy	USA	CEO of Xerox	Corporate turnaround, women in tech	Revived Xerox during financial crisis; advocated for diversity in executive roles
Carmen Velasco	Bolivia	Microfinance Leader	Financial inclusion, women's credit access	Co-founded Pro Mujer, providing microloans and healthcare to underserved Latin American women
Ellen Johnson Sirleaf	Liberia	Economist, President	Women's economic empowerment	Promoted infrastructure and education for women as part of post-war recovery strategy
Cher Wang	Taiwan	Tech Entrepreneur	Innovation, women in technology	Co-founded HTC; one of the first women to lead a major tech hardware company
Sara Blakely	USA	Entrepreneur, Inventor	Female-led startups, product innovation	Founded Spanx with $5,000; became youngest self-made female billionaire
Ngozi Okonjo-Iweala	Nigeria	Economist, WTO Director-General	Global finance, debt relief	First African woman to lead the World Trade Organization; led

Name	Country	Role	Focus Areas	Notable Contribution
				anti-poverty financial reforms at the World Bank
Gita Gopinath	India	Economist, IMF Leader	International trade, macroeconomics	First female Chief Economist of the International Monetary Fund (IMF)

Chapter 7: Women Who Transformed Media and Representation (1980s to 2000s)

Name	Country	Role	Focus Areas	Notable Contribution
Oprah Winfrey	USA	TV Host, Producer, CEO	Storytelling, media ownership, empowerment	Built a media empire centered on authenticity and emotional depth; first Black female billionaire in media
Barbara Walters	USA	Broadcast Journalist	Network news, political reporting	First female co-anchor of a U.S. network evening news broadcast; co-creator of *The View*
Nora Ephron	USA	Screenwriter, Director	Romantic comedy, female voice in film	Wrote and directed classics like *Sleepless in Seattle* and *Julie & Julia*, blending wit with emotional insight
Madonna	USA	Musician, Cultural Icon	Sexuality, female agency in pop culture	Redefined the role of women in entertainment through performance, control of image, and reinvention
Christiane Amanpour	UK/Iran	Foreign Correspondent	War reporting, global affairs	Prominent CNN journalist known for fearless coverage in conflict zones, with a focus on women's issues

Shonda Rhimes	USA	TV Producer, Writer	Diversity, strong female leads	Created hit series like *Grey's Anatomy*, *Scandal*, and *How to Get Away with Murder* — breaking new ground for representation
Tracee Ellis Ross	USA	Actress, Producer, Activist	Race, body positivity, hair politics	Starred in *Girlfriends* and *Black-ish*; co-founded Pattern Beauty to celebrate natural hair
Ava DuVernay	USA	Director, Producer	Social justice, women of color in film	First Black woman to direct a film nominated for Best Picture at the Oscars (*Selma*)
Jane Campion	New Zealand	Film Director	Feminine perspective, emotional realism	Directed *The Piano*; first woman to win the Palme d'Or at Cannes
Roxane Gay	USA	Author, Critic	Feminism, media critique, intersectionality	Authored *Bad Feminist*; influential voice on the intersection of pop culture and gender politics

Chapter 8: Pioneers of Intersectional Feminism and Inclusive Activism (1960s to 2000s)

Name	Country	Role	Focus Areas	Notable Contribution
Kimberlé Crenshaw	USA	Legal Scholar, Professor	Intersectionality, critical race theory	Coined the term *intersectionality*; co-founder of the African American Policy Forum
Bell Hooks	USA	Author, Feminist Theorist	Race, gender, class, education	Wrote *Ain't I a Woman?*, *Feminism is for Everybody*; redefined feminist thought through

Name	Country	Role	Focus	Contribution
				love and justice
Audre Lorde	USA	Poet, Essayist, Activist	Black feminism, queer theory	Authored *Sister Outsider*, emphasized difference as a source of strength
Gloria Anzaldúa	USA	Chicana Writer, Scholar	Border identity, language, queer feminism	Wrote *Borderlands/La Frontera*, explored hybridity and intersectional identity
Angela Davis	USA	Scholar, Activist	Prison abolition, race, gender	Leading voice on structural oppression; linked feminism to broader systems of power
Cherríe Moraga	USA	Playwright, Essayist	Queer Chicana feminism, bilingual identity	Co-edited *This Bridge Called My Back*, a foundational text of intersectional feminist thought
Patricia Hill Collins	USA	Sociologist, Author	Black feminist thought, knowledge production	Wrote *Black Feminist Thought*, expanded the concept of the matrix of domination
Laverne Cox	USA	Actress, Activist	Trans rights, media representation	First openly transgender person nominated for a Primetime Emmy; global advocate for inclusive feminism
Maya Angelou	USA	Author, Poet	Intersection of race, trauma, resilience	Authored *I Know Why the Caged Bird Sings*, explored survival and voice through literature
Gloria Steinem	USA	Journalist, Organizer	Feminist organizing, allyship	Co-founder of *Ms.* magazine; later embraced intersectional advocacy with women of

color and Indigenous women

Chapter 9: Women Who Changed the Tech World (1940s to Today)

Name	Country	Role	Focus Areas	Notable Contribution
Ada Lovelace	UK	Mathematician, Early Programmer	Algorithm design, theoretical computing	Wrote the first algorithm intended for a machine — recognized as the world's first computer programmer
Grace Hopper	USA	Computer Scientist, Rear Admiral	Programming languages, software development	Invented the first compiler; contributed to COBOL, a foundational programming language
Radia Perlman	USA	Network Engineer	Computer networking, internet infrastructure	Invented the spanning tree protocol, which made Ethernet scalable
Shirley Ann Jackson	USA	Physicist, Researcher	Telecommunications, science leadership	Breakthroughs in theoretical physics and telecommunications; led major public policy reforms in STEM
Anita Borg	USA	Computer Scientist, Advocate	Tech workforce diversity, women's leadership	Founded the Grace Hopper Celebration of Women in Computing and the AnitaB.org Institute
Reshma Saujani	USA	Lawyer, Founder of Girls Who Code	Coding education, tech pipeline equity	Empowered hundreds of thousands of girls to enter tech through Girls

				Who Code
Whitney Wolfe Herd	USA	Tech Entrepreneur	Feminist app development, user empowerment	Founder and CEO of Bumble; youngest woman to take a company public in the U.S.
Dr. Fei-Fei Li	USA/China	AI Researcher, Professor	Computer vision, ethical AI	Led ImageNet project; advocate for human-centered and inclusive artificial intelligence
Tracy Chou	USA	Software Engineer, Inclusion Advocate	Diversity in tech, workplace equity	Launched Project Include; vocal leader in Silicon Valley's push for transparency and change
Funke Opeke	Nigeria	Engineer, Telecom Executive	Broadband infrastructure, connectivity access	Founded MainOne, improving internet access across West Africa

Chapter 10: Global Feminist Leaders and Movements (1990s to Today)

Name / Movement	Region	Role	Focus Areas	Notable Contribution
Wangari Maathai	Kenya	Environmentalist, Nobel Laureate	Ecofeminism, reforestation	Founded the Green Belt Movement; mobilized women to plant more than 51 million trees
Tarana Burke	USA	Activist	Sexual violence, survivor advocacy	Founded the original *Me Too* movement in 2006 to support survivors of sexual abuse
Oby	Nigeria	Political	Girls'	Co-founded *Bring*

Ezekwesili		Leader, Activist	education, anti-corruption	*Back Our Girls* campaign to raise awareness about abducted Nigerian schoolgirls
Nemonte Nenquimo	Ecuador	Indigenous Leader	Land rights, climate justice	Led legal victory protecting 500,000 acres of Amazon rainforest from oil drilling
Gloria Steinem	USA	Writer, Organizer	Transnational feminism	Bridged Western feminism with global movements; advocated for intersectional, international feminism
Alicia Garza, Patrisse Cullors, Opal Tometi	USA	Organizers	Racial justice, Black liberation	Co-founded *Black Lives Matter*, a global network demanding justice and systemic reform
#NiUnaMenos	Latin America	Grassroots Movement	Anti-femicide, gender-based violence	Originated in Argentina; now spans dozens of countries in Latin America and beyond
#MahsaAmini Movement	Iran/Global	Feminist Protest Wave	Bodily autonomy, anti-theocracy	Sparked by the death of Mahsa Amini, this movement catalyzed a feminist uprising under authoritarian repression
Girls Not Brides	Global	Coalition Network	Ending child marriage	Works in over 100 countries to prevent child marriage and protect girls' rights and futures
MADRE	Global (HQ in USA)	International	Feminist aid,	Provides direct support and funding to women-led

MARIA L. ELLIS

Organi-zation	peace-building	grassroots groups in crisis and conflict zones

312

APPENDIX III: CULTURAL AND ECONOMIC INNOVATORS (CHAPTERS 11 TO 14)

Here you will find tables documenting women's influence in cultural industries, economic innovation, and cooperative models of work. From corporate pioneers to grassroots entrepreneurs, these catalogs trace the diverse ways women shaped markets, communities, and creative spaces. Together, they highlight the breadth of women's impact beyond traditional political narratives.

Chapter 11: Global Leaders and Advocates in Reproductive Health and Rights

Name / Organization	Region	Role	Focus Areas	Notable Contribution
Dr. Nafis Sadik	Pakistan / UN	Physician, UNFPA Director	Family planning, population policy	First woman to lead a major UN program; key figure in the 1994 Cairo conference on reproductive rights
Loretta Ross	USA	Activist, Scholar	Reproductive justice, human rights	Co-founder of SisterSong; helped shape the reproductive justice framework
SisterSong Women of Color Reproductive Justice Collective	USA	Grassroots Coalition	Reproductive justice, intersectional health	Led the national conversation linking reproductive rights with racial, economic, and gender justice
Dr. Denis Mukwege	DRC	Gynecologist,	Sexual violence in	Nobel Peace Prize laureate for his

		Humanitarian	conflict, maternal health	work treating survivors of sexual violence in the Democratic Republic of Congo
Catriona Cairns and Marge Berer	Global	Advocates, Publishers	Safe abortion, global policy reform	Founders of *Reproductive Health Matters*, a journal central to global policy shifts on abortion and reproductive rights
Women on Web / Women on Waves	International	Telemedicine and Activist Network	Safe abortion access, digital health	Pioneered safe abortion access via ships and online platforms in countries with restrictive laws
Obstetric Fistula Foundation	Sub-Saharan Africa	Nonprofit	Maternal health, surgical care	Provides life-saving surgery and support to women with fistula, a preventable childbirth injury caused by inadequate care
Marie Stopes International (now MSI Reproductive Choices)	Global	NGO	Contraception, safe abortion, women's health	Offers reproductive health services in over thirty-seven countries, focusing on underserved populations
The Afiya Center	USA (Texas)	Black Women–Led Organization	HIV, reproductive justice, health access	Addresses the needs of Black women in Texas through education, policy advocacy, and direct services
Center for Reproductive Rights	Global (HQ in USA)	Legal Advocacy Group	Reproductive law, litigation	Uses courts and human rights law to advance reproductive freedom globally, including landmark wins at

| | | | | the UN and regional courts |

Chapter 12: Emerging Leaders: Voices Shaping the Future

Name	Country	Role	Focus Areas	Notable Contribution
Amanda Gorman	USA	Poet, Activist	Art as advocacy, racial justice	Youngest inaugural poet in U.S. history; uses poetry to advance civic engagement and equity
Vanessa Nakate	Uganda	Climate Justice Leader	Environmental justice, youth advocacy	Founder of the Rise Up Movement; amplifies African voices in climate conversations
Aya Chebbi	Tunisia	Diplomat, Youth Envoy	African feminist leadership, diplomacy	First African Union Youth Envoy; advocate for Pan-Africanism and intergenerational dialogue
Gita Gopinath	India	Economist, Policy Leader	Gender and global economics	First woman Chief Economist at the International Monetary Fund (IMF)
Alice Wong	USA	Disability Rights Activist	Intersectional feminism, accessibility	Founder of Disability Visibility Project; amplifies disabled voices through media and storytelling
Zahra Langhi	Libya	Peace Builder, Scholar	Gender and peacebuilding, Islamic feminism	Co-founder of the Libyan Women's Platform for Peace; works to integrate women in post-conflict rebuilding
Nadya Okamoto	USA	Entrepreneur, Advocate	Menstrual equity, youth organizing	Founded PERIOD, a global nonprofit fighting period poverty and stigma
Sayaka	Japan	Novelist,	Gender	Award-winning author

Murata		Cultural Critic	norms, nonconformity	challenging societal expectations of women in modern Japan

Chapter 13: Women Peacebuilders and Grassroots Organizers in Conflict Zones

Name / Group	Country / Region	Role	Focus Areas	Notable Contribution
Leymah Gbowee	Liberia	Peace Activist, Nobel Laureate	Interfaith organizing, nonviolent protest	Led Women of Liberia Mass Action for Peace, pressuring warlords into negotiations and ending civil war
Ellen Johnson Sirleaf	Liberia	Politician, President	Post-war reconstruction, women's leadership	First elected female head of state in Africa; promoted gender equity and national healing
Panzi Hospital and Dr. Denis Mukwege	DRC	Medical Humanitarian Team	Sexual violence treatment, trauma care	Provided physical and psychological care for thousands of rape survivors; survivors trained as advocates
Waad al-Kateab	Syria	Filmmaker, Journalist	Documentation, storytelling	Directed *For Sama*, a harrowing account of motherhood during siege in Aleppo, which reached global audiences
Yazidi Women's Movement	Iraq / Diaspora	Survivors, Organizers	Recovery from captivity, cultural justice	Led global awareness campaigns after ISIS genocide; some women ran for parliament or pursued international advocacy

Gulalai Ismail	Pakistan	Human Rights Advocate	Extremism resistance, girls' education	Founded Aware Girls; faced exile for speaking out against religious extremism and violence against women
Women in Black	International (Started in Israel/Palestine conflict)	Peace Network	Anti-war protest, civil disobedience	Global network of silent vigils for peace and justice, particularly against militarization and occupation
Rwandan Women's Councils	Rwanda	Community Leaders	Reconciliation, post-genocide healing	Helped reintegrate genocide survivors, facilitated peace dialogues, and filled key roles in rebuilding local governance
Ukrainian Women Veteran Movement	Ukraine	Soldiers, Advocates	Military inclusion, post-service support	Campaigns for recognition of women veterans, mental health services, and greater representation in defense policy
Razan Zaitouneh *(disappeared 2013)*	Syria	Lawyer, Activist	Human rights documentation	Co-founder of the Syrian Violations Documentation Center; kidnapped for her work amid the civil war

Chapter 14: Women Economic Leaders and Global Financial Changemakers

Name / Organization	Region	Role	Focus Areas	Notable Contribution
Esther Duflo	Global (France/USA)	Economist,	Poverty	Co-founded J-PAL, transformed

		Nobel Laureate	alleviation, development economics	development policy with evidence-based interventions for women's empowerment
Ngozi Okonjo-Iweala	Nigeria / Global	Economist, WTO Director-General	Trade equity, development finance	First woman and first African to lead the World Trade Organization; former Nigerian Finance Minister
Ellevest – Sallie Krawcheck	USA	Fintech Entrepreneur	Women's wealth building, financial literacy	Built a women-centered investment platform; advocates for gender-specific financial strategies
WIEGO (Women in Informal Employment: Globalizing and Organizing)	Global South	Research and Advocacy Network	Informal labor, urban policy	Provides data, policy, and support for street vendors, domestic workers, and home-based workers globally
SheTrades (International Trade Centre)	Global	UN-led Initiative	Women-led businesses in global markets	Connects women entrepreneurs to buyers, investors, and policymakers worldwide
Rosalind Brewer	USA	CEO, Walgreens Boots Alliance	Retail leadership, corporate diversity	One of the first Black women CEOs of a Fortune 500 company; focuses on equity and ESG integration
Ana Patricia Botín	Spain / Global	Executive Chair, Banco Santander	Banking innovation, gender	Leads major EU banking group with gender-inclusive policy and

			equity in finance	sustainability focus
Maria Teresa Kumar	USA / Latinx Community	CEO, Voto Latino	Civic engagement, economic access	Connects Latina voters and entrepreneurs with education, investment, and tech opportunities
Dr. Jennifer Riria	Kenya	Microfinance Leader	Women's banking, education, and microenterprise	CEO of Kenya Women Holding; developed innovative savings and credit programs for rural women

APPENDIX IV: CONTEMPORARY GLOBAL MOVEMENTS (CHAPTERS 15 TO 22)

This appendix compiles data-rich tables covering the twenty-first century, including political leaders, spiritual figures, educators, and activists at the forefront of global change. It reflects the diversity and interconnectedness of women's movements today, providing a reference point for the stories explored in the later chapters.

Chapter 15: Global Faith Leaders and Feminist Theologians

Name / Group	Country / Tradition	Role	Focus Areas	Notable Contribution
Phyllis Trible	USA / Christianity	Biblical Scholar	Feminist theology, Hebrew Bible	Reinterpreted biblical stories from a feminist lens; challenged traditional readings of Eve and other female figures
Rabbi Sally Priesand	USA / Judaism	Rabbi	Religious leadership, gender equality	First woman ordained as a rabbi in the U.S. (1972); paved the way for women in rabbinic roles
Sister Joan Chittister	USA / Catholicism	Benedictine Nun, Author	Justice, peace, women's rights	Vocal critic of patriarchy in the Catholic Church; advocate for religious reform and women's

Name	Region / Religion	Role	Focus	Contributions
Mata Amritanandamayi (Amma)	India / Hinduism	Guru, Humanitarian	Compassion, spiritual service	empowerment Known as "the hugging saint," Amma has built hospitals, schools, and disaster relief programs across India and the world
Pema Chödrön	USA / Buddhism	Buddhist Nun, Teacher	Meditation, mindfulness, compassion	Popularized Tibetan Buddhist teachings in the West; author of *When Things Fall Apart*
Dr. Nontando Hadebe	South Africa / Catholicism	Theologian, Scholar	African theology, gender justice	Promotes contextual theology in Africa; advocates for women's inclusion in religious leadership
Womanist Theologians (e.g. Katie Cannon, Emilie Townes)	USA / Christianity	Scholars, Ministers	Race, gender, and faith	Developed womanist theology to reflect the lived spiritual experience of Black women in America
Musawah Movement	Global / Islam	Collective Initiative	Family law reform, equality in Muslim societies	Global movement for justice in Muslim families using Islamic sources and gender-equitable interpretations
Rev. Dr. Serene Jones	USA / Christianity	President, Union Theological Seminary	Feminist theology, public theology	First female president of a major U.S. seminary; public advocate for progressive Christian values and inclusivity

Chapter 16: Trailblazing Women Athletes and Advocates for Gender Equity in Sports

Name	Sport / Country	Notable Achievements	Advocacy Impact
Billie Jean King	Tennis / USA	Won thirty-nine Grand Slam titles; defeated Bobby Riggs in "Battle of the Sexes" (1973)	Founded the Women's Tennis Association and Women's Sports Foundation; championed Title IX and equal pay
Serena Williams	Tennis / USA	Twenty-three Grand Slam singles titles; one of the most decorated athletes in history	Advocated for racial and gender equality, maternal health, and body positivity
Megan Rapinoe	Soccer / USA	Two-time World Cup Champion and Olympic gold medalist	Vocal advocate for LGBTQ+ rights and equal pay in sports; led legal battle for U.S. Women's National Team pay equity
Simone Biles	Gymnastics / USA	Most decorated gymnast in World Championships history	Redefined athlete mental health norms by withdrawing from Olympic events in 2021 to prioritize wellness
Caster Semenya	Track and Field / South Africa	Olympic gold medalist in 800m	Challenged World Athletics' gender regulations; became a global advocate for bodily

			autonomy and dignity
Ibtihaj Muhammad	Fencing / USA	First hijabi U.S. Olympian; bronze medalist in 2016	Advocated for religious inclusion and representation; launched modest fashion line and wrote children's books
Naomi Osaka	Tennis / Japan	Four-time Grand Slam champion	Used her platform to speak out on racial justice and mental health; withdrew from tournaments to protect her well-being
Tatyana McFadden	Paralympic Track / USA	Seventeen Paralympic medals; won all four major marathons in the same year multiple times	Fought for wheelchair accessibility in schools; champion for disability rights
Katie Taylor	Boxing / Ireland	Olympic gold medalist; multiple-time lightweight world champion	Helped legalize and promote women's boxing at the elite level
Manisha Malhotra	Tennis / India	Fed Cup team member; Commonwealth Games medalist	Works with Olympic Gold Quest to support rural and underprivileged female athletes in India

Chapter 17: Women Environmental Leaders and Movements for Climate Justice

Name	Country /Region	Role	Focus Areas	Notable Contributions
Wangari Maathai	Kenya	Environmentalist, Nobel Laureate	Reforestation, women's empowerment	Founded the Green Belt Movement; planted over 50 million trees; first African woman to win the Nobel Peace Prize
Berta Cáceres	Honduras	Indigenous activist	Anti-dam, Indigenous land rights	Co-founded COPINH; assassinated after opposing a hydroelectric project threatening Lenca territory
Nemonte Nenquimo	Ecuador	Indigenous leader	Amazon rainforest protection	Won a major legal victory safeguarding Waorani land from oil exploitation
Christiana Figueres	Costa Rica	Climate diplomat	Global climate policy	Led the negotiations of the 2015 Paris Climate Agreement as Executive Secretary of the UNFCCC
Greta Thunberg	Sweden	Youth climate activist	Global climate justice	Founded "Fridays for Future" movement; catalyzed global school climate strikes
Vanessa Nakate	Uganda	Climate activist	African climate equity	Advocates for visibility of African voices in climate discourse; founded Rise Up Movement
Sunita Narain	India	Environmentalist, Policy Expert	Water, air pollution, equity in climate policy	Director of Centre for Science and Environment; critic of Western-centric climate frameworks

Lois Gibbs	USA	Community organizer	Environmental health, toxic waste	Led Love Canal movement; influenced creation of Superfund to clean hazardous waste sites
Tara Houska	USA (Ojibwe)	Indigenous attorney and activist	Land defense, fossil fuel resistance	Founder of Giniw Collective; involved in protests against Line 3 pipeline in Minnesota
Isatou Ceesay	The Gambia	Recycler and entrepreneur	Waste management, women's empowerment	Founded Women's Initiative the Gambia; known as "Queen of Recycling" for turning plastic waste into reusable goods

Chapter 18: Notable Digital Feminist Leaders

Name	Country / Region	Role	Contribution
Tarana Burke	USA	Founder of #MeToo	Launched the #MeToo movement to center survivors of sexual violence – especially women of color – in conversations on justice and healing.
Anita Sarkeesian	USA / Canada	Media critic, founder of Feminist Frequency	Exposed sexism in video games and online culture; endured severe harassment while sparking industry-wide

Dr. Safiya Noble	USA	Scholar, Author of *Algorithms of Oppression*	conversations. Investigated algorithmic bias and how search engines reinforce racism and sexism.
Diana J. Greene Foster	USA	Demographer, Lead on the Turnaway Study	Used digital platforms to disseminate research on abortion access and its social effects.
Krytyka Polityczna (Agata Diduszko-Zyglewska and others)	Poland	Feminist journalists and activists	Mobilized digital campaigns against Poland's abortion restrictions using viral protest media.
Amani Al-Khatahtbeh	USA	Founder of MuslimGirl.com	Created the first online platform dedicated to the voices of Muslim women, breaking stereotypes through digital storytelling.

Hashtag Movements that Shaped Digital Feminism

Hashtag	Origin	Focus	Impact
#MeToo	USA	Sexual violence and survivor justice	Millions worldwide shared their stories, sparking investigations, firings, and policy change in multiple industries.

#NiUnaMenos	Argentina	Femicide and gender-based violence	Ignited mass protests in Latin America and institutional reforms to combat femicide.
#SayHerName	USA	Police brutality against Black women	Raised awareness of cases often left out of racial justice discourse; amplified intersectional activism.
#BringBackOurGirls	Nigeria	Mass abduction of schoolgirls	Galvanized global awareness and pressure to act against Boko Haram; highlighted gendered conflict.
#FreePeriods	UK / Global	Menstrual justice	Pushed for free access to period products in schools and broke taboos around menstruation.
#WhyIStayed	Global	Domestic violence	Gave voice to survivors and educated the public on why leaving abusive relationships is complex.

Trailblazing Women in Tech and Digital Equity

Name	Affiliation	Area of Impact	Legacy
Kimberly Bryant	Black Girls Code	Tech education and racial equity	Empowered thousands of young Black girls to pursue careers in tech through

Reshma Saujani	Girls Who Code	Coding and confidence for girls	coding camps and mentorship. Created one of the largest pipelines for closing the gender gap in tech and leadership.
Joy Buolamwini	Algorithmic Justice League	AI ethics and facial recognition	Revealed racial and gender bias in facial recognition systems; influenced corporate accountability.
Tracy Chou	Project Include	Inclusion in Silicon Valley	Built tools and communities advocating for transparency and equity in hiring and culture.
Radhika Nagpal	Harvard University / Computer Science	Swarm robotics and inclusive science	Broke stereotypes in engineering and AI while mentoring women in STEM globally.

Chapter 19: Female Political Leaders, Movements, and Milestones in Global Politics

Pioneering Female Political Leaders

Name	Country	Position	Legacy
Ellen Johnson Sirleaf	Liberia	President (2006 to 2018)	Africa's first elected female head of state; Nobel Peace Prize winner; focused on post-war reconciliation and women's inclusion.
Michelle Bachelet	Chile	President, UN High Commissioner for Human Rights	Twice elected as Chile's President; led key reforms on education, labor, and reproductive rights.
Jacinda Ardern	New Zealand	Prime Minister (2017 to 2023)	Redefined compassionate leadership during global crises; emphasized empathy, inclusion, and transparency.
Kamala Harris	United States	Vice President (2021 to 2025)	First woman, first Black and South Asian person to hold the vice presidency in U.S.

history.

Major Global Gender and Governance Milestones

Year	Milestone	Description
2000	UNSCR 1325 on Women, Peace, and Security	Recognized the role of women in conflict prevention and peacebuilding; urged inclusion in peace processes.
2011	UN Women created	Consolidated global efforts to empower women and promote gender equality through policy, funding, and advocacy.
2017 to Present	#SheDecides / #NotTheCost	Campaigns against gender-based violence in politics and support for bodily autonomy and female political leadership.

Chapter 20: Data Snapshot – Women in Politics Today

Indicator	Finding (2024)	Source
Women in national parliaments (global average)	26.7 percent	Inter-Parliamentary Union
Countries with parliamentary gender quotas	137	UN Women
Corruption levels	States with >30 percent women in parliament have significantly lower corruption	World Bank
Peace agreements	Inclusion of women increases the	UN Women

| | likelihood of agreements lasting more than fifteen years by 35 percent | |
| Gender-balanced cabinets | Only twenty-three countries have achieved parity | IPU / UN Women |

Chapter 21: Cultural Icons Embracing Feminine Power

Name	Field	Contribution
Michelle Obama	Politics, Advocacy	Redefined the role of First Lady with strength, elegance, and emotional intelligence; her memoir *Becoming* models vulnerability as leadership.
Zendaya	Entertainment	Embodies both softness and strength in her performances and fashion; uses her platform to speak about self-worth and identity.
Jacinda Ardern	Politics	As Prime Minister of New Zealand, led with compassion and competence, balancing empathy and decisiveness.
Rihanna	Business, Music	Combines fierce independence with glamorous femininity; redefined beauty standards through Fenty Beauty's inclusive vision.
Adele	Music	Her emotionally raw lyrics, vulnerability,

		and unapologetic self-expression resonate across generations.
Emma Watson	Activism, Film	Feminist advocate and UN Women ambassador who balances intellect, empathy, and grace.

Thinkers and Writers on Femininity

Name	Field	Perspective
Bell Hooks	Feminist Theory	Wrote extensively on love, feminism, and how patriarchy damages both women and men. Her work reclaims emotional depth as power.
Audre Lorde	Poetry, Activism	Declared the erotic as power – femininity as intuitive, sensual, and revolutionary.
Esther Perel	Psychotherapy	Explores the balance between love, desire, and power in modern relationships, embracing complexity in feminine identity.
Clarissa Pinkola Estés	Jungian Psychology	*Women Who Run With the Wolves* explores the wild woman archetype as an expression of deep, instinctual femininity.

Fashion and Femininity: Icons of Style and Substance

Name	Industry	Impact
Diane von Fürstenberg	Fashion	Created the iconic wrap dress – merging comfort, professionalism, and feminine

Meghan Markle	Public Life	elegance. Blends modern royal style with humanitarian advocacy, challenging traditional norms with subtle strength.
Frida Kahlo	Art	Though earlier in history, Kahlo's bold, unfiltered self-representation continues to inspire women to own their image and pain.

Contemporary Voices Redefining Femininity Online

Platform	Voice / Creator	Message
Instagram / Podcasts	@themantraco, Glennon Doyle (*We Can Do Hard Things*)	Emphasize authenticity, intuition, and emotional honesty as feminine strengths.
YouTube / TikTok	Nabela Noor, Sofie Dossi	Promote body positivity, cultural identity, and creativity — on their terms.
Books and Blogs	Brianna Wiest (*The Mountain Is You*), Sarah Blondin (*Heart Minded*)	Write on feminine healing, self-awareness, and spiritual resilience.

Global Feminine Traditions

Culture	Feminine Archetype / Practice
India	The goddess Saraswati (knowledge, wisdom) and Lakshmi (abundance, beauty) represent divine feminine power.
Japan	*Yamato Nadeshiko* – the ideal of inner strength and quiet dignity in women, evolving into modern self-expression.
West Africa	Female griots (oral historians) preserve community wisdom through storytelling and music.
Latin America	Marianismo and evolving interpretations of

spiritual motherhood influence feminine identity and resistance.

Chapter 22: Notable Female Religious Leaders and Reformers

Name	Faith Tradition	Region	Contribution
Sally Priesand	Judaism	United States	First woman ordained as a rabbi in the U.S. (1972); paved the way for female leadership in liberal Jewish denominations.
Mary Daly	Christianity (Catholic)	United States	Radical feminist philosopher and theologian; critiqued patriarchal structures in Christianity and proposed a feminist spiritual ethos.
Mpho Tutu van Furth	Anglican Christianity	South Africa / Netherlands	Ordained priest and daughter of Desmond Tutu; challenged church policy on LGBTQ+ clergy and same-sex marriage.
Pema Chödrön	Tibetan Buddhism	United States	Buddhist nun and author of *When Things Fall Apart*; popularized mindfulness and resilience teachings

Name	Faith / Philosophy	Country	Focus
			for Western audiences.
Sr. Teresa Forcades	Catholicism	Spain	Feminist nun, medical doctor, and theologian advocating for reproductive rights, public health, and democratic socialism.
Traci Blackmon	Protestant Christianity	United States	Minister and activist at the intersection of faith and racial justice; vocal in the Ferguson and Black Lives Matter movements.

Spiritual Thinkers and Feminist Theologians

Name	Faith / Philosophy	Key Work / Role	Focus
Letty Russell	Christianity	*Church in the Round*	Feminist liberation theology emphasizing community and inclusion
Phyllis Trible	Christianity	*Texts of Terror*	Reinterpreted Bible stories of women's suffering through feminist critique
Delores S. Williams	Womanist Theology	*Sisters in the Wilderness*	Focused on survival, resilience, and Hagar's story as a theological lens
Fatima Mernissi	Islam	*The Veil and the Male Elite*	Critiqued patriarchal misreadings of Islamic

			texts; advocated Muslim feminism
Rita Nakashima Brock	Interfaith / Feminist Theology	Co-founder of Soul Repair Center	Explores spiritual trauma and recovery, especially for veterans

Faith-Based Feminist and Interfaith Movements

Movement / Organization	Region	Focus	Impact
Women of the Wall	Israel	Judaism and religious freedom	Advocates for women's right to pray with Torah and wear prayer shawls at the Western Wall
Catholics for Choice / Católicas por el Derecho a Decidir	Global / Latin America	Reproductive rights and Catholic ethics	Challenges Church teachings on contraception and abortion from a pro-choice, faith-affirming lens
Mujeristas Theology	Latin America and U.S.	Latina feminist theology	Centers the experiences of Latinas in theology, often from working-class and immigrant backgrounds
Musawah	Muslim-majority countries	Equality in Muslim family law	International movement advocating for justice and reform in Muslim legal frameworks
WCC	Global	Christian	Amplifies

Ecumenical Women's Network		feminist unity	women's voices in the World Council of Churches and interfaith collaboration
Nuns on the Bus	United States	Catholic social justice activism	Women religious who travel and advocate for healthcare, immigration reform, and economic justice

APPENDIX V: SELECTED BIBLIOGRAPHY

This book draws from a wide body of historical, journalistic, and academic sources. Below is a curated list of foundational texts and references:

- Angela Davis, Women, Race, and Class
- Bell Hooks, Feminism is for Everybody
- Malala Yousafzai, I Am Malala
- Michelle Obama, Becoming
- Gloria Steinem, My Life on the Road
- Chimamanda Ngozi Adichie, We Should All Be Feminists
- Sara Ahmed, Living a Feminist Life
- Judith Butler, Gender Trouble
- Roxane Gay, Bad Feminist
- Audre Lorde, Sister Outsider
- Rebecca Solnit, The Mother of All Questions
- Amina Wadud, Qur'an and Woman
- Mary Beard, Women and Power
- Beverly Guy-Sheftall (Ed.), Words of Fire: An Anthology of African American Feminist Thought
- Fatima Mernissi, The Veil and the Male Elite
- Carol Gilligan, In a Different Voice

APPENDIX VI:
READER'S REFLECTION GUIDE

The progress of women over the past century is not only history to be remembered – it is a living legacy to be carried forward. As you close this book, take time to reflect on the questions below and consider how the stories you've read connect to your own journey, your community, and the future you want to help build.

Art and Representation

- How have the women artists, writers, and cultural figures in this book reshaped how you think about femininity, identity, and creativity?
- In your own life, how do you challenge or reinforce the images of women you encounter daily?

Activism and Politics

- Which activist stories resonated most with you, and why?
- How can you use your own voice, vote, or platform to amplify issues of equality and justice?

Education and Economics

- How has access to education or financial independence influenced your own opportunities or those around you?
- What role can you play – whether as a mentor, employer, teacher, or advocate – in ensuring equal access for others?

Environment and Technology

- The women environmentalists and digital activists in this book highlight how interconnected justice issues are. Where do you see yourself making a difference – in local sustainability efforts, digital spaces, or policy advocacy?

- How can you help ensure that innovation and technology are designed with inclusion in mind?

Spirituality and Belief

- How have belief systems shaped your understanding of gender roles?

- What traditions, rituals, or values do you carry forward, and which do you feel called to challenge or reinterpret?

Looking Ahead

- After reading these chapters, what barriers do you see in your community or industry that still need to be broken?

- What single step can you take – this month, this year – to contribute to a more equitable future?

Remember: The story of women's progress is not finished. It continues with each of us – our choices, our courage, and our commitment to equity in both private and public life.

APPENDIX VII:
READER'S DISCUSSION GUIDE

1. Rediscovering Legacy

- How does reframing women's history as central rather than secondary change the way we think about modern progress?

2. Activism and Agency

- What common strategies did women activists across regions (e.g., Latin America, Africa, Asia, U.S.) use to gain visibility and influence?

- How do these strategies compare to activism today?

3. Education as a Doorway

- Why is education consistently described as the foundation for women's empowerment?

- How do cultural or political contexts shape women's access to education differently around the world?

4. Sports and Equality

- Title IX transformed U.S. athletics – but what can we learn from global examples like women's football in Europe or cricket in India?

- What does equity in sports teach us about broader struggles for gender equality?

5. Political Leadership

- The book highlights leaders like Ellen Johnson Sirleaf and Jacinda Ardern. How did their leadership styles differ from traditional political models, and what impact did this have on institutions?

- Do you think women's representation in politics changes the outcomes of governance? Why or why not?

6. Economics and Labor

- From cooperatives in Ghana to SEWA in India, collective economic models empowered women. What strengths do these models have compared to traditional market structures?

- How can these lessons be applied in today's global economy?

7. Media and Representation

- How do concepts like the "female gaze" change the way we view films, advertisements, and pop culture?

- Can you think of recent examples where women's media representation shifted public perception or policy?

8. Technology and Digital Feminism

- Movements like #MeToo and #NiUnaMenos spread rapidly online. What advantages and limitations do digital activism have compared to traditional street protests?

9. Intersectionality

- Kimberlé Crenshaw's concept of intersectionality reshaped feminist discourse. Which of the case studies in this book best illustrates intersectionality in action?

- How can this lens be applied to challenges facing women in your own community?

10. Environment and Sustainability

- Women leaders at Standing Rock or in climate negotiations show how environmental justice and gender justice intersect. Why do you think women often stand at the forefront of environmental activism?

11. Faith and Belief

- How have women across different faith traditions reinterpreted religion to empower rather than restrict?

- Do you see belief as more often a barrier to or a catalyst for women's equality?

12. The Road Ahead

- After finishing the book, what do you think are the most urgent barriers women still face globally?

- What concrete steps can individuals, organizations, or governments take to advance gender equality in the next decade?

A LETTER TO THE
NEXT GENERATION

Dear Future Leaders, Dreamers, and Change-Makers,

As I write these final words, I think of you.

I think of your questions, your courage, your curiosity. I think of the world you are already shaping – one more interconnected, more complex, and, I believe, more full of possibility than ever before.

This book was written not only to honor the past but to offer it to you as a mirror and a compass. Inside these pages are the lives of women who dared to ask difficult questions, speak inconvenient truths, and break through walls they were never supposed to touch. These were not superheroes. They were artists, mothers, students, farmers, legislators, athletes, healers, and warriors. They stumbled. They sacrificed. They endured.

And still – they rose.

The path forward will not be easy. Some of the same struggles these women faced will still challenge you: inequality, discrimination, violence, fear, doubt. But you will have something they did not – a fuller record of their resistance, a louder chorus of allies, and the clarity that comes from standing on the shoulders of those who came before.

You are not starting from scratch. You are continuing a legacy.

So, I write to remind you:

- Your voice matters. Even when it shakes, especially when it challenges power, always when it speaks your truth.

- Your body is not a battleground – it is your home. Treat it with dignity, demand it be honored, and defend the right of others to do the same.

- Your ideas are needed. Let them be bold. Let them be messy. Let them be different from mine.

- Your solidarity is power. Change does not happen alone. It happens when people, across generations and identities, say: "We deserve better – and we are willing to build it."

If you are tired, rest. But do not retreat.

If you are unsure, look to the stories of those who have already carved paths through fire. Then take a deep breath, gather your people, and walk your own.

There will be new barriers ahead. But I trust you will face them with brilliance, compassion, and the quiet, steady power of those who know that liberation is not a dream – it is a commitment.

The world needs your leadership.

Lead with love.

With hope and gratitude,
Maria L. Ellis, BBA, MBA

ACKNOWLEDGMENTS

This book would not exist without the voices, visions, and victories of countless women – named and unnamed – whose lives have inspired this work. I am deeply grateful to:

- The curators, artists, and scholars behind the Radical! Women exhibition at the Belvedere in Vienna, whose thoughtful presentation sparked the very first seed of this project.

- The women activists, educators, athletes, politicians, and spiritual leaders whose courage forms the heart of every chapter.

- The researchers, journalists, and archivists whose tireless work has preserved the stories that too often go untold.

- My family, who has always supported my writing, my curiosity, and my passion for justice.

- My readers – especially the next generation – who I hope will carry this story forward and write their own.

To every woman who ever thought her story didn't matter: it does. This book is for you.

ABOUT THE AUTHOR

Maria L. Ellis, BBA, MBA, is a seasoned investor, business leader, and educator with a deep passion for helping others build lasting wealth through real estate. With decades of experience spanning finance, entrepreneurship, and strategic investing, Maria has mentored countless individuals to take control of their financial futures and invest with clarity, confidence, and purpose.

She is the founder of a family real estate investment firm, where she and her team acquire, manage, and grow multifamily portfolios across thriving U.S. markets. Known for her practical wisdom, compassionate leadership, and values-based approach, Maria believes that real estate is not just about properties – it's about people, impact, and legacy.

Maria is also a published author of multiple books on entrepreneurship, wellness, longevity, and women's empowerment. Her writing reflects her life's mission: to educate, inspire, and empower others to live fully and invest wisely.

When she's not negotiating deals or guiding investors, Maria enjoys traveling with her family, mentoring the next generation, and living a purpose-driven life filled with service, joy, and growth.

Connect with Maria:
Email: mellis@fsacap.com
Mobile: 973-216-4181

ABOUT ELLIS PUBLISHING HOUSE

Ellis Publishing House presents the work and vision of bestselling author and educator Maria L. Ellis, BBA, MBA. Founded to bring clear, useful ideas to a wide readership, the imprint focuses on practical nonfiction with enduring value—finance and business, health and longevity, leadership, caregiving, real estate, and poetry—alongside the signature *Journey to Wellness, Freedom, and Legacy* series. Editions are available in English and Spanish across print, eBook, and audio.

Maria's career spans international banking, investment advising, and financial planning, experience that informs her grounded approach to money, leadership, and long-term well-being. A graduate of the Harvard Business School Owner/President Management program, she holds business degrees from the University of Massachusetts Amherst and has served in leadership and advisory roles across education and nonprofit boards. Her books and talks emphasize clarity, compassion, and action—helping readers make better decisions for themselves, their families, and their communities.

Ellis Publishing House exists to advance that mission: books that translate expertise into everyday tools, invite thoughtful reflection, and encourage readers to build not only success but also significance. The catalog includes guides to financial freedom, family business legacy planning, entrepreneurial health, longevity, real-estate investing, leadership, caregiving, and a poetry collection that celebrates life on earth.

In all of its publishing, Ellis Publishing House favors ideas with measurable impact, stories with heart, and designs made to last—work shaped by Maria L. Ellis's commitment to service, integrity, and accessible excellence.

OTHER BOOKS BY
ELLIS PUBLISHING HOUSE

Achieve Financial Freedom: The Road Map to Financial Success by Maria L. Ellis, BBA, MBA

Family Business Legacy Plan: The Ultimate Guide to Creating a Legacy for Your Family without Paying too Much in Taxes by Maria L. Ellis, BBA, MBA

Redefining Entrepreneurial Success: A Guide to a Healthy and Holistic Lifestyle by Maria L. Ellis, BBA, MBA

Longevity: Reinvent Yourself at Any Age by Maria L. Ellis, BBA, MBA

Life on Earth: Poetic Perspectives by Maria L. Ellis, BBA, MBA

Golf: A Course in Business: A Few Lessons Golf Can Teach Us About Management & Entrepreneurship by Maria L. Ellis, BBA, MBA

From Operator to Entrepreneur: Unlocking the Power of Visionary Leadership by Maria L. Ellis, BBA, MBA

Stolen Memories: A Journey Through Alzheimer's by Maria L. Ellis, BBA, MBA

Designing Your Longevity: A Personalized Blueprint for Thriving Longer with Energy, Purpose, and Vitality by Maria L. Ellis, BBA, MBA

Investing in Multifamily Real Estate: A Guide to Investing for Income, Impact, and Generational Wealth by Maria L. Ellis, BBA, MBA

FINAL CALL TO ACTION

The stories in this book are not meant to be admired from a distance – they are meant to be a spark.

You don't have to be famous or fearless to make a difference. You only need to start.

Here's how you can act:

- Learn more about women's history where you live – who are the pioneers in your own community?

- Support women-led organizations and movements – especially those working at the grassroots level.

- Mentor someone younger. Share your story, listen to theirs.

- Speak up when others can't. Use your voice and your platform, no matter how small.

- Vote for leaders who advocate gender equity. Run for office, if you're called to.

- Challenge norms in your workplace, school, or faith community. Don't wait for permission.

- Honor intersectionality – recognize that gender justice must include racial, economic, LGBTQ+, and disability justice.

- Create something – write, paint, teach, build, organize. Culture is changed by creators.

The world we want isn't far off – it's being made every day in choices like these.

You are part of this movement. Keep going.

www.ingramcontent.com/pod-product-compliance
Lightning Source LLC
Chambersburg PA
CBHW051410050726
47595CB00010B/4003